THE FIRST HEBREW PRIMER

THIRD EDITION

ANSWER BOOK

•

Ethelyn Simon
Dorey Brandt-Finell

•

EKS Publishing Co., Oakland, California

Editor
Alan K. Lipton

Technical Consultant
Joseph Anderson

Book Design
Irene Imfeld

EKS Publishing Co.

P.O. Box 9750
Berkeley, CA 94709-0750
e-mail: orders@ekspublishing.com
Phone (510) 251-9100 • Fax (510) 251-9102

www.ekspublishing.com

Seventh Printing, October 2008
ISBN 978-0-939144-16-7

INTRODUCTION

This answer book was prepared to make *The First Hebrew Primer* the most effective teaching tool possible. Beneficial to students who are using the *Primer* in classes, these answers are indispensable for students working alone. All students should work through exercises independently and refer to this guide to check their answers and correct any errors.

Biblical Hebrew does not directly translate into correct, idiomatic English. We have stayed as close to the literal Hebrew as possible in our translations of *Primer* exercises. This choice will make some sentences sound awkward, but will make it easy for students to analyze Hebrew phrases and sentences word for word.

The *Answer Book* does not provide translations for biblical quotes. We hope that students will use their new language skills to produce a translation that can be checked against an English-language Bible. Students may consult a variety of English versions. To be useful, a translation must be modern and complete. We recommend the Revised Standard Version, the New International Version, or the New JPS (Jewish Publication Society) Translation.

Hebrew has a smaller vocabulary than English, so more than one English word may be used to translate a Hebrew one. Sometimes, to clarify a grammatical point, we offer multiple English translations. At other times, we choose one English word where another would be equally correct. The varying nuances of Hebrew make interpreting the Hebrew Bible a fascinating experience. We hope this *Answer Book* will enrich your Hebrew studies.

EKS Publishing is the premier publisher of Hebrew educational materials. In addition to the books listed below, EKS offers audio CDs and cassettes, flashcards, charts, posters, and magnets for students of Hebrew. For a complete catalog call **877-7-HEBREW** or visit our website: **www.ekspublishing.com**.

For Adults
Teach Yourself to Read Hebrew
The First Hebrew Primer
The First Hebrew Reader
Prayerbook Hebrew the Easy Way
The Beginner's Dictionary of Prayerbook Hebrew
HebrewTalk: 101 Hebrew Roots and
    the Stories They Tell

For Children
The Bedtime Sh'ma
Siddur Shabbat b'Yachad
In the Beginning
The Tower of Babel
Noah's Ark
Lech Lecha
Rebecca
Jacob's Travels
Joseph the Dreamer
Og the Terrible Series: Comic Book Adventures
    in Prayerbook Hebrew

Jewish Practice
Give Me Your Hand: Guidelines for Visiting the Sick
K'vod Hamet: A Guide for the Bereaved
Chesed shel Emet: Guidelines for Taharah
A Place in the Tent: Intermarriage and
    Conservative Judaism

Chapter 4

Exercise 1

1. stood 2. son 3. he 4. heard 5. man 6. house
7. Abraham 8. king 9. guarded 10. David
11. word, thing 12. remembered 13. ruled
14. young man 15. the young man

Exercise 2

We are translating the first sentence of this exercise
with all of its possibilities. Each of the other sentences
will only be translated with its simplest form, although
other translations will be equally acceptable.

1. Abraham stood. Abraham did stand. Abraham was
standing. Abraham has stood. Abraham had stood.
2. Abraham heard. 3. The king ruled. 4. A son stood.
5. David guarded. 6. He ruled. 7. A house stood.
8. A young man remembered. 9. A man guarded.

Exercise 3

1. A young man heard. The young man heard.
2. A son stood. The son stood. 3. A man guarded.
The man guarded. 4. A king ruled. The king ruled.
5. David remembered a word. The man remembered
a word. 6. He guarded a house. The king guarded a
house.

Exercise 4

הַנַּעַר, הַבַּיִת, הַבֵּן, הַדָּבָר, הַמֶּלֶךְ

Exercise 5

1. נַעַר שָׁמַע. הַנַּעַר שָׁמַע. 2. מֶלֶךְ מָלַךְ. הַמֶּלֶךְ
מָלַךְ. 3. הַבֵּן עָמַד. הַבֵּן זָכַר. 4. הָאִישׁ שָׁמַר.
הָאִישׁ שָׁמַר. 5. הַנַּעַר שָׁמַר. נַעַר שָׁמַר. 6. מֶלֶךְ
זָכַר. הַמֶּלֶךְ זָכַר.

Exercise 6

1. Abraham heard a word. 2. David ruled. 3. The
young man remembered a word. 4. A son guarded.
5. The king stood. 6. He remembered a house. 7. The
man heard a word. 8. The house stood. 9. The king
ruled.

Exercise 7

1. הָאִישׁ עָמַד. 2. הָאִישׁ שָׁמַר בַּיִת. 3. דָּוִד שָׁמַע
דָּבָר. 4. הוּא מָלַךְ. 5. אַבְרָהָם זָכַר דָּבָר.
6. הַבֵּן שָׁמַע. 7. מֶלֶךְ שָׁמַר. 8. הַבַּיִת עָמַד.
9. הַנַּעַר זָכַר. 10. הַמֶּלֶךְ שָׁמַע.

Chapter 5

Oral Review

1. David remembered. He remembered. He
remembered a word. 2. He guarded. A young man
guarded. The young man guarded a house. 3. A man
stood. A young man stood. The young man stood.
4. The man ruled. The son ruled. The son heard.
5. The man heard a word. Abraham heard a word.
The young man heard a word. 6. A king guarded. A
king guarded a son. David, the king, guarded a son.
7. Abraham stood. Abraham remembered. Abraham
heard a man. 8. A man guarded a house. The man
ruled. The man stood. 9. A house stood. The house
stood. The house stood. 10. A son remembered a man.
The son heard a king. The king guarded. 11. He
heard a young man. He guarded a son. He ruled.
12. The king ruled. The king ruled. David
remembered.

Exercise 1

1. a son (m) 2. a daughter (f) 3. a man (m) 4. a
woman (f) 5. Abraham (m) 6. a young man (m) 7. a
young woman (f) 8. a king (m) 9. a family (f) 10. a
father (m) 11. an animal (f) 12. Jerusalem (f) 13. a
word (m) 14. a house (m) 15. Egypt (f)

Exercise 2

1. he walked, she walked, ה.ל.ךְ 2. he stood, she
stood, ע.מ.ד 3. he guarded, she guarded, שׁ.מ.ר
4. he heard, she heard, שׁ.מ.ע 5. he remembered,
she remembered, ז.כ.ר 6. he ruled, she ruled, מ.ל.ךְ

Exercise 3

1. David remembered. 2. Abraham stood. 3. Sarah
stood. 4. A father guarded. 5. The young woman
guarded. 6. The woman heard. 7. Ruth remembered.
8. He went. 9. She went.

Exercise 4

1. שָׁמַע, David heard. 2. שָׁמְעָה, Ruth heard. 3. זָכַר,
The son remembered. 4. שָׁמְרָה, A daughter guarded.
5. הָלַךְ, A young man walked. 6. מָלְכָה, The family
ruled. 7. עָמַד, The house stood. 8. מָלַךְ, A man
ruled.

Exercise 5

1. The young woman went and she stood. 2. The king
ruled and he remembered. 3. Sarah guarded and she
stood. 4. David stood and he ruled. 5. The family
ruled and it remembered a son. 6. Sarah remembered

1

(Exercise 5 continued)

a word and a son.   7. Abraham listened and he remembered, and he went.   8. The animal stood, and it went.

Exercise 6

1. The young man stood.

2. David listened to the young woman.

א. שָׂרָה שָׁמְעָה אֶל הַנַּעֲרָה.   ב. הִיא שָׁמְעָה אֶל הַנַּעֲרָה.   ג. הַבֵּן שָׁמַע אֶל הַנַּעֲרָה.   ד. הַמִּשְׁפָּחָה שָׁמְעָה אֶל הַנַּעֲרָה.   ה. הוּא שָׁמַע אֶל הַנַּעֲרָה.   ו. אִשָּׁה מִמִּצְרַיִם שָׁמְעָה אֶל הַנַּעֲרָה.

3. Abraham remembered a word from the king.

א. הִיא זָכְרָה דָּבָר מִן הַמֶּלֶךְ.   ב. הַבֵּן זָכַר דָּבָר מִן הַמֶּלֶךְ.   ג. רוּת זָכְרָה דָּבָר מִן הַמֶּלֶךְ.   ד. הַנַּעֲרָה זָכְרָה דָּבָר מִן הַמֶּלֶךְ.   ה. הָאִישׁ זָכַר דָּבָר מִן הַמֶּלֶךְ.   ו. הָאִשָּׁה זָכְרָה דָּבָר מִן הַמֶּלֶךְ.

4. A king stood, and he ruled, and he listened to the family.

א. עָמַד הָאָב, וְהוּא מָלַךְ, וְהוּא שָׁמַע אֶל הַמִּשְׁפָּחָה.   ב. עָמְדָה שָׂרָה, וְהִיא מָלְכָה, וְהִיא שָׁמְעָה אֶל הַמִּשְׁפָּחָה.   ג. עָמַד הָאִישׁ מִירוּשָׁלַם, וְהוּא מָלַךְ, וְהוּא שָׁמַע אֶל הַמִּשְׁפָּחָה.   ד. עָמְדָה הִיא, וְהִיא מָלְכָה, וְהִיא שָׁמְעָה אֶל הַמִּשְׁפָּחָה.   ה. עָמַד דָּוִד, וְהוּא מָלַךְ, וְהוּא שָׁמַע אֶל הַמִּשְׁפָּחָה.

5. The man guarded an animal, and he went to Egypt.

א. שָׁמְרָה שָׂרָה בְּהֵמָה, וְהִיא הָלְכָה אֶל מִצְרַיִם.   ב. שָׁמַר נַעַר מִן הַבַּיִת בְּהֵמָה, וְהוּא הָלַךְ אֶל מִצְרַיִם.   ג. שָׁמְרָה הַבַּת בְּהֵמָה, וְהִיא הָלְכָה אֶל מִצְרַיִם.   ד. שָׁמְרָה הַנַּעֲרָה בְּהֵמָה, וְהִיא הָלְכָה אֶל מִצְרַיִם.

6. The young woman listened to the father, and she walked to Jerusalem and to the young man.

א. דָּוִד שָׁמַע אֶל הָאָב, וְהוּא הָלַךְ אֶל יְרוּשָׁלַם וְאֶל הַנַּעַר.   ב. הָאִישׁ מִמִּצְרַיִם שָׁמַע אֶל הָאָב, וְהוּא הָלַךְ אֶל יְרוּשָׁלַם וְאֶל הַנַּעַר.   ג. הָאִשָּׁה שָׁמְעָה אֶל הָאָב, וְהִיא הָלְכָה אֶל יְרוּשָׁלַם וְאֶל הַנַּעַר.   ד. הַמֶּלֶךְ שָׁמַע אֶל הָאָב, וְהוּא הָלַךְ אֶל יְרוּשָׁלַם וְאֶל הַנַּעַר.

Exercise 7

1. The man guarded a king and the woman guarded an animal.

A. הָאִישׁ שָׁמַר.   B. הָאִישׁ שָׁמַר מֶלֶךְ.   C. הָאִשָּׁה שָׁמְרָה מֶלֶךְ.   D. הָאִשָּׁה שָׁמְרָה בְּהֵמָה.   E. הָאִישׁ שָׁמַר בְּהֵמָה וְהָאִשָּׁה שָׁמְרָה מֶלֶךְ.   F. הָאִישׁ שָׁמַר דָּבָר וְהָאִשָּׁה שָׁמְרָה דָּבָר.

2. The king ruled from Jerusalem and he listened to David. OR The king from Jerusalem ruled and he listened to David.

A. מָלַךְ הַמֶּלֶךְ.   B. מָלַךְ הַמֶּלֶךְ מִירוּשָׁלַם.   C. מָלַךְ הַמֶּלֶךְ וְהוּא שָׁמַע.   D. הָאִישׁ שָׁמַע דָּבָר.   E. הָאִישׁ שָׁמַע אֶל דָּוִד.   F. הָאִישׁ מִירוּשָׁלַם שָׁמַע אֶל הַמֶּלֶךְ.

3. Ruth remembered a young man from Egypt and she walked to Jerusalem.

A. רוּת זָכְרָה נַעַר.   B. נַעַר מִמִּצְרַיִם זָכַר נַעֲרָה.   C. רוּת הָלְכָה אֶל מִצְרַיִם.   D. הִיא זָכְרָה נַעֲרָה מִמִּצְרַיִם.   E. נַעַר זָכַר נַעֲרָה מִירוּשָׁלַם וְהוּא הָלַךְ אֶל מִצְרַיִם.

Exercise 8

1. The father guarded a son and a daughter and he heard a word from Jerusalem.   2. Ruth stood and she remembered a man and a woman from Egypt and she listened to the young man and she went to the young man.   3. The family stood and it guarded a house and it ruled.   4. The father guarded and the woman stood and the daughter went to Egypt.   5. The king ruled from Jerusalem and he remembered an animal from Egypt and he went to Egypt and he guarded an animal. 6. The young man remembered a young woman from Jerusalem, and he remembered a young woman from Egypt, and he went to...Jerusalem.

Chapter 6

Oral Review

1. He went. She went to Jerusalem. The woman from Egypt went to Jerusalem. The daughter from Egypt went and she remembered.   2. The family remembered a word. The family guarded a thing. She remembered a word. The family remembered and it guarded.
3. The man heard a word. The man listened to the father. The man listened to the father from Egypt. A man listened to the father from Egypt and he went.

(Oral Review continued)

4. Sarah stood and Ruth guarded a thing. The daughter from Egypt stood and the son from Jerusalem guarded. The daughter from Egypt stood and she guarded. The son from Jerusalem stood and he ruled. 5. David ruled from Egypt. David ruled from Egypt and the father ruled from Jerusalem.

David ruled from Egypt and he went to Jerusalem. He went to Jerusalem and he guarded a man.

Exercise 1

1. מְלָכִים – kings 2. עַמִּים – peoples 3. דְּרָכִים – roads 4. נְעָרִים – young men 5. brothers – אַחִים 6. נָשִׁים – women 7. אָבוֹת – fathers 8. עָרִים – cities 9. הָרִים – mountains 10. דְּבָרִים – words 11. נְעָרוֹת – young women 12. בְּהֵמוֹת – animals 13. יָמִים – days 14. בָּתִּים – houses 15. בָּנוֹת – daughters 16. אֲנָשִׁים – men 17. עֲבָדִים – slaves 18. בָּנִים – sons 19. מִשְׁפָּחוֹת – families 20. אֲרָצוֹת – lands

Exercise 2

1. kings 2. young women 3. young men
4. mountains 5. families 6. cities 7. lands 8. days
9. slaves 10. words 11. roads 12. daughters
13. animals 14. nations 15. women 16. sons
17. brothers 18. houses 19. fathers 20. men

Exercise 3

1. אַחִים   2. נְעָרִים   3. נְעָרוֹת   4. עַמִּים   5. בָּנִים
6. בְּהֵמוֹת   7. אָבוֹת   8. הָרִים   9. יָמִים
10. מִשְׁפָּחוֹת   11. דְּרָכִים   12. אֲנָשִׁים   13. עָרִים
14. בָּתִּים   15. בָּנוֹת   16. דְּבָרִים   17. עֲבָדִים
18. נָשִׁים   19. אֲרָצוֹת   20. מְלָכִים

Exercise 4

1. The father remembered a day in Moab. The fathers remembered a day in Moab. The woman remembered a day in a house. The women remembered a day in the house. 2. The son crossed over a road. The sons crossed over roads. The daughters crossed over roads. The daughter crossed over roads and mountains. 3. Abraham sent a young woman to a city. Sarah sent a young man to the city. They (m) sent a young man to Jerusalem. They (f) sent young men to the cities. 4. The slave stood there and he remembered a nation. The slaves stood there and they remembered nations. Mountains stood and the people crossed over from there. The cities stood and the people went (to) there. 5. Abraham ruled as a king. Abraham ruled as the king. The sons walked like the men. The daughters walked like the women. 6. He heard an animal in the country. She heard animals in a country. They (m) heard women in the lands. They (f) heard women in the mountains.

Exercise 5

1. A. שָׁמַר, The brother guarded. B. שָׁמְרָה, Ruth guarded. C. שָׁמְרוּ, The sons guarded. D. שָׁמְרוּ, The young women guarded. 2. A. עָמַד, The king stood in the city. B. עָמְדוּ, The young men stood in (on) the mountain. C. עָמְדוּ, The daughters stood in the road. D. עָמְדָה, The animal stood in (on) the land. 3. A. הָלְכָה, A young woman went to a king and she listened to the servant there. B. הָלְכוּ, Young women went to the king and they listened to the servants there. C. הָלְכוּ, Abraham and David went to Moab and they listened to the brothers. D. הָלַךְ, A man went to Egypt and he remembered cities and mountains. 4. A. שָׁלְחוּ, The women sent cattle to the men in the city. B. שָׁלַח, The people sent slaves to the king in Jerusalem and they listened to the king there. C. שָׁלְחָה, The family sent things to the children and they (שָׁלְחוּ) sent cattle to the family. D. שָׁלְחוּ, The brothers sent a thing to the father and the father crossed over to Jerusalem.

Exercise 6

1. Abraham went to a city like Jerusalem and he ruled.

A. אַבְרָהָם הָלַךְ אֶל עִיר.   B. הוּא הָלַךְ אֶל עִיר כִּירוּשָׁלַ͏ִם.   C. הוּא הָלַךְ אֶל עִיר וְהוּא מָלַךְ שָׁם.
D. אַבְרָהָם וְדָוִד הָלְכוּ אֶל הָעִיר וְהֵם מָלְכוּ שָׁם.
E. שָׂרָה הָלְכָה אֶל עִיר כִּירוּשָׁלַ͏ִם.

2. Today the nation from Moab crossed over with kings from the mountains on (in) the road to Jerusalem.

A. הַיּוֹם הָעָם עָבַר בַּמְּלָכִים.   B. הַיּוֹם הַמְּלָכִים עָבְרוּ בָּעָם מֵהֶהָרִים.   C. הַיּוֹם הָעָם עָבַר הַר בַּדֶּרֶךְ אֶל יְרוּשָׁלַ͏ִם.   D. הַיּוֹם הַבְּהֵמוֹת עָבְרוּ דֶּרֶךְ בָּאֲנָשִׁים מִירוּשָׁלַ͏ִם.   E. הָאֲנָשִׁים מִמּוֹאָב עָבְרוּ בְּנָשִׁים בַּדֶּרֶךְ אֶל יְרוּשָׁלַ͏ִם.

Exercise 7

1. David ruled in Jerusalem, and the people listened to David.

א. הַנְּעָרִים מָלְכוּ בִּירוּשָׁלַם, וְהָעָם שָׁמַע לַנְּעָרִים.
ב. שָׂרָה מָלְכָה בִּירוּשָׁלַם, וְהָעָם שָׁמַע לְשָׂרָה.
ג. הַבָּנוֹת מָלְכוּ בִּירוּשָׁלַם, וְהָעָם שָׁמַע לַבָּנוֹת.
ד. הַבֵּן מָלַךְ בִּירוּשָׁלַם, וְהָעָם שָׁמַע לַבֵּן.

2. Today the fathers guarded cattle in the land, and the women sent things to the fathers there.

א. הַיּוֹם שָׁמְרוּ הָאָבוֹת בְּהֵמוֹת בָּאָרֶץ, וּבָנִים מִן הַמִּשְׁפָּחָה שָׁלְחוּ דְּבָרִים לָאָבוֹת שָׁם. ב. הַיּוֹם שָׁמְרוּ הָאָבוֹת בְּהֵמוֹת בָּאָרֶץ, וְרוּת שָׁלְחָה דְּבָרִים לָאָבוֹת שָׁם. ג. הַיּוֹם שָׁמְרוּ הָאָבוֹת בְּהֵמוֹת בָּאָרֶץ, וְהָעֶבֶד בַּבַּיִת שָׁלַח דְּבָרִים לָאָבוֹת שָׁם. ד. הַיּוֹם שָׁמְרוּ הָאָבוֹת בְּהֵמוֹת בָּאָרֶץ, וַאֲנָשִׁים שָׁלְחוּ דְּבָרִים לָאָבוֹת שָׁם.

3. The father heard a word, and he guarded a daughter from Egypt.

א. הַנַּעֲרָה שָׁמְעָה דָּבָר, וְהִיא שָׁמְרָה בַּת מִמִּצְרַיִם.
ב. הָעֲבָדִים שָׁמְעוּ דָּבָר, וְהֵם שָׁמְרוּ בַּת מִמִּצְרַיִם.
ג. רוּת וְשָׂרָה שָׁמְעוּ דָּבָר, וְהֵנָּה שָׁמְרוּ בַּת מִמִּצְרַיִם.
ד. אִישׁ מִמּוֹאָב שָׁמַע דָּבָר, וְהוּא שָׁמַר בַּת מִמִּצְרַיִם.

4. The sons walked on a road to the mountains and they crossed over to the city.

א. הַבֵּן הָלַךְ בְּדֶרֶךְ אֶל הֶהָרִים וְהוּא עָבַר לָעִיר.
ב. הַבַּת הָלְכָה בְּדֶרֶךְ אֶל הֶהָרִים וְהִיא עָבְרָה לָעִיר.
ג. הַמִּשְׁפָּחָה הָלְכָה בְּדֶרֶךְ אֶל הֶהָרִים וְהִיא עָבְרָה לָעִיר. ד. הַנָּשִׁים הָלְכוּ בְּדֶרֶךְ אֶל הֶהָרִים וְהֵנָּה עָבְרוּ לָעִיר. ה. הָעָם הָלַךְ בְּדֶרֶךְ אֶל הֶהָרִים וְהוּא עָבַר לָעִיר.

5. The daughter went to the house from the city, she listened to the father, and she stood in the house as a daughter.

א. הָאִישׁ הָלַךְ לַבַּיִת מִן הָעִיר, שָׁמַע לָאָב, וְהוּא עָמַד בַּבַּיִת כְּאִישׁ. ב. הַנָּשִׁים הָלְכוּ לַבַּיִת מִן הָעִיר, שָׁמְעוּ לָאָב, וְהֵנָּה עָמְדוּ בַּבַּיִת כְּנָשִׁים. ג. הָאֲנָשִׁים הָלְכוּ לַבַּיִת מִן הָעִיר, שָׁמְעוּ לָאָב, וְהֵם עָמְדוּ בַּבַּיִת

כַּאֲנָשִׁים. ד. הִיא הָלְכָה לַבַּיִת מִן הָעִיר, שָׁמְעָה לָאָב, וְהִיא עָמְדָה בַּבַּיִת כְּבַת.

6. The fathers heard women, and they crossed over from the land, and they went in the mountains.

א. הָאָב שָׁמַע נָשִׁים, וְהוּא עָבַר מִן הָאָרֶץ, וְהוּא הָלַךְ בֶּהָרִים. ב. הִיא שָׁמְעָה נָשִׁים, וְהִיא עָבְרָה מִן הָאָרֶץ, וְהִיא הָלְכָה בֶּהָרִים. ג. הִיא שָׁלְחָה נָשִׁים, וְהִיא עָבְרָה מִן הָאָרֶץ, וְהִיא הָלְכָה בֶּהָרִים. ד. הָאָב שָׁלַח נָשִׁים, וְהוּא עָבַר מִן הָאָרֶץ, וְהוּא הָלַךְ בֶּהָרִים.

Exercise 8

1. David ruled in Jerusalem. He remembered a woman in the land and he sent things to the woman. The woman remembered, and she went on the road to the city and to the king. They ruled in Jerusalem. 2. The nation crossed over from Egypt, it crossed over mountains and countries. It crossed over with the cattle and with the slaves, and it crossed over to the cities in Moab and it has stood there until today. 3. In the country stood a city, and in the city stood a house, and in the house stood a father and young women and slaves and cattle and things. The father went, the young women went, the slaves went, the cattle went, and the things stood there in the house. 4. The slaves listened to the man in Egypt, and they crossed over to the mountains with the things from the houses in Egypt. They walked on the road to Moab and they guarded things on the road. 5. Abraham, a man from Moab, went to Sarah, a woman from Egypt, and they crossed to Moab. The family from Egypt remembered and it sent slaves and cattle to Sarah and Abraham in Moab.

Chapter 7

Oral Review

1. The brother went to the land. The brothers went to the city. They crossed over to the city. The young women crossed over to the land. 2. A man sent an animal to Moab. Men sent animals to Moab. A woman sent a slave to Moab. Women sent slaves to Moab. 3. Daughters from Egypt crossed over to Jerusalem. Sons from Egypt crossed over to Jerusalem. Sons and daughters stood in Egypt. They crossed over to Egypt and they stood in Egypt. 4. On the road to the mountains stood a young man. On the road to the mountains stood a young man and a young woman. They stood and they heard animals in the mountains. On the way to the city, they remembered days in the mountains. 5. The king ruled in Jerusalem. He ruled in the city and the brothers ruled in the mountains. The king guarded people and the brothers guarded animals. They sent cattle to the city and he sent the people to the mountains.

Exercise 1

1. זָכַרְתָּ – you remembered, מָלַכְתָּ – you ruled
2. זָכַרְתְּ – you remembered, מָלַכְתְּ – you ruled
3. זָכַר – he remembered, מָלַךְ – he ruled
4. זָכְרָה – she remembered, מָלְכָה – she ruled
5. זָכַרְנוּ – we remembered, מָלַכְנוּ – we ruled
6. זְכַרְתֶּם – you remembered, מְלַכְתֶּם – you ruled
7. זְכַרְתֶּן – you remembered, מְלַכְתֶּן – you ruled
8. זָכְרוּ – they remembered, מָלְכוּ – they ruled
9. זָכְרוּ – they remembered, מָלְכוּ – they ruled

Exercise 2

אֲנִי יָשַׁבְתִּי, אַתָּה יָשַׁבְתָּ, אַתְּ יָשַׁבְתְּ, הוּא יָשַׁב, הִיא
יָשְׁבָה, אֲנַחְנוּ יָשַׁבְנוּ, אַתֶּם יְשַׁבְתֶּם, אַתֶּן יְשַׁבְתֶּן, הֵמָּה
יָשְׁבוּ, הֵנָּה יָשְׁבוּ

אֲנִי לָקַחְתִּי, אַתָּה לָקַחְתָּ, אַתְּ לָקַחְתְּ, הוּא לָקַח, הִיא
לָקְחָה, אֲנַחְנוּ לָקַחְנוּ, אַתֶּם לְקַחְתֶּם, אַתֶּן לְקַחְתֶּן, הֵמָּה
לָקְחוּ, הֵנָּה לָקְחוּ

Exercise 3

1. I walked, I remembered, I crossed over, I sat, I took, I ate, I said, I heard   2. you ruled (*m sg*), you stood, you guarded, you sent, you heard, you took, you said, you sat   3. you remembered (*f sg*), you sat, you ruled, you said, you stood, you ate, you heard, you guarded   4. he sent, he took, he said, he crossed over, he walked, he ate, he sat, he heard   5. she stood, she sent, she said, she crossed over, she remembered, she guarded, she took, she ate   6. we heard, we ate, we sent, we guarded, we took, we sat, we said, we crossed over   7. you ruled (*m pl*), you heard, you walked, you sent, you said, you took, you remembered, you stood   8. you sat (*f pl*), you sent, you ate, you remembered, you walked, you guarded, you took, you heard   9. they walked, they guarded, they crossed over, they heard, they sent, they stood, they ate, they ruled

Exercise 4

1. אַתֶּם   2. הֵם, הֵמָּה   3. הִיא   4. אַתֶּן   5. הוּא
6. הֵנָּה   7. אַתֶּם   8. הִיא   9. הֵם, הֵמָּה

Exercise 5

1. you heard (*m sg*), they heard, he heard, I heard , we heard, you heard (*m pl*), you heard (*f sg*), she heard   2. I ate, she ate, you ate (*m pl*), we ate, he ate, you ate (*f sg*), they ate, you ate (*m sg*)   3. they walked, you walked (*m pl*), I walked, you walked (*m sg*), she walked, we walked, you walked (*f sg*), he walked   4. you stood (*m pl*), we stood, he stood, they stood, you stood (*m sg*), she stood, you stood (*f sg*), I stood   5. you took (*f sg*), we took, she took, you took (*m pl*), they took, you took (*m sg*), he took, I took   6. he crossed over, you crossed over (*f sg*), you crossed over (*m pl*), she crossed over, I crossed over, you crossed over (*m sg*), we crossed over, they crossed over

Exercise 6

1. I stood in front of the mountain. We stood in front of the mountains.   2. You sat on the animal today. You (*pl*) sat on the animals today.   3. The woman ate bread from the house. The women ate bread from the houses.   4. I guarded a road from Jerusalem to Egypt. We guarded roads from the cities to the mountains.   5. The king sent bread to the servant. The kings sent things to the servants.   6. You remembered a young woman in the land and you went (to) there. You and David remembered a young woman in the land and you went (to) there.

Exercise 7

1. אֲנַחְנוּ, אֲנַחְנוּ, We listened to the father and we sat in the city.   2. אַתָּה, You said, "The family crossed over from Moab and it settled in Egypt."   3. אֲנִי, אַתָּה, You took from the bread in the house and I did not remember.   4. הֵמָּה, The sons ruled over the people, and they sent slaves to Jerusalem.   5. אַתֶּם, אֲנַחְנוּ, You crossed over roads and we walked on the roads.   6. הוּא, The man ate bread today, and he sat in front of the house.

Exercise 8

1. A. אָמְרוּ, The brothers said, "We guarded slaves in the city." B. אָמַרְתָּ, You said, "I guarded a slave in the city." C. אָמַרְתְּ, You said, "He guarded slaves in the land." D. אָמַרְנוּ, We said, "We guarded cattle in the mountain." E. אָמְרָה, The daughter said, "I guarded cities and lands as a king." 2. A. לָקַח, The man took brothers to the king and they stood there. B. לְקַחְתֶּם, You took bread to the servant in the house. C. לָקַחְנוּ, We took things to the people in the city. D. לָקְחוּ, Sarah and Ruth took cattle to Egypt. E. לָקַחְתְּ, You took bread and you ate there in front of the family. 3. A. אָכְלָה, אָכַלְנוּ, The animals ate in the mountains, and we sat and we ate in the city. B. אָכַלְתְּ, You ate bread in Jerusalem today, and you did not remember sons and daughters in the house. C. אָכַלְתִּי, I ate on the way to Moab, and I did not sit today. D. אָכַלְתָּ, אָכְלוּ, You ate today, and the young men did not eat. E. אָכְלוּ, אָכְלוּ, אָכְלוּ, The kings ate as kings today,

(Exercise 8 continued)

and the cattle ate as cattle, and the young men ate as animals.   4. A. עָבַרְתִּי, I did not cross over to Egypt, and I did not remember men there.   B. עָבְרוּ, The men crossed over from Egypt to Moab, and they took women and cattle from there.   C. עָבַר, A man crossed over to the land and he guarded animals there.   D. עָבַרְתָּ, You crossed over a road and you took a young woman for a wife.   E. עָבְרָה, Ruth crossed over to Moab and she resided there and did not remember a family in Jerusalem.

Exercise 9

1. You took bread from Jerusalem and you walked on the road to the mountain.

א. הוּא לָקַח לֶחֶם מִירוּשָׁלַם וְהוּא הָלַךְ בַּדֶּרֶךְ לָהָר.   ב. הֵמָּה לָקְחוּ לֶחֶם מִירוּשָׁלַם וְהֵמָּה הָלְכוּ בַּדֶּרֶךְ לָהָר.   ג. אָנֹכִי לָקַחְתִּי לֶחֶם מִירוּשָׁלַם וְאָנֹכִי הָלַכְתִּי בַּדֶּרֶךְ לָהָר.   ד. אַתְּ לָקַחְתְּ לֶחֶם מִירוּשָׁלַם וְאַתְּ הָלַכְתְּ בַּדֶּרֶךְ לָהָר.   ה. אֲנַחְנוּ לָקַחְנוּ לֶחֶם מִירוּשָׁלַם וַאֲנַחְנוּ הָלַכְנוּ בַּדֶּרֶךְ לָהָר.   ו. אַתָּה לָקַחְתָּ לֶחֶם מִירוּשָׁלַם וְאַתָּה הָלַכְתָּ בַּדֶּרֶךְ לָהָר.

2. I stood on the road in the mountains and I ate bread from the city and I remembered men there.

א. אַתְּ עָמַדְתְּ עַל הַדֶּרֶךְ בֶּהָרִים וְאַתְּ אָכַלְתְּ לֶחֶם מִן הָעִיר וְאַתְּ זָכַרְתְּ אֲנָשִׁים שָׁם.   ב. אֲנַחְנוּ עָמַדְנוּ עַל הַדֶּרֶךְ בֶּהָרִים וַאֲנַחְנוּ אָכַלְנוּ לֶחֶם מִן הָעִיר וַאֲנַחְנוּ זָכַרְנוּ אֲנָשִׁים שָׁם.   ג. הַבָּנִים עָמְדוּ עַל הַדֶּרֶךְ בֶּהָרִים וְהֵמָּה אָכְלוּ לֶחֶם מִן הָעִיר וְהֵמָּה זָכְרוּ אֲנָשִׁים שָׁם.   ד. שָׂרָה עָמְדָה עַל הַדֶּרֶךְ בֶּהָרִים וְהִיא אָכְלָה לֶחֶם מִן הָעִיר וְהִיא זָכְרָה אֲנָשִׁים שָׁם.   ה. אַתָּה עָמַדְתָּ עַל הַדֶּרֶךְ בֶּהָרִים וְאַתָּה אָכַלְתָּ לֶחֶם מִן הָעִיר וְאַתָּה זָכַרְתָּ אֲנָשִׁים שָׁם.

3. You said to the king: "I listened to the man and you did not listen to the man."

א. הוּא אָמַר לַמֶּלֶךְ: "שָׁמַעְתִּי לָאִישׁ וְאַתָּה לֹא שָׁמַעְתָּ לָאִישׁ."   ב. אַתֶּם אֲמַרְתֶּם לַמֶּלֶךְ: "שָׁמַעְנוּ לָאִישׁ וְאַתָּה לֹא שָׁמַעְתָּ לָאִישׁ."   ג. הָאַחִים אָמְרוּ לַמֶּלֶךְ: "שָׁמַעְנוּ לָאִישׁ וְאַתָּה לֹא שָׁמַעְתָּ לָאִישׁ."   ד. אֲנִי אָמַרְתִּי לַמֶּלֶךְ: "שָׁמַעְתִּי לָאִישׁ וְאַתָּה לֹא שָׁמַעְתָּ לָאִישׁ."

ה. אֲנַחְנוּ אָמַרְנוּ לַמֶּלֶךְ: "שָׁמַעְנוּ לָאִישׁ וְאַתָּה לֹא שָׁמַעְתָּ לָאִישׁ."

4. You crossed over from Jerusalem to Egypt today, and you did not settle there.

א. אֲנַחְנוּ עָבַרְנוּ מִירוּשָׁלַם אֶל מִצְרַיִם הַיּוֹם, וְלֹא יָשַׁבְנוּ שָׁם.   ב. הַמִּשְׁפָּחָה עָבְרָה מִירוּשָׁלַם אֶל מִצְרַיִם הַיּוֹם, וְלֹא יָשְׁבָה שָׁם.   ג. הָעָם עָבַר מִירוּשָׁלַם אֶל מִצְרַיִם הַיּוֹם, וְלֹא יָשַׁב שָׁם.   ד. הָאֲנָשִׁים עָבְרוּ מִירוּשָׁלַם אֶל מִצְרַיִם הַיּוֹם, וְלֹא יָשְׁבוּ שָׁם.   ה. אַתָּה עָבַרְתָּ מִירוּשָׁלַם אֶל מִצְרַיִם הַיּוֹם, וְלֹא יָשַׁבְתָּ שָׁם.   ו. אֲנִי עָבַרְתִּי מִירוּשָׁלַם אֶל מִצְרַיִם הַיּוֹם, וְלֹא יָשַׁבְתִּי שָׁם.   ז. הַנָּשִׁים עָבְרוּ מִירוּשָׁלַם אֶל מִצְרַיִם הַיּוֹם, וְלֹא יָשְׁבוּ שָׁם.

5. Abraham said to the children in Moab: "I crossed over to Jerusalem from the mountains and I ate there."

א. אָמַר אַבְרָהָם אֶל הַבָּנִים בְּמוֹאָב: "עָבַרְנוּ אֶל יְרוּשָׁלַם מִן הֶהָרִים וַאֲנַחְנוּ אָכַלְנוּ שָׁם."   ב. אָמַר אַבְרָהָם אֶל הַבָּנִים בְּמוֹאָב: "הוּא עָבַר אֶל יְרוּשָׁלַם מִן הֶהָרִים וְהוּא אָכַל שָׁם."   ג. אָמַר אַבְרָהָם אֶל הַבָּנִים בְּמוֹאָב: "הִיא עָבְרָה אֶל יְרוּשָׁלַם מִן הֶהָרִים וְהִיא אָכְלָה שָׁם."   ד. אָמַר אַבְרָהָם אֶל הַבָּנִים בְּמוֹאָב: "הֵמָּה עָבְרוּ אֶל יְרוּשָׁלַם מִן הֶהָרִים וְהֵמָּה אָכְלוּ שָׁם."

6. I said to the people: "I did not take bread from the slaves."

א. אֲנַחְנוּ אָמַרְנוּ אֶל הָעָם: "לֹא לָקַחְנוּ לֶחֶם מִן הָעֲבָדִים."   ב. אַתָּה אָמַרְתָּ אֶל הָעָם: "לֹא לָקַחְתִּי לֶחֶם מִן הָעֲבָדִים."   ג. הֵמָּה אָמְרוּ אֶל הָעָם: "לֹא לָקַחְנוּ לֶחֶם מִן הָעֲבָדִים."   ד. הוּא אָמַר אֶל הָעָם: "לֹא לָקַחְתִּי לֶחֶם מִן הָעֲבָדִים."   ה. אַתֶּם אֲמַרְתֶּם אֶל הָעָם: "לֹא לָקַחְנוּ לֶחֶם מִן הָעֲבָדִים."   ו. הִיא אָמְרָה אֶל הָעָם: "לֹא לָקַחְתִּי לֶחֶם מִן הָעֲבָדִים."   ז. אַתְּ אָמַרְתְּ אֶל הָעָם: "לֹא לָקַחְתִּי לֶחֶם מִן הָעֲבָדִים."

7. You listened to David and you sent daughters before the king.

א. אָנֹכִי שָׁמַעְתִּי לְדָוִד וְאָנֹכִי שָׁלַחְתִּי בָּנוֹת לִפְנֵי הַמֶּלֶךְ.   ב. הוּא שָׁמַע לְדָוִד וְהוּא שָׁלַח בָּנוֹת לִפְנֵי הַמֶּלֶךְ.   ג. הִיא שָׁמְעָה לְדָוִד וְהִיא שָׁלְחָה בָּנוֹת לִפְנֵי הַמֶּלֶךְ.   ד. הֵמָּה שָׁמְעוּ לְדָוִד וְהֵמָּה שָׁלְחוּ בָּנוֹת לִפְנֵי הַמֶּלֶךְ.

(Exercise 9 continued)

ה. אֲנַחְנוּ שָׁמַעְנוּ לְדָוִד וַאֲנַחְנוּ שָׁלַחְנוּ בָּנוֹת לִפְנֵי הַמֶּלֶךְ.

Exercise 10

1. I ruled over the people, and over the land, and I listened to the father.

A. אֲנִי מָלַכְתִּי עַל הָעָם. B. אַתָּה מָלַכְתָּ עַל הָעָם. C. אַתֶּם מְלַכְתֶּם עַל הָאָרֶץ. D. אַתֶּם מְלַכְתֶּם עַל הָאָרֶץ וְאַתֶּם שְׁמַעְתֶּם לָאָבוֹת. E. אַתְּ מְלַכְתְּ עַל הָאָרֶץ וְאַתְּ שְׁמַעְתְּ לְעָם.

2. We sent things to the children, and we did not send a thing to the family.

A. אֲנַחְנוּ שָׁלַחְנוּ דְּבָרִים לַבָּנִים. B. אֲנַחְנוּ לֹא שָׁלַחְנוּ דְּבָרִים לַבָּנִים. C. אַתֶּם לֹא שְׁלַחְתֶּם דְּבָרִים לַמִּשְׁפָּחָה. D. אֲנִי שָׁלַחְתִּי לֶחֶם לַנְּעָרִים, וְלֹא שָׁלַחְתִּי לֶחֶם לַנְּעָרוֹת. E. אַתְּ שָׁלַחַתְּ דְּבָרִים לַמִּשְׁפָּחָה, וְלֹא שָׁלַחַתְּ דְּבָר לַבָּנִים.

3. You said to the brother: "You stood before the people in the land."

A. אָמַרְתְּ לָאָח: "אֲנִי עָמַדְתִּי לִפְנֵי הָעָם בָּאָרֶץ." B. אָמַרְתִּי לָאָח: "אַתָּה עָמַדְתָּ לִפְנֵי הָעָם בָּעִיר." C. אָמַרְנוּ לָאָח: "אַתָּה עָמַדְתָּ לִפְנֵי הַמִּשְׁפָּחָה בַּבַּיִת." D. אָמְרוּ לְאִשָּׁה: "אַתְּ עָמַדְתְּ לִפְנֵי הָעָם." E. הִיא אָמְרָה לְאַבְרָהָם: "אֲנַחְנוּ עָמַדְנוּ לִפְנֵי הָעָם בְּמוֹאָב."

Exercise 11

Sue and Lou sat in the house and they said...
Sue: "Lou, you took bread from the house and you ate from the bread!"
Lou: "No, I did not take bread from the house! You took bread from the house!"
Sue: "No Lou, you took (it)!"
Lou: "You took (it)!"
Sue: "You!"
Lou: "You!"
The father heard and he said: "Sue, Lou did not take bread from the house. Lou, Sue did not take bread from the house. You did not take bread from the house. I took bread from the house!"
Sue and Lou: "Oh, you ate from the bread!" Sue and Lou sat there, and they did not say a word.

Chapter 8

Oral Review

1. I sat. I sat on the road from Moab to Egypt. 2. You ate. You ate today before the king. 3. You took. You took sons from the fathers. 4. He said. He said: "I did not remember a young woman from Jerusalem."
5. She sent. She did not send bread to the house.
6. We crossed over. We crossed over from the city to the mountains. 7. You stood. You stood on the land.
8. They took. They took animals from the fathers, and they did not say a word. 9. You stood on the mountain. You stood on the mountain and there you remembered a woman. 10. He guarded cattle and he ate bread. We guarded cattle and we ate bread. 11. She crossed over from Egypt and she walked to Moab. They crossed over from Egypt and they walked to Moab.

Exercise 1

1. I, a voice 2. D, the voice 3. D, the war 4. I, a judgement 5. D, the gates 6. I, a field 7. I, water 8. D, the water 9. I, a gate 10. D, the fields 11. D, Jerusalem 12. D, the mountains 13. D, Egypt 14. I, a people 15. I, a word 16. D, the animals 17. I, a country 18. D, the city 19. D, Ruth 20. D, the family 21. D, the thing 22. I, a woman 23. D, David 24. D, Moab

Exercise 2

1. The father crossed over a field. 2. The father crossed over the field. 3. The men guarded land. 4. The men guarded the land 5. The men guarded Moab. 6. You ate bread. 7. You ate the bread. 8. We remembered a woman. 9. We remembered Sarah. 10. We remembered Sarah and Ruth. 11. I sent brothers. 12. I sent the brothers.

Exercise 3

1. You took water from the house. 2. אֵת, The slaves sent the cattle to the field. 3. אֵת, The father heard the voice in the mountain. 4. אֵת, אֵת, The young men remembered Abraham and the woman. 5. A son ate bread and he stood and he walked. 6. אֵת, אֵת, We passed through the gates and the roads. 7. You were the men who sat among the fields.

Exercise 4

מ.ל.ך -- אֲנִי מָלַכְתִּי, אַתָּה מָלַכְתָּ, אַתְּ מָלַכְתְּ, הוּא מָלַךְ, הִיא מָלְכָה, אֲנַחְנוּ מָלַכְנוּ, אַתֶּם מְלַכְתֶּם, אַתֶּן מְלַכְתֶּן, הֵם מָלְכוּ   ה.י.ה -- אֲנִי הָיִיתִי, אַתָּה הָיִיתָ,

(Exercise 4 continued)

אַתְּ הָיִית, הוּא הָיָה, הִיא הָיְתָה, אֲנַחְנוּ הָיִינוּ, אַתֶּן הֱיִיתֶן, הֵם הָיוּ

Exercise 5

1. I guarded, I was, I did, I saw, I walked, I remembered, I heard   2. you guarded (*m sg*), you were, you did, you saw, you stood, you sent, you crossed over   3. you guarded (*f sg*), you were, you did, you saw, you ruled, you took, you said   4. he guarded, he was, he did, he saw, he sat, he heard, he ate, he remembered   5. she guarded, she was, she did, she saw, she stood, she took, she remembered   6. we guarded, we were, we did, we saw, we sent, we ate, we crossed over   7. you guarded (*m pl*), you were, you did, you saw, you ruled, you said, you heard   8. they guarded, they were, they ruled, they did, they saw, they walked, they took, they sat

Exercise 6

1. A. רָאִיתִי, I saw the road. B. רָאִיתָ, What did you see today? C. רָאִית, You saw Ruth. D. רָאָה, He saw young women from the family. E. רָאֲתָה, She saw a woman on the gate. F. רָאִינוּ, We saw David. G. רְאִיתֶם, You saw the land. H. רָאוּ, They saw Moab. 2. A. הָיָה, The servant was in the house. B. הָיִיתָ, You were in the city today. C. הָיְתָה, She was with the slaves in the field. D. הָיִיתִי, I was the king in Moab. E. הָיוּ, There were daughters in front of the gates. F. הָיִינוּ, We were the young men in Jerusalem. 3. A. עָשִׂיתָ, You made bread in front of the people. B. עָשׂוּ, The kings made war with the people from Egypt. C. עָשִׂינוּ, We made the things that we sent. D. עָשְׂתָה, There was a war in the house, and Sarah made a judgement between the father and the daughter.

Exercise 7

1. I walked between the gates to the city, and I was there until today.   2. There was a father and a daughter in the house. The daughter said to the father: "What did you hear in the city?"   3. You were in the land, and you ate the bread and you took the things. 4. I ruled over the land from the mountains until (to) the water, and I made a judgement there.   5. You did what you said, and we did not do what we said.   6. I took a young woman for a wife and she did not sit in the house. She walked on the road from the house to the father. I did not see the young woman until today. 7. The children stood on the mountain, and they heard a voice, and they did not see a man.

Exercise 8

1. Before the war, there was no bread in the land, and we ate the cattle in the fields.

א. לִפְנֵי הַמִּלְחָמָה, לֹא הָיָה לֶחֶם בָּאָרֶץ, וְאַתָּה אָכַלְתָּ אֶת הַבְּהֵמוֹת בַּשָּׂדוֹת. ב. לִפְנֵי הַמִּלְחָמָה, לֹא הָיָה לֶחֶם בָּאָרֶץ, וְהֵם אָכְלוּ אֶת הַבְּהֵמוֹת בַּשָּׂדוֹת. ג. לִפְנֵי הַמִּלְחָמָה, לֹא הָיָה לֶחֶם בָּאָרֶץ, וַאֲנִי אָכַלְתִּי אֶת הַבְּהֵמוֹת בַּשָּׂדוֹת. ד. לִפְנֵי הַמִּלְחָמָה, לֹא הָיָה לֶחֶם בָּאָרֶץ, וְאַתְּ אָכַלְתְּ אֶת הַבְּהֵמוֹת בַּשָּׂדוֹת. ה. לִפְנֵי הַמִּלְחָמָה, לֹא הָיָה לֶחֶם בָּאָרֶץ, וְהוּא אָכַל אֶת הַבְּהֵמוֹת בַּשָּׂדוֹת.

2. You sat with the brothers in the field and you saw the young men who guarded the cattle.

א. הוּא יָשַׁב עִם הָאַחִים בַּשָּׂדֶה וְהוּא רָאָה אֶת הַנְּעָרִים אֲשֶׁר שָׁמְרוּ אֶת הַבְּהֵמוֹת. ב. אֲנַחְנוּ יָשַׁבְנוּ עִם הָאַחִים בַּשָּׂדֶה וַאֲנַחְנוּ רָאִינוּ אֶת הַנְּעָרִים אֲשֶׁר שָׁמְרוּ אֶת הַבְּהֵמוֹת. ג. אַתָּה יָשַׁבְתָּ עִם הָאַחִים בַּשָּׂדֶה וְאַתָּה רָאִיתָ אֶת הַנְּעָרִים אֲשֶׁר שָׁמְרוּ אֶת הַבְּהֵמוֹת. ד. הַבַּת יָשְׁבָה עִם הָאַחִים בַּשָּׂדֶה וְהִיא רָאֲתָה אֶת הַנְּעָרִים אֲשֶׁר שָׁמְרוּ אֶת הַבְּהֵמוֹת. ה. הֵם יָשְׁבוּ עִם הָאַחִים בַּשָּׂדֶה וְהֵם רָאוּ אֶת הַנְּעָרִים אֲשֶׁר שָׁמְרוּ אֶת הַבְּהֵמוֹת. ו. אַתֶּם יְשַׁבְתֶּם עִם הָאַחִים בַּשָּׂדֶה וְאַתֶּם רְאִיתֶם אֶת הַנְּעָרִים אֲשֶׁר שָׁמְרוּ אֶת הַבְּהֵמוֹת.

3. David ruled over the people and he made war with the kings in Egypt, and he was like a father to the people.

א. אֲנַחְנוּ מָלַכְנוּ עַל הָעָם וַאֲנַחְנוּ עָשִׂינוּ מִלְחָמָה עִם הַמְּלָכִים בְּמִצְרַיִם, וַאֲנַחְנוּ הָיִינוּ כְּאָבוֹת לָעָם. ב. הַמְּלָכִים מָלְכוּ עַל הָעָם וְהֵם עָשׂוּ מִלְחָמָה עִם הַמְּלָכִים בְּמִצְרַיִם, וְהֵם הָיוּ כְּאָבוֹת לָעָם. ג. אַתֶּם מְלַכְתֶּם עַל הָעָם וְאַתֶּם עֲשִׂיתֶם מִלְחָמָה עִם הַמְּלָכִים בְּמִצְרַיִם, וְאַתֶּם הֱיִיתֶם כְּאָבוֹת לָעָם. ד. אַתָּה מָלַכְתָּ עַל הָעָם וְאַתָּה עָשִׂיתָ מִלְחָמָה עִם הַמְּלָכִים בְּמִצְרַיִם, וְאַתָּה הָיִיתָ כְּאָב לָעָם. ה. אָנֹכִי מָלַכְתִּי עַל הָעָם וְאָנֹכִי עָשִׂיתִי מִלְחָמָה עִם הַמְּלָכִים בְּמִצְרַיִם, וְאָנֹכִי הָיִיתִי כְּאָב לָעָם.

4. There was water between Moab and Egypt.

(Exercise 8 continued)

א. הָיוּ מִלְחָמוֹת בֵּין מוֹאָב וּבֵין מִצְרַיִם. ב. הָיָה (הָיְתָה) דֶּרֶךְ בֵּין מוֹאָב וּבֵין מִצְרַיִם. ג. הָיְתָה מִלְחָמָה בֵּין מוֹאָב וּבֵין מִצְרַיִם. ד. הָיָה שָׂדֶה בֵּין מוֹאָב וּבֵין מִצְרַיִם.

5. "What did you do today?" "I sent the things which I took from the house."

א. "מָה הֵמָּה עָשׂוּ הַיּוֹם?" "הֵמָּה שָׁלְחוּ אֶת הַדְּבָרִים אֲשֶׁר לָקְחוּ מִן הַבַּיִת." ב. "מָה הָאִשָּׁה עָשְׂתָה הַיּוֹם?" "הִיא שָׁלְחָה אֶת הַדְּבָרִים אֲשֶׁר לָקְחָה מִן הַבַּיִת." ג. "מָה אַתֶּם עֲשִׂיתֶם הַיּוֹם?" "שָׁלַחְנוּ אֶת הַדְּבָרִים אֲשֶׁר לָקַחְנוּ מִן הַבַּיִת." ד. "מָה אֲנַחְנוּ עָשִׂינוּ הַיּוֹם?" "שָׁלַחְנוּ אֶת הַדְּבָרִים אֲשֶׁר לָקַחְנוּ מִן הַבַּיִת." ה. "מָה הוּא עָשָׂה הַיּוֹם?" "הוּא שָׁלַח אֶת הַדְּבָרִים אֲשֶׁר לָקַח מִן הַבַּיִת."

6. I walked from the mountains to the city where I resided, and I saw things that I did not remember.

א. הָלַכְתָּ מִן הֶהָרִים אֶל הָעִיר אֲשֶׁר יָשַׁבְתָּ שָׁם, וּדְבָרִים רָאִיתָ אֲשֶׁר לֹא זָכַרְתָּ. ב. הֵם הָלְכוּ מִן הֶהָרִים אֶל הָעִיר אֲשֶׁר יָשְׁבוּ שָׁם, וּדְבָרִים רָאוּ אֲשֶׁר לֹא זָכְרוּ. ג. הָלַכְנוּ מִן הֶהָרִים אֶל הָעִיר אֲשֶׁר יָשַׁבְנוּ שָׁם, וּדְבָרִים רָאִינוּ אֲשֶׁר לֹא זָכַרְנוּ. ד. הָלְכָה מִן הֶהָרִים אֶל הָעִיר אֲשֶׁר יָשְׁבָה שָׁם, וּדְבָרִים רָאֲתָה אֲשֶׁר לֹא זָכְרָה. ה. הוּא הָלַךְ מִן הֶהָרִים אֶל הָעִיר אֲשֶׁר יָשַׁב שָׁם, וּדְבָרִים רָאָה אֲשֶׁר לֹא זָכַר. ו. הֲלַכְתֶּם מִן הֶהָרִים אֶל הָעִיר אֲשֶׁר יְשַׁבְתֶּם שָׁם, וּדְבָרִים רְאִיתֶם אֲשֶׁר לֹא זְכַרְתֶּם.

Exercise 9

1. You were in the city and you saw the war and you made a judgement.

A. אַתֶּם הֱיִיתֶם בָּעִיר. B. אַתֶּם רְאִיתֶם אֶת הַמִּלְחָמָה וְאַתֶּם עֲשִׂיתֶם מִשְׁפָּט. C. אַתֶּם הֱיִיתֶם בַּמִּלְחָמָה בָּעִיר. D. אַתֶּם רְאִיתֶם אֶת הַשְּׁעָרִים וְאֶת הָעִיר. E. אַתֶּם לֹא עֲשִׂיתֶם מִלְחָמָה בָּעִיר.

2. The people who stood in front of the gate said: "David was a king in Moab, and he ruled over the people until today."

A. הָעָם עָמַד לִפְנֵי הַשַּׁעַר. B. דָּוִד הָיָה מֶלֶךְ, וְהוּא מָלַךְ בְּמוֹאָב עַד הַיּוֹם. C. אָמַר הָעָם: "דָּוִד הַמֶּלֶךְ עָמַד לִפְנֵי הַשַּׁעַר וְהוּא שָׁמַר יְרוּשָׁלַם." D. דָּוִד אֲשֶׁר מָלַךְ עַל הָעָם עַד הַיּוֹם, הָלַךְ לִירוּשָׁלַם וְהוּא לָקַח עֲבָדִים. E. אָמַר דָּוִד: "הָעָם אֲשֶׁר עָמַד לִפְנֵי הַמֶּלֶךְ, יָשַׁב בִּירוּשָׁלַם וְהוּא שָׁמַר אֶת הַשְּׁעָרִים שָׁם."

A TALL TALE: The Young Man Who Said Wolf

In those days the people who resided in the city sent the young man David to the field. David guarded the cattle in the field.

The people said to David: "On other days the wolves ate the cattle and there was famine in the land."

David listened to the people in the city, and every day he took the cattle to the field. He guarded the cattle from the wolves and he remembered what the people in the city had said. David stood in the field...he sat in the field...he did not see wolves and he did not hear wolves. He heard the cattle. David said words to the cattle because there were no people there.

The cattle said: "Moo...moo..."

In the field there were cattle and there were no wolves.

Then David did a bad thing. He crossed over from the field to the city. He went to the people.

He said to the people: "Wolf! Wolf!"

The people from the city went with David to the field and they did not see a wolf there.

David said: "Oh! The wolf was in the field and she went."

The people crossed over from the field to the city.

On another day David took the cattle to the field. There were no wolves in the field. David went to the people in the city and he said: "Wolf! A wolf in the field!"

The people said: "What did you say? You were in the field and you saw a wolf?"

David said: "Wolf! A wolf in the field!"

The people went with David to the field and they did not see a wolf there. The people did not say a thing to David. They crossed over from the field to the city.

On another day David stood and he guarded the cattle in the field. He did not hear a thing. Then David saw wolves. The wolves were in the field!! And they were eating from the cattle there. David crossed over from the field to the city.

9

(A TALL TALE continued)

And he said to the people: "Wolves! Wolves! Wolves in the field!"

The people stood there and they did not go.

David said to the people: "Today, today I saw wolves in the field! The wolves were eating from the cattle!"

The people remembered what David said on other days.

They said to David: "We remembered that you said: 'Wolf! Wolf!', and then we crossed over to the field and the wolves were not there."

The people did not go with David to the field and then the wolves ate the cattle.

There was a famine in the land...

Chapter 9

Oral Review

1. Sue and Lou sat in the house, and the father was not in the house.   2. And in the house there was bread which the father had made.   3. Sue and Lou saw the bread and they remembered what the father had said. 4. He had said: "I made the bread for the king."   5. "I did not make the bread for Sue and Lou."   6. Sue saw the bread and Lou saw Sue.   7. Lou said: "No, Sue! The bread was for the king, and the bread was not for a son and a daughter!"   8. Sue saw the bread and she took the bread.   9. Lou said: "No! No!"   10. Sue ate from the bread.   11. Sue said: "Mmm..."   12. Lou said: "The father said no, Sue!"   13. Sue ate the bread, until there was no bread.   14. She said: "Mfmfmfmf..." 15. Lou said: "What, Sue? What did you say?" 16. Sue said: "Achachachach!" And Sue was sick. 17. The father went to the house and he said to Sue. 18. "I made the bread for the king and you ate the bread, and you were sick."   19. Lou and the father went to the city and they ate with the king.   20. Sue sat in the house, and she was sick.

Exercise 1

1. a slave of a king   2. the slave of the king   3. a name of a city   4. the name of the city   5. the name of Jerusalem   6. a hand of a master   7. the hand of the master   8. the hand of Moses   9. a heart of a young man   10. the heart of the young man   11. the head of the cattle   12. a man of peace   13. the judgement of the master   14. the hand of Sarah   15. the people of the land   16. a land of peace   17. the peace of the heart   18. the heart of the brother   19. the brother of the family   20. a family of a man   21. the master of everything   22. the king of Moab   23. all of the field 24. a field of war   25. the voice of the nations   26. the ancestor of the woman   27. the name of the gate

Exercise 2

1. the head of the city of Moses   2. the voice of the father of Abraham   3. the heart of the wife of David 4. the name of the son of the king of Egypt   5. the cattle of the house of the daughter of Abraham   6. all of the judgement of the land

Exercise 3

1.אִישׁ הַר   2.אִישׁ הָהָר   3.שַׁעַר הָעִיר   4.דְּבַר
שָׁלוֹם   5.שֵׁם הָעֶבֶד   6.אֵשֶׁת מֹשֶׁה   7.קוֹל הַבַּת
8.אֲבִי הַבָּנִים   9.שְׂדֵה אַבְרָהָם   10.מִשְׁפַּחַת הָאַחִים
11.בֵּית הַמֶּלֶךְ   12.כָּל הַנָּשִׁים

Exercise 4

1. The son of the man remembered the water in Moab.
2. The daughter of the man remembered everything.
3. The father of the sons took the sons in hand.
4. The family of David crossed over near the house of Abraham.   5. The head of all the slaves sent the woman in front of the master.   6. Who was the wife of Adam? The wife of Adam was Sarah.   7. What was the name of the father of Ruth? The name of the father of Ruth was David.

Exercise 5

1.הָלַךְ   2.עָבַר   3.שָׁלַח   4.שָׁמְעָה   5.אָכְלָה
6.מָלַךְ

Exercise 6

1. I remembered, I did, I went up, I saw, I knew, I said, I ruled   2. you sent (*m sg*), you did, you went up, you were, you knew, you said, you ruled   3. you sat (*f sg*), you did, you went up, you saw, you knew, you walked, you heard   4. he guarded, he did, he went up, he was, he knew, he took, he sat, he heard   5. she ruled, she did, she went up, she saw, she knew, she heard, she remembered   6. we stood, we did, we went up, we were, we knew, we ate, we guarded   7. you said (*m pl*), you did, you went up, you saw, you knew, you took, you walked   8. they crossed over, they went up, they were, they sent, they knew, they ate, they took, they remembered

Exercise 7

1. A. יָדַע, Adam knew that the cattle stood next to the water. B. יָדַעְתִּי, I knew the name of the man who sat next to the family. C. יָדַע, He knew everything about all of the men in the house. D. יָדַעְנוּ, We knew all of the nations who went to the war. E. יְדַעְתֶּם, You knew the voice of the man that you heard on the road.

(Exercise 7 continued)

2. A. עָלָה, The father of Sarah went up on the mountain as far as the top of the mountain. B. עָלְתָה, The daughter of Abraham went up from the field to the gate of Jerusalem with all of the family. C. עָלִינוּ, We went up on the mountain and we guarded the road all day. D. עָלִיתָ, You went up to the city with Moses because there was no bread in the house. E. עָלִיתִי, I went up from Egypt and I saw the land of Moab.

Exercise 8

Next to the gate Adam said to Sarah: "What did we do? We went up from the field to the city, and everything was there. And we saw things which were not in the field, and we did not know what the things were. We listened to all of the people in the city, and also we saw the king! We ate the bread of the city, and it was not like the bread of the field. Also we saw women in the city who were not like women in the field. We settled in the city until today!"

A. אָמַר אָדָם אֶל שָׂרָה: "עָלִינוּ לָעִיר וְשָׁם יָשַׁבְנוּ."
B. הַכֹּל הָיָה בָּעִיר עַל יַד הַשַּׁעַר. C. אֲנַחְנוּ רָאִינוּ דְּבָרִים בַּשָּׂדֶה וְלֹא יָדַעְנוּ מָה הָיוּ הַדְּבָרִים.
D. אָכַלְנוּ אֶת לֶחֶם הָעִיר וְגַם רָאִינוּ אֶת הַכֹּל שָׁם.
E. כָּל הָאֲנָשִׁים בָּעִיר לֹא הָיוּ כַּאֲנָשִׁים בִּירוּשָׁלַם.
F. הָאֲנָשִׁים בָּעִיר רָאוּ אֶת הַנָּשִׁים אֲשֶׁר הָיוּ בַּשָּׂדוֹת. G. מִי רָאִיתָ? רָאִיתִי אֶת הַמֶּלֶךְ וְגַם כָּל בֵּית הַמֶּלֶךְ. H. אֲנִי גַּם זָכַרְתִּי אֶת מֶלֶךְ מוֹאָב וְהוּא לֹא הָיָה כְּמֶלֶךְ מִצְרַיִם.

Exercise 9

1. I walked with the family between the gates on the road of Egypt, and I knew that there was bread and water on the road.

A. אַתָּה הָלַכְתָּ עִם הַמִּשְׁפָּחָה בֵּין הַשְּׁעָרִים בְּדֶרֶךְ מִצְרַיִם, וְאַתָּה יָדַעְתָּ כִּי הָיוּ בַּדֶּרֶךְ לֶחֶם וּמַיִם.
B. מֹשֶׁה הָלַךְ עִם הַמִּשְׁפָּחָה בֵּין הַשְּׁעָרִים בְּדֶרֶךְ מִצְרַיִם, וְהוּא יָדַע כִּי הָיוּ בַּדֶּרֶךְ לֶחֶם וּמַיִם.
C. אֲנַחְנוּ הָלַכְנוּ עִם הַמִּשְׁפָּחָה בֵּין הַשְּׁעָרִים בְּדֶרֶךְ מִצְרַיִם, וַאֲנַחְנוּ יָדַעְנוּ כִּי הָיוּ בַּדֶּרֶךְ לֶחֶם וּמַיִם.
D. אַתֶּם הֲלַכְתֶּם עִם הַמִּשְׁפָּחָה בֵּין הַשְּׁעָרִים בְּדֶרֶךְ מִצְרַיִם, וְאַתֶּם יְדַעְתֶּם כִּי הָיוּ בַּדֶּרֶךְ לֶחֶם וּמַיִם.
E. הֵם הָלְכוּ עִם הַמִּשְׁפָּחָה בֵּין הַשְּׁעָרִים בְּדֶרֶךְ מִצְרַיִם, וְהֵם יָדְעוּ כִּי הָיוּ בַּדֶּרֶךְ לֶחֶם וּמַיִם. F. הִיא

הָלְכָה עִם הַמִּשְׁפָּחָה בֵּין הַשְּׁעָרִים בְּדֶרֶךְ מִצְרַיִם, וְהִיא יָדְעָה כִּי הָיוּ בַּדֶּרֶךְ לֶחֶם וּמַיִם.

2. The servant of the brother ate all of the bread in the house, until the brother sent the servant from there.

A. עֶבֶד הַנָּשִׁים אָכַל אֶת כָּל הַלֶּחֶם בַּבַּיִת, עַד אֲשֶׁר הַנָּשִׁים שָׁלְחוּ אֶת הָעֶבֶד מִשָּׁם. B. עֶבֶד הָאֲדוֹנִים אָכַל אֶת כָּל הַלֶּחֶם בַּבַּיִת, עַד אֲשֶׁר הָאֲדוֹנִים שָׁלְחוּ אֶת הָעֶבֶד מִשָּׁם. C. עֶבֶד שָׂרָה אָכַל אֶת כָּל הַלֶּחֶם בַּבַּיִת, עַד אֲשֶׁר שָׂרָה שָׁלְחָה אֶת הָעֶבֶד מִשָּׁם.
D. עֶבֶד אַבְרָהָם אָכַל אֶת כָּל הַלֶּחֶם בַּבַּיִת, עַד אֲשֶׁר אַבְרָהָם שָׁלַח אֶת הָעֶבֶד מִשָּׁם.

3. You went up from the city as far as the house of Abraham among the mountains, and you did not cross over from there because everything was like a house of a king there.

A. אָנֹכִי עָלִיתִי מִן הָעִיר עַד בֵּית אַבְרָהָם בֵּין הֶהָרִים, וְלֹא עָבַרְתִּי מִשָּׁם כִּי הַכֹּל הָיָה כְּבֵית מֶלֶךְ שָׁם.
B. הֵמָּה עָלוּ מִן הָעִיר עַד בֵּית אַבְרָהָם בֵּין הֶהָרִים, וְלֹא עָבְרוּ מִשָּׁם כִּי הַכֹּל הָיָה כְּבֵית מֶלֶךְ שָׁם.
C. אֲנַחְנוּ עָלִינוּ מִן הָעִיר עַד בֵּית אַבְרָהָם בֵּין הֶהָרִים, וְלֹא עָבַרְנוּ מִשָּׁם כִּי הַכֹּל הָיָה כְּבֵית מֶלֶךְ שָׁם.
D. אַתָּה עָלִיתָ מִן הָעִיר עַד בֵּית אַבְרָהָם בֵּין הֶהָרִים, וְלֹא עָבַרְתָּ מִשָּׁם כִּי הַכֹּל הָיָה כְּבֵית מֶלֶךְ שָׁם.
E. הַמִּשְׁפָּחָה עָלְתָה מִן הָעִיר עַד בֵּית אַבְרָהָם בֵּין הֶהָרִים, וְלֹא עָבְרָה מִשָּׁם כִּי הַכֹּל הָיָה כְּבֵית מֶלֶךְ שָׁם. F. דָּוִד עָלָה מִן הָעִיר עַד בֵּית אַבְרָהָם בֵּין הֶהָרִים, וְלֹא עָבַר מִשָּׁם כִּי הַכֹּל הָיָה כְּבֵית מֶלֶךְ שָׁם.

4. Between the nation of Moab and the nation of Egypt there was peace, and you crossed over on the road to Egypt and you ate bread with the people there.

A. בֵּין עַם מוֹאָב וּבֵין עַם מִצְרַיִם הָיָה שָׁלוֹם, וְעִם הָאָרֶץ עָבַר בַּדֶּרֶךְ אֶל מִצְרַיִם וְעִם הָאָרֶץ אָכַל לֶחֶם עִם הָאֲנָשִׁים שָׁם. B. בֵּין עַם מוֹאָב וּבֵין עַם מִצְרַיִם הָיָה שָׁלוֹם, וַאֲנִי עָבַרְתִּי בַּדֶּרֶךְ אֶל מִצְרַיִם וַאֲנִי אָכַלְתִּי לֶחֶם עִם הָאֲנָשִׁים שָׁם. C. בֵּין עַם מוֹאָב וּבֵין עַם מִצְרַיִם הָיָה שָׁלוֹם, וּמִשְׁפַּחַת אָחִי דָּוִד עָבְרָה בַּדֶּרֶךְ אֶל מִצְרַיִם וְהַמִּשְׁפָּחָה אָכְלָה לֶחֶם עִם הָאֲנָשִׁים שָׁם. D. בֵּין עַם מוֹאָב וּבֵין עַם מִצְרַיִם הָיָה שָׁלוֹם, וַאֲנַחְנוּ עָבַרְנוּ בַּדֶּרֶךְ אֶל מִצְרַיִם וַאֲנַחְנוּ אָכַלְנוּ לֶחֶם

(Exercise 9 continued)

ה. בֵּין עַם מוֹאָב וּבֵין עַם מִצְרַיִם   עִם הָאֲנָשִׁים שָׁם.
הָיָה שָׁלוֹם, וְהָאָבוֹת עָבְרוּ בַּדֶּרֶךְ אֶל מִצְרַיִם וְהֵם
אָכְלוּ לֶחֶם עִם הָאֲנָשִׁים שָׁם.

5. Who was the head of the city, and what did he do?

מִי הָיָה אֲדוֹן הַכֹּל, וּמָה עָשָׂה הוּא?   ב. מִי הָיְתָה בַּת
אָדָם, וּמָה עָשְׂתָה הִיא?   ג. מִי הָיוּ הָאַחִים, וּמָה עָשׂוּ
הֵמָה?   ד. מִי הָיוּ הַמִּשְׁפָּחוֹת, וּמָה עָשׂוּ הֵנָּה?

6. "Who went up between the gates as far as the field of
Egypt?" "I went up to there, and I made a judgement."

א. "מִי עָלָה בֵּין הַשְּׁעָרִים עַד שְׂדֵה מִצְרַיִם?" "אַתְּ
עָלִית לְשָׁם, וְאַתְּ עָשִׂית מִשְׁפָּט."   ב. "מִי עָלָה בֵּין
הַשְּׁעָרִים עַד שְׂדֵה מִצְרַיִם?" "מֹשֶׁה וּבֶן אַבְרָהָם עָלוּ
לְשָׁם, וְהֵם עָשׂוּ מִשְׁפָּט."   ג. "מִי עָלָה בֵּין הַשְּׁעָרִים
עַד שְׂדֵה מִצְרַיִם?" "אֲנַחְנוּ עָלִינוּ לְשָׁם, וַאֲנַחְנוּ עָשִׂינוּ
מִשְׁפָּט."   ד. "מִי עָלָה בֵּין הַשְּׁעָרִים עַד שְׂדֵה
מִצְרַיִם?" "אַתָּה עָלִיתָ לְשָׁם, וְאַתָּה עָשִׂיתָ מִשְׁפָּט."
ה. "מִי עָלָה בֵּין הַשְּׁעָרִים עַד שְׂדֵה מִצְרַיִם?" "בַּת
רֹאשׁ הָעֲבָדִים עָלְתָה לְשָׁם, וְהִיא עָשְׂתָה מִשְׁפָּט."

A TALL TALE: A Love Story

There was a king who ruled in Jerusalem. Every man
in the city listened to the voice of (obeyed) the king, and
also he was lord of every man in the land. The people
in the land did everything that the king said. In the
house of the king there was everything...but there was
not a woman there because the king had not taken a
young woman for a wife. And also there were no sons
and daughters in the house of the king.

The king walked in Jerusalem every day and he saw
young women there, and he had not taken a young
woman from Jerusalem for a wife. Then he crossed
over from Jerusalem to all of the land. He went up
among the mountains, and also passed near the water,
and also went to all of the cities in the land. The king
saw young women on the mountains, and also near the
water, and also in all of the cities, and he did not take
a young woman from the mountains, and he did not take
a young woman who resided (lived) near the water, and
he did not take a young woman from the cities for a
wife.

The king said: "What did I do? I saw all of the young
women in the land, and I have not seen a young woman
for me."

There was a day on which (when) the king was sitting
in the house in Jerusalem, and from the house he saw a
young woman who walked on the road in front of the
house. The heart of the king went up.

He said: "Who did I see?"

The king went to the road which was in front of the
house, and he did not see the young woman on the road.
The king walked in all of Jerusalem, and the young
woman was not there.

The king said to the servants: "Who did know the name
of the young woman? And who did know the house of
the young woman? Who did know the father of the
young woman?"

And there was not a servant among all of the servants
who knew the name of the young woman and the house
of the young woman and the father of the young
woman.

The king walked in Jerusalem all day and there was no
peace in the head of the king. And there was war in
the heart of the king. Then the king sat down next to
the road.

Then from among the houses the king heard a voice.

The head of the king went up, and he saw a young
woman between the houses, and the heart of the king
went up, because she was the young woman! The king
took the hand of the young woman, and she took the
hand of the king, and they walked to the house of the
king. And he took the young woman for a wife, and
they lived in the house of the king with sons and
daughters until today.

Chapter 10

Oral Review

1. Who knew the name of the man who crossed over to
Jerusalem? I knew the name of the man who crossed
over to Jerusalem. 2. What did the head of the land
say to the lord of the slaves in Egypt? The head of the
land said to the lord of the slaves: "I heard the voice
of the slaves." 3. Who went up to the heart of the
mountains because there was war in the city? Moses
and I went up to the heart of the mountains because
there was war in the city. 4. What did the father of the
house send to the king? The father of the house sent a
word of peace to the house of the king. 5. Who saw all
of the people who sat in the house next to the field of
Moses? The young man of the king saw all of the people
who resided in the house next to the field of Moses.
6. What did I do with all of the cattle which were in
front of the gate of the city? I ate all of the cattle which
were in front of the gate of the city. 7. Who stood
between the father of the house and the daughter of the
house? The woman of the house stood there and she
guarded over the daughter. 8. Who took the hand of

(Oral Review continued)

the young woman in front of the brother of David? Adam took the hand of the young woman and also the heart of the young woman there in front of the brother of David.   9. Who crossed over to the city of peace and who heard the voice of the lord of everything? Moses crossed over to the city of peace and also heard the voice of the lord of everything.   10. What did the people of the land remember on the road to the mountain of Egypt? The people of the land remembered that there was no water on the road and also not in the mountains.

Exercise 1

1. a man of a place, the man of the place, men of a place, the men of the place   2. the eye of Adam, the eye of Moses, the eyes of Adam, the eyes of Moses   3. a chief of cities, the chief of the cities, chiefs of cities, the chiefs of the cities   4. a house of a desert, the house of the desert, houses of desert, the houses of the desert   5. a family of a priest, the family of the priest, families of a priest, the families of the priest   6. a soul of a brother, the soul of Jacob, the faces of the brother, the faces of Jacob

Exercise 2

1. to the mountain of the desert   2. to the mountains of the desert   3. from the hand of Moses   4. from the hands of Moses   5. in the eyes of Rachel   6. as the tents of Egypt   7. in the days of the kings   8. with a heart of gold   9. for the master of everything   10. to the place of the war   11. from the women of Jacob   12. for the vessels of the tent

Exercise 3

4. בְּנֵי הַשַּׂר   3. בְּנֵי שַׂר   2. בֶּן הַשַּׂר   1. בֶּן שַׂר

7. אָהֳלֵי הַמָּקוֹם   6. מְקוֹם הָאֹהָלִים   5. בְּנֵי הַשָּׂרִים

10. נֶפֶשׁ רָחֵל   9. נַפְשׁוֹת יְרוּשָׁלַיִם   8. עֵינֵי הַכֹּהֵן

13. לֵב הַמָּקוֹם   12. כְּלֵי הַבַּיִת   11. כֹּהֲנֵי הַמִּדְבָּר

15. בְּיַד יַעֲקֹב   14. לְהָרֵי זָהָב

Exercise 4

1. he stood, he was, he saw, he knew, he did, he went up, he crossed over, he ate, he walked, he sent   2. they stood, we stood, I stood, she stood, he stood, you stood (*m sg*), you stood (*m pl*), you stood (*f sg*)   3. he was, I was, we were, they were, she was, you were (*m sg*), you were (*f sg*), you were (*m pl*)   4. we saw, I saw, he saw, they saw, you saw (*m sg*), you saw (*m pl*), she saw, you saw (*f sg*)   5. I knew, you knew (*f sg*), she knew, you knew (*m pl*), they knew, you knew (*m sg*), he knew, we knew   6. he did, you did (*m sg*), we did, you did (*m pl*), they did, I did, she did, you did (*f sg*)   7. you went up (*m pl*), they went up, we went up, he went up, she went up, you went up (*f sg*), I went up, you went up (*m sg*)

Exercise 5

1. David walked towards the mountain and he saw the implements of gold and everything that there was. כְּלֵי הַזָּהָב   2. The daughter of Ruth saw the son of Abraham. בֶּן אַבְרָהָם, בַּת רוּת   3. Thus said Moses to the children of Moab: "You went up from Egypt." בְּנֵי מוֹאָב   4. All of the people remembered the water of Egypt on the road toward the desert. כָּל הָאֲנָשִׁים, מֵי מִצְרַיִם   5. We crossed over with the family of David toward Jerusalem and there we settled in the land of Moab until today. בְּאֶרֶץ מוֹאָב, מִשְׁפַּחַת דָּוִד   6. You heard the voice of the cattle today in the fields of Sarah and you saw the tents of Moab. אָהֳלֵי מוֹאָב   בִּשְׂדֵי שָׂרָה, קוֹל הַבְּהֵמָה   7. Thus the people of the desert made the vessel of gold in front of the eyes of the priests. עֵינֵי הַכֹּהֲנִים, אַנְשֵׁי הַמִּדְבָּר

Exercise 6

1. The priests of the place guarded the vessels of gold from the people of the desert.

א. כֹּהֵן הַמָּקוֹם שָׁמַר אֶת כְּלֵי הַזָּהָב מִן אַנְשֵׁי הַמִּדְבָּר.

ב. אֲנַחְנוּ שָׁמַרְנוּ אֶת כְּלֵי הַזָּהָב מִן אַנְשֵׁי הַמִּדְבָּר.

ג. אַתָּה שָׁמַרְתָּ אֶת כְּלֵי הַזָּהָב מִן אַנְשֵׁי הַמִּדְבָּר.

ד. אַתֶּם שְׁמַרְתֶּם אֶת כְּלֵי הַזָּהָב מִן אַנְשֵׁי הַמִּדְבָּר.

ה. אֵשֶׁת אַבְרָהָם שָׁמְרָה אֶת כְּלֵי הַזָּהָב מִן אַנְשֵׁי הַמִּדְבָּר.

2. Thus Abraham said to the children of Ruth: "I went up to the top of the mountains and from the tent I took the implements of the war and I also guarded the implements of the war from the waters of Moab."

א. כֹּה אָמַר אַבְרָהָם אֶל בְּנֵי רוּת: "אֲנַחְנוּ עָלִינוּ אֶל רֹאשׁ הֶהָרִים וּמִן הָאֹהֶל לָקַחְנוּ אֶת כְּלֵי הַמִּלְחָמָה וְגַם שָׁמַרְנוּ אֶת כְּלֵי הַמִּלְחָמָה מִן מֵי מוֹאָב."   ב. כֹּה אָמַר אַבְרָהָם אֶל בְּנֵי רוּת: "הֵמָּה עָלוּ אֶל רֹאשׁ הֶהָרִים וּמִן הָאֹהֶל לָקְחוּ אֶת כְּלֵי הַמִּלְחָמָה וְגַם שָׁמְרוּ אֶת כְּלֵי הַמִּלְחָמָה מִן מֵי מוֹאָב."   ג. כֹּה אָמַר אַבְרָהָם אֶל בְּנֵי רוּת: "אַתֶּם עֲלִיתֶם אֶל רֹאשׁ הֶהָרִים וּמִן הָאֹהֶל לְקַחְתֶּם אֶת כְּלֵי הַמִּלְחָמָה וְגַם שְׁמַרְתֶּם אֶת כְּלֵי הַמִּלְחָמָה מִן מֵי מוֹאָב."   ד. כֹּה אָמַר אַבְרָהָם אֶל בְּנֵי רוּת: "הִיא עָלְתָה אֶל רֹאשׁ הֶהָרִים וּמִן הָאֹהֶל לָקְחָה

(Exercise 6 continued)

אֶת כְּלֵי הַמִּלְחָמָה וְגַם שָׁמְרָה אֶת כְּלֵי הַמִּלְחָמָה מִן מֵי מוֹאָב." ה. כֹּה אָמַר אַבְרָהָם אֶל בְּנֵי רוּת: "הַכֹּהֲנִים עָלוּ אֶל רֹאשׁ הֶהָרִים וּמִן הָאֹהֶל לָקְחוּ אֶת כְּלֵי הַמִּלְחָמָה וְגַם שָׁמְרוּ אֶת כְּלֵי הַמִּלְחָמָה מִן מֵי מוֹאָב." ו. כֹּה אָמַר אַבְרָהָם אֶל בְּנֵי רוּת: "אֲבִי דָוִד עָלָה אֶל רֹאשׁ הֶהָרִים וּמִן הָאֹהֶל לָקַח אֶת כְּלֵי הַמִּלְחָמָה וְגַם שָׁמַר אֶת כְּלֵי הַמִּלְחָמָה מִן מֵי מוֹאָב."

3. You went toward the city and there you ruled over the people of the place and you did not know another war (war any more).

א. אֲנִי הָלַכְתִּי הָעִירָה וְשָׁם מָלַכְתִּי עַל אַנְשֵׁי הַמָּקוֹם וְלֹא יָדַעְתִּי עוֹד מִלְחָמָה. ב. שָׂרֵי הָעָם הָלְכוּ הָעִירָה וְשָׁם מָלְכוּ עַל אַנְשֵׁי הַמָּקוֹם וְלֹא יָדְעוּ עוֹד מִלְחָמָה. ג. הוּא הָלַךְ הָעִירָה וְשָׁם מָלַךְ עַל אַנְשֵׁי הַמָּקוֹם וְלֹא יָדַע עוֹד מִלְחָמָה. ד. הִיא הָלְכָה הָעִירָה וְשָׁם מָלְכָה עַל אַנְשֵׁי הַמָּקוֹם וְלֹא יָדְעָה עוֹד מִלְחָמָה. ה. אֲנַחְנוּ הָלַכְנוּ הָעִירָה וְשָׁם מָלַכְנוּ עַל אַנְשֵׁי הַמָּקוֹם וְלֹא יָדַעְנוּ עוֹד מִלְחָמָה. ו. אַתֶּם הֲלַכְתֶּם הָעִירָה וְשָׁם מְלַכְתֶּם עַל אַנְשֵׁי הַמָּקוֹם וְלֹא יְדַעְתֶּם עוֹד מִלְחָמָה.

4. The children of Moab crossed over from place to place, went up toward the land and they settled in Jerusalem.

א. אָנֹכִי עָבַרְתִּי מִמָּקוֹם לְמָקוֹם, עָלִיתִי אַרְצָה וְאָנֹכִי יָשַׁבְתִּי בִּירוּשָׁלַם. ב. שַׂר הַמִּלְחָמָה עָבַר מִמָּקוֹם לְמָקוֹם, עָלָה אַרְצָה וְהוּא יָשַׁב בִּירוּשָׁלַם. ג. בֶּהֱמַת יַעֲקֹב עָבְרָה מִמָּקוֹם לְמָקוֹם, עָלְתָה אַרְצָה וְהִיא יָשְׁבָה בִּירוּשָׁלַם. ד. אֲנַחְנוּ עָבַרְנוּ מִמָּקוֹם לְמָקוֹם, עָלִינוּ אַרְצָה וַאֲנַחְנוּ יָשַׁבְנוּ בִּירוּשָׁלַם. ה. אַתֶּם עֲבַרְתֶּם מִמָּקוֹם לְמָקוֹם, עֲלִיתֶם אַרְצָה וְאַתֶּם יְשַׁבְתֶּם בִּירוּשָׁלַם. ו. אַתָּה עָבַרְתָּ מִמָּקוֹם לְמָקוֹם, עָלִיתָ אַרְצָה וְאַתָּה יָשַׁבְתָּ בִּירוּשָׁלַם.

5. The priests remembered that the name of the son of Abraham was David and the name of the daughter of Abraham was Ruth and they also knew that the children of Abraham went as far as the gates.

א. שָׂרָה זָכְרָה כִּי שֵׁם בֶּן אַבְרָהָם הָיָה דָוִד וְשֵׁם בַּת אַבְרָהָם הָיָה רוּת וְגַם יָדְעָה כִּי בְּנֵי אַבְרָהָם הָלְכוּ עַד הַשְּׁעָרִים. ב. הוּא זָכַר כִּי שֵׁם בֶּן אַבְרָהָם הָיָה

דָוִד וְשֵׁם בַּת אַבְרָהָם הָיָה רוּת וְגַם יָדַע כִּי בְּנֵי אַבְרָהָם הָלְכוּ עַד הַשְּׁעָרִים. ג. אֲנַחְנוּ זָכַרְנוּ כִּי שֵׁם בֶּן אַבְרָהָם הָיָה דָוִד וְשֵׁם בַּת אַבְרָהָם הָיָה רוּת וְגַם יָדַעְנוּ כִּי בְּנֵי אַבְרָהָם הָלְכוּ עַד הַשְּׁעָרִים. ד. אֲנִי זָכַרְתִּי כִּי שֵׁם בֶּן אַבְרָהָם הָיָה דָוִד וְשֵׁם בַּת אַבְרָהָם הָיָה רוּת וְגַם יָדַעְתִּי כִּי בְּנֵי אַבְרָהָם הָלְכוּ עַד הַשְּׁעָרִים.

6. The daughter of Sarah knew everything about everything and she did not listen to the voice of (obey) the father and she did not guard over the bread and over the water and the cattle of the field ate everything.

א. בֶּן שָׂרָה יָדַע אֶת הַכֹּל עַל הַכֹּל וְלֹא שָׁמַע בְּקוֹל הָאָב וְלֹא שָׁמַר עַל הַלֶּחֶם וְעַל הַמַּיִם וּבְהֵמוֹת הַשָּׂדֶה אָכְלוּ אֶת הַכֹּל. ב. בְּנֵי שָׂרָה יָדְעוּ אֶת הַכֹּל עַל הַכֹּל וְלֹא שָׁמְעוּ בְּקוֹל הָאָב וְלֹא שָׁמְרוּ עַל הַלֶּחֶם וְעַל הַמַּיִם וּבְהֵמוֹת הַשָּׂדֶה אָכְלוּ אֶת הַכֹּל. ג. אָנֹכִי יָדַעְתִּי אֶת הַכֹּל עַל הַכֹּל וְלֹא שָׁמַעְתִּי בְּקוֹל הָאָב וְלֹא שָׁמַרְתִּי עַל הַלֶּחֶם וְעַל הַמַּיִם וּבְהֵמוֹת הַשָּׂדֶה אָכְלוּ אֶת הַכֹּל. ד. אַתֶּם יְדַעְתֶּם אֶת הַכֹּל עַל הַכֹּל וְלֹא שְׁמַעְתֶּם בְּקוֹל הָאָב וְלֹא שְׁמַרְתֶּם עַל הַלֶּחֶם וְעַל הַמַּיִם וּבְהֵמוֹת הַשָּׂדֶה אָכְלוּ אֶת הַכֹּל. ה. אֲנַחְנוּ יָדַעְנוּ אֶת הַכֹּל עַל הַכֹּל וְלֹא שָׁמַעְנוּ בְּקוֹל הָאָב וְלֹא שָׁמַרְנוּ עַל הַלֶּחֶם וְעַל הַמַּיִם וּבְהֵמוֹת הַשָּׂדֶה אָכְלוּ אֶת הַכֹּל. ו. אַתָּה יָדַעְתָּ אֶת הַכֹּל עַל הַכֹּל וְלֹא שָׁמַעְתָּ בְּקוֹל הָאָב וְלֹא שָׁמַרְתָּ עַל הַלֶּחֶם וְעַל הַמַּיִם וּבְהֵמוֹת הַשָּׂדֶה אָכְלוּ אֶת הַכֹּל.

A TALL TALE: Three Pigs

In the days of the kings, there were three pigs in the land. All of the pigs made houses. The first pig made a house of grass because he saw grass in the field of the king. And he lived in a house of grass.

The second pig made a house of wood because there was wood near the tents of the chiefs of the king. And he lived in a house of wood.

The third pig remembered that there was gold on the top of the mountains. He went up to the top of the mountains of (the) gold and he also took the gold from the mountain. He crossed over with the gold to the field of the king. The third pig made a house from gold. He resided in the house of (the) gold.

Also an animal lived in the field of the king. The first pig stood in the field. He saw the animal and he went toward the house. He sat in the house because he knew who ate pigs—animals ate pigs!

(A TALL TALE continued)

The animal walked until the house of the first pig and it stood in front of the house. And it said: "Every day I have eaten a pig. Today I have not yet eaten a pig."

Thus said the animal: "Huff."

And it said: "Puff."

And also it sent a wind between the grass of the house. And the house did not stand any more. And the animal ate the first pig.

On another day the second pig stood in the field. He saw the animal and also he went toward the house. He sat in the house because he knew who ate pigs–animals!

The animal went up to (until) the house of the second pig and it stood in front of the house.

And it said: "I have not yet eaten a pig today."

And thus said the animal: "Huff."

And it said: "Puff."

Still the house stood.

Again the animal said: "Huff-puff, and huff-puff, and huff-puff."

It sent the wind between the wood of the house. And then the house did not stand any more. And the animal ate the second pig.

On another day the third pig stood in the field. He saw the animal which ate the first pig and the second pig. And also he went toward the house. He sat in the house and he remembered that a house of gold stood forever.

The animal crossed over as far as the house of the third pig, as far as the house of gold.

Thus said the animal: "I ate the first pig. I ate the second pig. And I have not yet eaten a pig today."

And then the animal said: "Huff."

And it said: "Puff."

And the house still stood.

Again the animal said: "Huff" and again "Puff."

Still the house stood! The third pig heard the breath of the animal next to the house. He knew that the animal ate the first pig and the second pig. And then the pig took a dish of gold. He crossed over from the house with the dish of gold. The pig sent the dish of gold to the head of the animal and the animal was not standing any more. And then the pig ate the animal.

The third pig lived there in the house of gold until today.

Chapter 11

Oral Review

1. A tent of a chief stood in the field of Rachel near the desert. The tent of the chief stood in the field of Rachel near the desert. Tents of chiefs stood in the field of Rachel near the desert. The tents of the chiefs stood in the field of Rachel near the desert.   2. A man of peace guarded every soul in the city. The man of peace guarded all of the souls in the city. Men of peace guard every soul in the city. The men of peace guarded all of the souls in Jerusalem.   3. The eye of Rachel was on the face of Jacob. The eyes of Rachel were on the face of Jacob. The priest of the place sent bread toward the city. The priests of the place sent bread toward the city.   4. The son of Adam made a vessel of gold. The son of Jacob made the vessel of gold. The sons of Adam made vessels of gold. The sons of Jacob made the vessels of gold.   5. Thus said a servant of a king: "I made more bread." Thus said the servants of the king: "We made more bread." Thus said the wife of the king: "I made more bread." Thus said the wives of the king: We made more bread."

Exercise 1

1. I will remember, I will write, I will rule, I will open, I will send, I will hear, I remembered, I wrote   2. you will guard (*m sg*), you will rule, you will write, you will find, you will call, you will open, you guarded, you ruled   3. you will write (*f sg*), you will remember, you will guard, you will hear, you will send, you will call, you sent, you heard   4, he will rule, he will guard, he will remember, he will open, he will send, he will hear, he opened, he found   5. she will remember, she will write, she will rule, she will call, she will find, she will send, she stood, she crossed over   6. we will guard, we will rule, we will write, we will find, we will call, we will open, we knew, we sat   7. you will remember (*m pl*), you will write, you will rule, you will send, you will hear, you will find, you took, you opened   8. they will guard, they will remember, they will write, they will hear, they will find, they will call, they opened, they found

Exercise 2

מ.ל.ך, perfect – מָלַכְתִּי, מָלַכְתָּ, מָלַכְתְּ, מָלַךְ, מָלְכָה,
מָלַכְנוּ, מְלַכְתֶּם, מְלַכְתֶּן, מָלְכוּ, מָלְכוּ

מ.ל.ך, imperfect – אֶמְלֹךְ, תִּמְלֹךְ, תִּמְלְכִי, יִמְלֹךְ,
תִּמְלֹךְ, נִמְלֹךְ, תִּמְלְכוּ, תִּמְלֹכְנָה, יִמְלְכוּ, תִּמְלֹכְנָה

פ.ת.ח, perfect – פָּתַחְתִּי, פָּתַחְתָּ, פָּתַחְתְּ, פָּתַח, פָּתְחָה,
פָּתַחְנוּ, פְּתַחְתֶּם, פְּתַחְתֶּן, פָּתְחוּ, פָּתְחוּ

(Exercise 2 continued)

פ.ת.ח, imperfect – אֶפְתַּח, תִּפְתַּח, תִּפְתְּחִי, יִפְתַּח,
תִּפְתַּח, נִפְתַּח, תִּפְתְּחוּ, תִּפְתַּחְנָה, יִפְתְּחוּ, תִּפְתַּחְנָה

מ.צ.א, perfect – מָצָאתִי, מָצָאתָ, מָצָאת, מָצָא, מָצְאָה,
מָצָאנוּ, מְצָאתֶם, מְצָאתֶן, מָצְאוּ, מָצְאוּ

מ.צ.א, imperfect – אֶמְצָא, תִּמְצָא, תִּמְצְאִי, יִמְצָא,
תִּמְצָא, נִמְצָא, תִּמְצְאוּ, תִּמְצֶאנָה, יִמְצְאוּ, תִּמְצֶאנָה

Exercise 3

1. אֶשְׁמֹר, אֶפְתַּח, אֶשְׁלַח, אֶזְכֹּר   2. תִּכְתֹּב, תִּפְתַּח,
תִּשְׁמַע תִּמְצָא   3. תִּקְרְאִי, תִּשְׁלְחִי, תִּמְלְכִי, תִּמְצְאִי,
4. יִזְכֹּר, יִכְתֹּב, יִמְלֹךְ, יִקְרָא   5. תִּמְצָא, תִּקְרָא,
תִּשְׁמַע, תִּשְׁמֹר   6. נִפְתַּח, נִשְׁמֹר, נִשְׁמַע, נִקְרָא
7. תִּמְצְאוּ, תִּכְתְּבוּ, תִּקְרְאוּ, תִּמְלְכוּ   8. יִכְתְּבוּ, יִשְׁמְרוּ,
יִמְלְכוּ, יִזְכְּרוּ

Exercise 4

1. זָכַר, The son of Ruth remembered the women of Bethlehem. יִזְכֹּר, The son of Ruth will remember the women of Bethlehem.   2. שָׁמַעְתִּי, I heard the sound of the water between the trees and the desert. אֶשְׁמַע, I will hear the sound of the water between the trees and the desert.   3. כָּתַבְנוּ, We wrote in blood on a tree in Moab. נִכְתֹּב, We will write in blood on a tree in Moab.
4. מָצָא, Moses found blood on the sword and on the head of the chief. יִמְצָא, Moses will find blood on the sword and on the head of the chief.   5. שָׁמַרְתָּ, You guarded the silver of the king. תִּשְׁמֹר, You will guard the silver of the king.   6. פָּתְחָה, Rachel opened the gates of Bethlehem. תִּפְתַּח, Rachel will open the gates of Bethlehem.   7. מְלַכְתֶּם, You ruled over the heart of the people. תִּמְלְכוּ, You will rule over the heart of the people.   8. שָׁלְחָה, The family sent all of the blood of the animals to the priest. תִּשְׁלַח, The family will send all of the blood of the animals to the priest.   9. קָרָאת, You called the name of the daughter Sarah. תִּקְרְאִי, You will call the name of the daughter Sarah.

Exercise 5

1. If you (m sg)/she will guard the cattle of the family you/she will find peace and then you/she will not hear the sound of the city any more.

א. אִם יִשְׁמֹר אֶת בֶּהֱמַת הַמִּשְׁפָּחָה יִמְצָא שָׁלוֹם וְאָז לֹא
יִשְׁמַע עוֹד אֶת קוֹל הָעִיר.   ב. אִם אֶשְׁמֹר אֶת בֶּהֱמַת
הַמִּשְׁפָּחָה אֶמְצָא שָׁלוֹם וְאָז לֹא אֶשְׁמַע עוֹד אֶת קוֹל
הָעִיר.   ג. אִם נִשְׁמֹר אֶת בֶּהֱמַת הַמִּשְׁפָּחָה נִמְצָא
שָׁלוֹם וְאָז לֹא נִשְׁמַע עוֹד אֶת קוֹל הָעִיר.   ד. אִם
יִשְׁמְרוּ אֶת בֶּהֱמַת הַמִּשְׁפָּחָה יִמְצְאוּ שָׁלוֹם וְאָז לֹא
יִשְׁמְעוּ עוֹד אֶת קוֹל הָעִיר.   ה. אִם תִּשְׁמְרִי אֶת
בֶּהֱמַת הַמִּשְׁפָּחָה תִּמְצְאִי שָׁלוֹם וְאָז לֹא תִּשְׁמְעִי עוֹד
אֶת קוֹל הָעִיר.   ו. אִם תִּשְׁמְרוּ אֶת בֶּהֱמַת הַמִּשְׁפָּחָה
תִּמְצְאוּ שָׁלוֹם וְאָז לֹא תִּשְׁמְעוּ עוֹד אֶת קוֹל הָעִיר.

2. The servant of David knew that he would find silver in the mountains of Moab.

א. כֹּהֲנֵי בֵּית לֶחֶם יָדְעוּ כִּי הֵם יִמְצְאוּ כֶּסֶף בְּהָרֵי
מוֹאָב.   ב. אֵשֶׁת אַבְרָהָם יָדְעָה כִּי הִיא תִּמְצָא כֶּסֶף
בְּהָרֵי מוֹאָב.   ג. אַתֶּם יְדַעְתֶּם כִּי אַתֶּם תִּמְצְאוּ כֶּסֶף
בְּהָרֵי מוֹאָב.   ד. אֲנִי יָדַעְתִּי כִּי אֲנִי אֶמְצָא כֶּסֶף בְּהָרֵי
מוֹאָב.   ה. אַתָּה יָדַעְתָּ כִּי אַתָּה תִּמְצָא כֶּסֶף בְּהָרֵי
מוֹאָב.

3. She stood among the trees and there she ate bread.

א. הוּא יָשַׁב בֵּין הָעֵצִים וְהוּא אָכַל לֶחֶם שָׁם.   ב. הֵם
הָיוּ בֵּין הָעֵצִים וְהֵם אָכְלוּ לֶחֶם שָׁם.   ג. אֲנִי עָבַרְתִּי
בֵּין הָעֵצִים וַאֲנִי אָכַלְתִּי לֶחֶם שָׁם.   ד. אֲנַחְנוּ הָלַכְנוּ
בֵּין הָעֵצִים וַאֲנַחְנוּ אָכַלְנוּ לֶחֶם שָׁם.   ה. אַתֶּם עֲלִיתֶם
בֵּין הָעֵצִים וְאַתֶּם אֲכַלְתֶּם לֶחֶם שָׁם.

4. We took the vessels of the land, we made roads and houses in the desert and thus we said: "We will rule in the desert forever!"

א. הוּא לָקַח אֶת כְּלֵי הָאָרֶץ, עָשָׂה דְּרָכִים וּבָתִּים
בַּמִּדְבָּר וְכֹה אָמַר: "אֶמְלֹךְ בַּמִּדְבָּר לְעוֹלָם!"   ב. אַתֶּם
לְקַחְתֶּם אֶת כְּלֵי הָאָרֶץ, עֲשִׂיתֶם דְּרָכִים וּבָתִּים
בַּמִּדְבָּר וְכֹה אֲמַרְתֶּם: "נִמְלֹךְ בַּמִּדְבָּר לְעוֹלָם!"   ג. אֲנִי
לָקַחְתִּי אֶת כְּלֵי הָאָרֶץ, עָשִׂיתִי דְּרָכִים וּבָתִּים בַּמִּדְבָּר
וְכֹה אָמַרְתִּי: "אֶמְלֹךְ בַּמִּדְבָּר לְעוֹלָם!"   ד. אַתָּה
לָקַחְתָּ אֶת כְּלֵי הָאָרֶץ, עָשִׂיתָ דְּרָכִים וּבָתִּים בַּמִּדְבָּר
וְכֹה אָמַרְתָּ: "אֶמְלֹךְ בַּמִּדְבָּר לְעוֹלָם!"   ה. שָׂרֵי הַמָּקוֹם
לָקְחוּ אֶת כְּלֵי הָאָרֶץ, עָשׂוּ דְּרָכִים וּבָתִּים בַּמִּדְבָּר וְכֹה
אָמְרוּ: "נִמְלֹךְ בַּמִּדְבָּר לְעוֹלָם!"   ו. אֵשֶׁת יַעֲקֹב לָקְחָה

(Exercise 5 continued)

אֶת כְּלֵי הָאָרֶץ, עָשְׂתָה דְּרָכִים וּבָתִּים בַּמִּדְבָּר וְכֹה אָמְרָה: "אֶמְלֹךְ בַּמִּדְבָּר לְעוֹלָם!"

5. If the young man will write to a young woman, and then he will send silver and gold to the young woman, he will open up the heart of the young woman and the soul of the young woman forever.

א. אִם הָאַחִים יִכְתְּבוּ לַנַּעֲרָה, וְאָז יִשְׁלְחוּ כֶּסֶף וְזָהָב אֶל הַנַּעֲרָה, הֵם יִפְתְּחוּ אֶת לֵב הַנַּעֲרָה וְאֶת נֶפֶשׁ הַנַּעֲרָה לְעוֹלָם. ב. אִם אַתָּה תִּכְתֹּב לַנַּעֲרָה, וְאָז תִּשְׁלַח כֶּסֶף וְזָהָב אֶל הַנַּעֲרָה, אַתָּה תִּפְתַּח אֶת לֵב הַנַּעֲרָה וְאֶת נֶפֶשׁ הַנַּעֲרָה לְעוֹלָם. ג. אִם אֲנִי אֶכְתֹּב לַנַּעֲרָה, וְאָז אֶשְׁלַח כֶּסֶף וְזָהָב אֶל הַנַּעֲרָה, אֲנִי אֶפְתַּח אֶת לֵב הַנַּעֲרָה וְאֶת נֶפֶשׁ הַנַּעֲרָה לְעוֹלָם. ד. אִם אַתֶּם תִּכְתְּבוּ לַנַּעֲרָה, וְאָז תִּשְׁלְחוּ כֶּסֶף וְזָהָב אֶל הַנַּעֲרָה, אַתֶּם תִּפְתְּחוּ אֶת לֵב הַנַּעֲרָה וְאֶת נֶפֶשׁ הַנַּעֲרָה לְעוֹלָם.

6. David will open the tent and he will find blood on the sword of Jacob and then he will call the priests who were guarding the place.

א. הִיא תִּפְתַּח אֶת הָאֹהֶל וְהִיא תִּמְצָא דָּם עַל חֶרֶב יַעֲקֹב וְאָז תִּקְרָא אֶל הַכֹּהֲנִים אֲשֶׁר שָׁמְרוּ אֶת הַמָּקוֹם. ב. אָנֹכִי אֶפְתַּח אֶת הָאֹהֶל וְאָנֹכִי אֶמְצָא דָּם עַל חֶרֶב יַעֲקֹב וְאָז אֶקְרָא אֶל הַכֹּהֲנִים אֲשֶׁר שָׁמְרוּ אֶת הַמָּקוֹם. ג. אַתָּה תִּפְתַּח אֶת הָאֹהֶל וְאַתָּה תִּמְצָא דָּם עַל חֶרֶב יַעֲקֹב וְאָז תִּקְרָא אֶל הַכֹּהֲנִים אֲשֶׁר שָׁמְרוּ אֶת הַמָּקוֹם. ד. אַתֶּם תִּפְתְּחוּ אֶת הָאֹהֶל וְאַתֶּם תִּמְצְאוּ דָּם עַל חֶרֶב יַעֲקֹב וְאָז תִּקְרְאוּ אֶל הַכֹּהֲנִים אֲשֶׁר שָׁמְרוּ אֶת הַמָּקוֹם. ה. אֲנַחְנוּ נִפְתַּח אֶת הָאֹהֶל וַאֲנַחְנוּ נִמְצָא דָּם עַל חֶרֶב יַעֲקֹב וְאָז נִקְרָא אֶל הַכֹּהֲנִים אֲשֶׁר שָׁמְרוּ אֶת הַמָּקוֹם. ו. הֵם יִפְתְּחוּ אֶת הָאֹהֶל וְהֵם יִמְצְאוּ דָּם עַל חֶרֶב יַעֲקֹב וְאָז יִקְרְאוּ אֶל הַכֹּהֲנִים אֲשֶׁר שָׁמְרוּ אֶת הַמָּקוֹם.

Exercise 6

We will not provide translations for the quotes from the Bible in this answer book. We encourage you to look them up in your own Bible.

A TALL TALE: The Seed of Grain

(Adapted from The Little Red Hen)

One day a woman was walking on the road of the king and she found a seed of grain on the land. She took the seed and she walked toward the house. The family was in the house – the father, the son, and the daughter.

The woman said to the family: "I found a seed of grain on the road. Who will plant the seed?"

"Not I," said the father.
"Not I," said the son.
"Not I," said the daughter.

The woman said: "I will plant the seed."
And then she took the seed and she planted the seed in the field near the house.

When she saw the grain in the field the woman called to the family: "I saw grain in the field! Who will guard the grain from the animals?"

"Not I," said the father.
"Not I," said the son.
"Not I," said the daughter.

The woman said: "Then I will guard the grain."
And she sat in the field every day and she guarded the grain from the animals.

One day the woman saw that the grain in the field was good.
She called to the family: "I have seen that the grain in the field was good. Who will reap the grain?"

"Not I," said the father.
"Not I," said the son.
"Not I," said the daughter.

The woman said: "I found the seed of grain. I planted the seed and also I guarded the grain. And also I will reap the grain!"

And she took a sword and she walked to the field and then she reaped all of the grain which was in the field near the house.

The woman took the grain to the family who sat in the house.
And she said: "I reaped all of the grain. Who will make bread?"

Again the father said: "Not I."
Again the son said: "Not I."
Again the daughter said: "Not I."

The woman said: "Then I will make the bread."
And she took the grain and also made bread.

The woman saw that the bread was good.
And then she said to all of the family: "I saw that the bread was good. And I will eat the bread!"

(A TALL TALE continued)

"Also I!" said the father.
"Also I!" said the son.
"Also I!" said the daughter.

Thus the woman said: "You did not find and you did not plant the seed. You did not guard and you did not reap the grain. Also you did not make the bread. Only I planted the seed and only I guarded the grain and only I reaped the grain and only I made the bread. I and only I will eat the bread!"

And she ate all of the bread.

Chapter 12

Oral Review

1. Abraham called to David and David did not hear. Abraham will call to David and David will not hear. Naomi sent bread to the people of Israel because she obeyed the fathers. Naomi will send bread to the people of Israel because she will obey the fathers. The kings of Moab called to all of the people in the land and they ruled in Moab. The kings of Moab will call to all of the people of the land and they will rule forever. 2. I will open the gates and I will find money. You will open the gate of Bethlehem and you will find a sword. You will open (f sg) the gates of the wood and you will find Naomi. He will open the gates of the house and he will find the family. You (m sg)/she will open the gates of the field and you/she will find all of the cattle. 3. If we will write the words then we will remember what we said. If you will write (m pl) the words of Naomi then you will remember what she said. If they write the words of peace then they will not remember the implements of war and the blood. If we will write the words of the priests then we will remember again the roads of Jerusalem. If you do not write (m pl) again the words of the ancestors then you will not remember the days of Egypt.

Exercise 1

1. I will eat 2. you (m sg)/she will sit 3. you will go (f sg) 4. he will take 5. you (m sg)/she will know 6. we will say 7. you will eat (m pl) 8. they will go 9. he will know 10. I will say 11. he will sit 12. we will take

Exercise 2

1. ל.כ.א, I ate, I will eat 2. ק.ר.א, you called (m sg), you will call 3. כ.ת.ב, you wrote (f sg), you will write 4. א.מ.ר, he will say, he said 5. ש.מ.ר, you will guard (m sg), you guarded 6. ה.ל.ך, we walked, we

will walk 7. י.ד.ע, you will know (m pl), you knew 8. י.ש.ב, they sat, they will sit 9. ל.ק.ח, I will take, I took 10. פ.ת.ח, I will open, I opened 11. מ.ל.ך, you rule (m sg), you will rule 12. מ.צ.א, you found (f sg), you will find 13. ש.ל.ח, he will send, he sent 14. ז.כ.ר, she will remember, she remembered 15. ש.מ.ע, we heard, we will hear

Exercise 3

1. I will guard, I will sit, I will eat, I will take, I will open, I will say, I will know, I will go 2. you will rule (m sg), you will go, you will know, you will send, you will eat, you will sit, you will say, you will take 3. you will write (f sg), you will know, you will say, you will go, you will call, you will sit, you will take, you will eat 4. he will remember, he will go, he will know, he will say, he will take, he will rule, he will eat, he will sit 5. she will hear, she will sit, she will eat, she will go, she will say, she will know, she will open, she will take 6. we will sit, we will guard, we will take, we will say, we will send, we will go, we will eat, we will know 7. you will sit (m pl), you will go, you will know, you will eat, you will call, you will say, you will hear, you will take 8. they will remember, they will go, they will take, they will say, they will sit, they will find, they will know, they will eat

Exercise 4

1. קָרָאתָ אֶת שֵׁם בֶּן אַבְרָהָם. תִּקְרָא לָכֹהֵן.
2. אָכַלְתִּי לֶחֶם. אֲנִי לֹא אֹכַל בְּהֵמוֹת. 3. הוּא יָשַׁב בַּבַּיִת. הוּא יֵשֵׁב עַל הָהָר. 4. כְּתַבְתֶּם דָּבָר. תִּכְתְּבוּ דְבָרִים. 5. הֵם הָלְכוּ לָעִיר. הֵם יֵלְכוּ לָאָרֶץ. 6. אָמַרְנוּ: "יָדַעְנוּ מִלְחָמָה." נֹאמַר: "נֵדַע שָׁלוֹם."

Exercise 5

1. You guarded the vessels of Moses from the eyes of the people. You will guard the animals from the people of Moab. 2. The young man will open the gates of the city. Abraham opened the road to Jerusalem. 3. The children of Israel resided in the land of Egypt in the days of peace. The children of Israel will reside in the land of Israel forever. 4. We will hear the voice of the commanders and then we will take the swords and we will go to the war. We heard the voice of Rachel and then we took the silver and we went toward the mountain. 5. I went toward the house and there I found bread and water. I will go toward the house and there I will find all of the servants of the family. 6. You knew (f sg) that the wife of the king will rule forever and ever. You would know (f sg) because the daughter of David ruled until the days of the war.

Exercise 6

1. F   2. P   3. D   4. I   5. K   6. A   7. M   8. G   9. R
10. O   11. Q   12. N   13. H   14. B   15. L   16. J
17. E   18. C

Exercise 7

1. שָׁמַר, David guarded the gold which was in (on) the top of the mountain.   יִשְׁמֹר, David will guard the gold which was in (on) the top of the mountain.   2. הָלַכְתִּי, הָלַכְתָּ, I went to the chief of the city and you went to the son of the priest.   תֵּלֵךְ, אֵלֵךְ, I will go to the chief of the city and you will go to the son of the priest.

3. יָשְׁבוּ, The people of the desert sat with the family in the tent of Abraham.   יֵשְׁבוּ, The people of the desert will sit with the family in the tent of Abraham.

4. יְדַעְתֶּם, You knew the name of the servant and also the face of the lord.   תֵּדְעוּ, You will know the name of the servant and also the face of the lord.   5. לָקַחְנוּ, לָקַחַתְּ, We took the implements of the house from the field of Moab and you took (f sg) the implements of war from the desert.   נִקַּח, תִּקְּחִי, We will take the implements of the house from the field of Moab and you will take the implements of war from the desert.

6. אָכַל, אָכְלָה, Rachel ate bread and water next to Moses who did not eat bread and water.   יֹאכַל, תֹּאכַל, Rachel will eat bread and water next to Moses who will not eat bread and water.   7. אָמְרָה, אָמַר, Thus Jacob has said to Sarah and thus Sarah has said to Jacob.   תֹּאמַר, יֹאמַר, Thus Jacob would say to Sarah and thus Sarah would say to Jacob.

Exercise 8

1. David will go to the mountains and there he will find gold.

א. נֵלֵךְ אֶל הֶהָרִים וְשָׁם נִמְצָא זָהָב.   ב. יֵלְכוּ אַחֵי נָעֳמִי אֶל הֶהָרִים וְשָׁם יִמְצְאוּ זָהָב.   ג. תֵּלֵךְ אֶל הֶהָרִים וְשָׁם תִּמְצָא זָהָב.   ד. אֵלֵךְ אֶל הֶהָרִים וְשָׁם אֶמְצָא זָהָב.   ה. תֵּלֵךְ הִיא אֶל הֶהָרִים וְשָׁם תִּמְצָא זָהָב.

2. If you will open the gates of the place, then you will know all of the people who resided there.

א. אִם אֶפְתַּח אֶת שַׁעֲרֵי הַמָּקוֹם, אָז אֵדַע אֶת כָּל הָאֲנָשִׁים אֲשֶׁר יָשְׁבוּ שָׁם.   ב. אִם הוּא יִפְתַּח אֶת שַׁעֲרֵי הַמָּקוֹם, אָז יֵדַע אֶת כָּל הָאֲנָשִׁים אֲשֶׁר יָשְׁבוּ שָׁם.   ג. אִם רוּת תִּפְתַּח אֶת שַׁעֲרֵי הַמָּקוֹם, אָז תֵּדַע אֶת כָּל הָאֲנָשִׁים אֲשֶׁר יָשְׁבוּ שָׁם.   ד. אִם תִּפְתְּחוּ אֶת שַׁעֲרֵי הַמָּקוֹם, אָז תֵּדְעוּ אֶת כָּל הָאֲנָשִׁים אֲשֶׁר יָשְׁבוּ שָׁם.   ה. אִם נִפְתַּח אֶת שַׁעֲרֵי הַמָּקוֹם, אָז נֵדַע אֶת כָּל הָאֲנָשִׁים אֲשֶׁר יָשְׁבוּ שָׁם.

3. David will take the hands of Ruth, he will hear the voice of Ruth and then he will say: "I have seen the soul of the woman."

א. אֶקַּח אֶת יְדֵי רוּת, אֶשְׁמַע אֶת קוֹל רוּת וְאָז אֹמַר: "רָאִיתִי אֶת נֶפֶשׁ הָאִשָּׁה."   ב. תִּקַּח אֶת יְדֵי רוּת, תִּשְׁמַע אֶת קוֹל רוּת וְאָז תֹּאמַר: "רָאִיתִי אֶת נֶפֶשׁ הָאִשָּׁה."   ג. נִקַּח אֶת יְדֵי רוּת, נִשְׁמַע אֶת קוֹל רוּת וְאָז נֹאמַר: "רָאִינוּ אֶת נֶפֶשׁ הָאִשָּׁה."   ד. הֵם יִקְחוּ אֶת יְדֵי רוּת, יִשְׁמְעוּ אֶת קוֹל רוּת וְאָז יֹאמְרוּ: "רָאִינוּ אֶת נֶפֶשׁ הָאִשָּׁה."

4. The people of Egypt will take the daughters of Jerusalem to the field and there they will sit near the trees all (of the) day.

א. מֹשֶׁה יִקַּח אֶת בְּנוֹת יְרוּשָׁלַם אֶל הַשָּׂדֶה וְשָׁם יֵשְׁבוּ עַל יַד הָעֵצִים כָּל הַיּוֹם.   ב. נִקַּח אֶת בְּנוֹת יְרוּשָׁלַם אֶל הַשָּׂדֶה וְשָׁם נֵשֵׁב עַל יַד הָעֵצִים כָּל הַיּוֹם.   ג. תִּקַּח אֶת בְּנוֹת יְרוּשָׁלַם אֶל הַשָּׂדֶה וְשָׁם יֵשְׁבוּ עַל יַד הָעֵצִים כָּל הַיּוֹם.   ד. נָעֳמִי תִּקַּח אֶת בְּנוֹת יְרוּשָׁלַם אֶל הַשָּׂדֶה וְשָׁם תֵּשַׁבְנָה עַל יַד הָעֵצִים כָּל הַיּוֹם.

5. I will remember the names of the cities in the land because I will write the names in blood.

א. יִזְכֹּר אֲחִי דָּוִד אֶת שְׁמוֹת הֶעָרִים בָּאָרֶץ כִּי יִכְתֹּב אֶת הַשְּׁמוֹת בַּדָּם.   ב. תִּזְכְּרִי אֶת שְׁמוֹת הֶעָרִים בָּאָרֶץ כִּי תִּכְתְּבִי אֶת הַשְּׁמוֹת בַּדָּם.   ג. תִּזְכֹּר הִיא אֶת שְׁמוֹת הֶעָרִים בָּאָרֶץ כִּי תִּכְתֹּב אֶת הַשְּׁמוֹת בַּדָּם.   ד. יִזְכֹּר יַעֲקֹב אֶת שְׁמוֹת הֶעָרִים בָּאָרֶץ כִּי יִכְתֹּב אֶת הַשְּׁמוֹת בַּדָּם.

6. You will know (msg) the face of the chief because you saw the chief before today.

א. אֵדַע אֶת פְּנֵי הַשַּׂר כִּי רָאִיתִי אֶת הַשַּׂר לִפְנֵי הַיּוֹם.   ב. נֵדַע אֶת פְּנֵי הַשַּׂר כִּי רָאִינוּ אֶת הַשַּׂר לִפְנֵי הַיּוֹם.   ג. תֵּדְעִי אֶת פְּנֵי הַשַּׂר כִּי רָאִית אֶת הַשַּׂר לִפְנֵי הַיּוֹם.   ד. תֵּדְעוּ אֶת פְּנֵי הַשַּׂר כִּי רְאִיתֶם אֶת הַשַּׂר לִפְנֵי הַיּוֹם.

(Exercise 8 continued)

7. Who will rule before David and what will he know about everything?

א.אַתָּה תִּמְלֹךְ לִפְנֵי דָוִד וּמַה תֵּדַע עַל הַכֹּל?
ב.אַתֶּם תִּמְלְכוּ לִפְנֵי דָוִד וּמַה תֵּדְעוּ עַל הַכֹּל?
ג.מֹשֶׁה יִמְלֹךְ לִפְנֵי דָוִד וּמַה יֵדַע עַל הַכֹּל? ד.בְּנֵי
רָחֵל יִמְלְכוּ לִפְנֵי דָוִד וּמַה יֵדְעוּ עַל הַכֹּל? ה.אֲנִי
אֶמְלֹךְ לִפְנֵי דָוִד וּמַה אֵדַע עַל הַכֹּל?

8. They crossed over the water, they went up toward the mountain, they stood there and also they made implements of gold.

א.אֲנִי עָבַרְתִּי אֶת הַמַּיִם, עָלִיתִי הָהָרָה, עָמַדְתִּי שָׁם
וְגַם עָשִׂיתִי כְּלֵי זָהָב. ב.אֲנַחְנוּ עָבַרְנוּ אֶת הַמַּיִם,
עָלִינוּ הָהָרָה, עָמַדְנוּ שָׁם וְגַם עָשִׂינוּ כְּלֵי זָהָב. ג.הוּא
עָבַר אֶת הַמַּיִם, עָלָה הָהָרָה, עָמַד שָׁם וְגַם עָשָׂה כְּלֵי
זָהָב. ד.אַתָּה עָבַרְתָּ אֶת הַמַּיִם, עָלִיתָ הָהָרָה, עָמַדְתָּ
שָׁם וְגַם עָשִׂיתָ כְּלֵי זָהָב. ה.אַתֶּם עֲבַרְתֶּם אֶת הַמַּיִם,
עֲלִיתֶם הָהָרָה, עֲמַדְתֶּם שָׁם וְגַם עֲשִׂיתֶם כְּלֵי זָהָב.
ו.הִיא עָבְרָה אֶת הַמַּיִם, עָלְתָה הָהָרָה, עָמְדָה שָׁם וְגַם
עָשְׂתָה כְּלֵי זָהָב.

A TALL TALE: Lou and Sue Walked

Lou and Sue sat in the house.

Sue said: "Lou, we will walk to the field and there we will eat."

Lou said: "No! I will sit in the house and I will eat with the dishes near the family."

Sue: "We will take the family to the field, and we will sit among the trees, and we will eat there, and also we will enjoy."

Lou: "I will not go and also I will not enjoy."

Sue: "I will take bread and water, the father will take Coca Cola! We will hear the sound of the trees and it will open the soul and the heart."

Lou: "I was in the field, I sat among the trees, I ate there and I did not enjoy."

Sue: "I will go with the family and we will eat in the field."

Lou: "There were animals in the field and they ate all of the bread. Also today they will eat the bread."

Sue: "We will sit and we will eat in the tent."

Lou: "You do not know and you will not find the road to the field."

Sue: "O.K. Then you will go! And also you will find the road! And you will sit among the trees! And you will eat in the field! And then if you will not enjoy – you will not enjoy."

And then Lou walked and also found the road. And he sat among the trees. And he ate in the field. And he enjoyed!!

Chapter 13

Oral Review

1. I will go with Abraham, I will sit in the city and then I will eat bread. You (*m sg*)/she will go with Sarah, you/she will sit in the field, and then you/she will eat among the trees. You will go (*f sg*) with David, you will sit in the desert of Moab and then you will eat in the tent. Abraham will go with Rachel, he will sit in the place and then he will eat there. She will go with Moses, she will sit in (on) the land and then she will eat with the animals. 2. We will take the vessels of gold which we will find in the house. You will take (*m pl*) the daughters of Rachel whom you will find in the heart of the desert. They will take the people of Moab whom they will find next to the gate. 3. I will remember the way because I will know the place. You will remember (*m sg*) the priest because you will know the name of the man. You will remember (*f sg*) the children because you know the fathers. He will remember a sword and blood because he will know the war. You (*m sg*)/she will remember the days of Israel because you/she will know the words of David. 4. Thus we will say to the children of Israel: "Peace." Thus you will say (*m pl*) to the king: "We will go with Moses." Thus they will say to the brothers of Ruth: "Do not go from there." 5. If I will open the gate, they will know that I was in the house. If you will open (*m sg*) the gate, he will know that you were in the house. If we will open the gate, she will know that we were in the house. If they will open the gate, we will know that they were in the house.

Exercise 1

1. I am a mother. 2. Who are we? 3. This is the word. 4. This is the law. 5. These are the heavens. 6. What is this? 7. Here is the brother. 8. The spirit is in the heavens. 9. The seed is in the ground of the field. 10. The man is like Moses. 11. The name of the mother is Naomi. 12. The wind of the night is on the sea. 13. Here is the lord of Egypt. 14. The law is in Jerusalem. 15. The wind is on the face of the earth. 16. On all of the nights we are there.

Exercise 2

1. I will guard, I will eat, I will hear, I will send, I will say, I will be, I will call, I will walk 2. you will write (*m sg*), you will know, you will be, you will sit, you will

(Exercise 2 continued)

take, you will rule, you will find, you will open   3. you will hear (*f sg*), you will eat, you will open, you will guard, you will be, you will know, you will call, you will sit   4. he will remember, he will be, he will say, he will send, he will find, he will go, he will take, he will rule   5. she will go, she will say, she will remember, she will send, she will hear, she will eat, she will guard   6. we will open, we will find, we will write, we will take, we will sit, we will be, we will know, we will remember   7. you will sit (*m pl*), you will call, you will know, you will be, you will guard, you will open, you will eat, you will hear   8. they will rule, they will take, they will walk, they will find, they will send, they will be, they will say, they will remember

Exercise 3

1. Tonight there is wind. There was wind in the night. Tonight there will be wind.   2. There is not a seed like a seed in Egypt. There was not a seed like a seed in Egypt. There will not be a seed like a seed in Egypt.   3. On the way to the sea there are mountains and fields. On the way to the sea there were mountains and fields. On the way to the sea there will be mountains and fields.   4. If there is no bread there is no law. If there was no bread there was no law. If there will be no bread there will be no law.   5. The heart of the land of Israel is in Jerusalem. The heart of the land of Israel is in the heart of the people. The heart of the people of Israel is in the heavens.   6. In the days of the war there is no spirit of peace. In the days of the war there was no spirit of peace. In the days of the war there will be no spirit of peace.

Exercise 4

1. זֶה, זֹאת, אֵלֶּה, This is the father and this is the mother and these are the children.   2. זֶה, זֶה, This is the name of the man and this is the name of the woman.   3. זֹאת, This is the law forever and ever.   4. זֹאת, Behold this is the woman who wrote to every soul in Bethlehem.   5. אֵלֶּה, These are the hands which made vessels of silver.   6. זֶה, אֵלֶּה, This is the leader of the family and these are the children.   7. זֶה, זֹאת, This is the man and this is the earth.   8. זֶה, אֵלֶּה, These are the waters (this is the water) from the mountains and this is the wind from the sea.   9. זֶה, אֵלֶּה, This is the voice of the chiefs and these are the faces of the slaves.   10. זֶה, זֹאת, This is the day of judgement and this is the soul of the people.

Exercise 5

1.לֹא אֶכְתֹּב לְאֵשֶׁת הַבַּיִת וְהִיא לֹא תִכְתֹּב לַאֲדוֹן הַמָּקוֹם.

I will not write to the woman of the house and she will not write to the lord of the place.

2.לֹא עָלִינוּ יְרוּשָׁלַמָה וְאָז לֹא רָאִינוּ אֶת כֹּהֲנֵי הָעִיר.

We did not go up toward Jerusalem and then we did not see the priests of the city.

3.אֵין רוּחַ בַּשָּׁמַיִם בַּלַּיְלָה וְאֵין שָׁלוֹם בַּשָּׁמַיִם בַּיּוֹם.

There is no wind in the heavens in the night and there is no peace in the heavens in the day.

4.לֹא עָשִׂינוּ אֶת הַלֶּחֶם מֵהַזֶּרַע אֲשֶׁר לֹא מָצָאנוּ עַל הָאֲדָמָה.

We did not make the bread from the seed which we did not find on the ground.

5.אֹהֶל אַבְרָהָם אֵין עוֹד בַּמִּדְבָּר.

The tent of Abraham is not still in the desert.

6.רֹאשׁ הָעָם לֹא יִשְׁמֹר אֶת הַתּוֹרָה בְּכָל הַיָּמִים וּבְכָל הַלֵּילוֹת.

The leader of the people will not guard the law in all of the days and in all of the nights.

Exercise 6

We went from Egypt in the night, and in the day we crossed over toward the sea, we stood in front of the mountain and then we heard the words of the Torah from the heavens and these are words of justice and peace forever.

A.הָלְכוּ מִמִּצְרַיִם בַּלַּיְלָה.   B.עָבַרְתֶּם יָמָּה.   C.אָז עָמַדְנוּ לִפְנֵי הָהָר.   D.הֵם שָׁמְעוּ אֶת דִּבְרֵי הַתּוֹרָה מִן הַשָּׁמַיִם.   E.אֵלֶּה הָיוּ דִּבְרֵי מִשְׁפָּט וְשָׁלוֹם לְעוֹלָם.   F.דִּבְרֵי הַתּוֹרָה מִן הַשָּׁמַיִם.   G.דִּבְרֵי הַמִּשְׁפָּט לְעוֹלָם.   H.בַּלַּיְלָה וּבַיּוֹם עָבַרְנוּ יָמָּה.

Exercise 7

1. The eyes of the son of the king are on the daughters of the city.

21

(Exercise 7 continued)

עֵינֵי בֶן הַמֶּלֶךְ הָיוּ עַל בְּנוֹת הָעִיר. עֵינֵי בֶן הַמֶּלֶךְ יִהְיוּ עַל בְּנוֹת הָעִיר.

2. The name of the father is Jacob and the name of the mother is Ruth.

שֵׁם הָאָב הָיָה יַעֲקֹב וְשֵׁם הָאֵם הָיָה רוּת. שֵׁם הָאָב יִהְיֶה יַעֲקֹב וְשֵׁם הָאֵם יִהְיֶה רוּת.

3. The silver from the mountains is in the ground among the trees.

הַכֶּסֶף מִן הֶהָרִים הוּא הָיָה בָּאֲדָמָה בֵּין הָעֵצִים.
הַכֶּסֶף מִן הֶהָרִים הוּא יִהְיֶה בָּאֲדָמָה בֵּין הָעֵצִים.

4. We are slaves in the day and also in the night.

הָיִינוּ עֲבָדִים בַּיּוֹם וְגַם בַּלַּיְלָה. נִהְיֶה עֲבָדִים בַּיּוֹם וְגַם בַּלַּיְלָה.

5. There is no seed and there is no bread.

לֹא הָיָה זֶרַע וְלֹא הָיָה לֶחֶם. לֹא יִהְיֶה זֶרַע וְלֹא יִהְיֶה לֶחֶם.

6. Behold there is the blood of the sword on the face of the earth.

הִנֵּה דַּם הַחֶרֶב הָיָה עַל פְּנֵי הָאֲדָמָה. הִנֵּה דַּם הַחֶרֶב יִהְיֶה עַל פְּנֵי הָאֲדָמָה.

7. I am near the water and you are on the road.

אֲנִי הָיִיתִי עַל יַד הַמַּיִם וְאַתָּה הָיִיתָ בַּדֶּרֶךְ. אֲנִי אֶהְיֶה עַל יַד הַמַּיִם וְאַתָּה תִּהְיֶה בַּדֶּרֶךְ.

8. There is no justice in Jerusalem and there is no peace in the soul of the people.

לֹא הָיָה מִשְׁפָּט בִּירוּשָׁלַם וְלֹא הָיָה שָׁלוֹם בְּנֶפֶשׁ הָעָם.
לֹא יִהְיֶה מִשְׁפָּט בִּירוּשָׁלַם וְלֹא יִהְיֶה שָׁלוֹם בְּנֶפֶשׁ הָעָם.

9. This is the animal which ate everything.

זֹאת הָיְתָה הַבְּהֵמָה אֲשֶׁר אָכְלָה אֶת הַכֹּל. זֹאת תִּהְיֶה הַבְּהֵמָה אֲשֶׁר תֹּאכַל אֶת הַכֹּל.

10. These are the words which Abraham said to Sarah.

אֵלֶּה הָיוּ הַדְּבָרִים אֲשֶׁר אָמַר אַבְרָהָם לְשָׂרָה. אֵלֶּה יִהְיוּ הַדְּבָרִים אֲשֶׁר יֹאמַר אַבְרָהָם לְשָׂרָה.

Exercise 8

1. I saw the sword of gold, and then I went up with the sword toward the mountain.

א.רָאִיתָ אַתָּה אֶת חֶרֶב הַזָּהָב, וְאָז עָלִיתָ עִם הַחֶרֶב הָהָרָה. ב.רָאֲתָה הִיא אֶת חֶרֶב הַזָּהָב, וְאָז עָלְתָה עִם הַחֶרֶב הָהָרָה. ג.רָאִינוּ אֲנַחְנוּ אֶת חֶרֶב הַזָּהָב, וְאָז עָלִינוּ עִם הַחֶרֶב הָהָרָה. ד.רָאָה הוּא אֶת חֶרֶב הַזָּהָב, וְאָז עָלָה עִם הַחֶרֶב הָהָרָה. ה.רָאוּ הֵם אֶת חֶרֶב הַזָּהָב, וְאָז עָלוּ עִם הַחֶרֶב הָהָרָה.

2. Thus Moses said to the children of Israel: "This is the bread which you will eat in the desert."

א.כֹּה אָמַר מֹשֶׁה אֶל בְּנֵי יִשְׂרָאֵל: "זֶה הַלֶּחֶם אֲשֶׁר אֲנִי אֹכַל בַּמִּדְבָּר." ב.כֹּה אָמַר מֹשֶׁה אֶל בְּנֵי יִשְׂרָאֵל: "זֶה הַלֶּחֶם אֲשֶׁר אֲנַחְנוּ נֹאכַל בַּמִּדְבָּר." ג.כֹּה אָמַר מֹשֶׁה אֶל בְּנֵי יִשְׂרָאֵל: "זֶה הַלֶּחֶם אֲשֶׁר הֵם יֹאכְלוּ בַּמִּדְבָּר." ד.כֹּה אָמַר מֹשֶׁה אֶל בְּנֵי יִשְׂרָאֵל: "זֶה הַלֶּחֶם אֲשֶׁר הִיא תֹּאכַל בַּמִּדְבָּר." ה.כֹּה אָמַר מֹשֶׁה אֶל בְּנֵי יִשְׂרָאֵל: "זֶה הַלֶּחֶם אֲשֶׁר הוּא יֹאכַל בַּמִּדְבָּר."

3. I heard the wind of the night, I opened the gate, I walked to the sea and there I sat until today.

א.אֶשְׁמַע אֶת רוּחַ הַלַּיְלָה, אֶפְתַּח אֶת הַשַּׁעַר, אֵלֵךְ אֶל הַיָּם וְשָׁם אֵשֵׁב עַד הַיּוֹם. ב.שָׁמַע אֶת רוּחַ הַלַּיְלָה, פָּתַח אֶת הַשַּׁעַר, הָלַךְ אֶל הַיָּם וְשָׁם יָשַׁב עַד הַיּוֹם. ג.יִשְׁמַע אֶת רוּחַ הַלַּיְלָה, יִפְתַּח אֶת הַשַּׁעַר, יֵלֵךְ אֶל הַיָּם וְשָׁם יֵשֵׁב עַד הַיּוֹם. ד.שָׁמַעְנוּ אֶת רוּחַ הַלַּיְלָה, פָּתַחְנוּ אֶת הַשַּׁעַר, הָלַכְנוּ אֶל הַיָּם וְשָׁם יָשַׁבְנוּ עַד הַיּוֹם. ה.תִּשְׁמְעוּ אֶת רוּחַ הַלַּיְלָה, תִּפְתְּחוּ אֶת הַשַּׁעַר, תֵּלְכוּ אֶל הַיָּם וְשָׁם תֵּשְׁבוּ עַד הַיּוֹם. ו.שָׁמַעְתָּ אֶת רוּחַ הַלַּיְלָה, פָּתַחְתָּ אֶת הַשַּׁעַר, הָלַכְתָּ אֶל הַיָּם וְשָׁם יָשַׁבְתָּ עַד הַיּוֹם.

4. Behold you will be the priest and then you will know all of the words in the Torah.

א.הִנֵּה הוּא יִהְיֶה הַכֹּהֵן וְאָז יֵדַע אֶת כָּל הַדְּבָרִים בַּתּוֹרָה. ב.הִנֵּה אֲנַחְנוּ נִהְיֶה הַכֹּהֲנִים וְאָז נֵדַע אֶת כָּל הַדְּבָרִים בַּתּוֹרָה. ג.הִנֵּה אֲנִי אֶהְיֶה הַכֹּהֵן וְאָז אֵדַע

(Exercise 8 continued)

אֶת כָּל הַדְּבָרִים בַּתּוֹרָה. ד. הִנֵּה הֵם יִהְיוּ הַכֹּהֲנִים וְאָז יֵדְעוּ אֶת כָּל הַדְּבָרִים בַּתּוֹרָה. ה. הִנֵּה אַתֶּם תִּהְיוּ הַכֹּהֲנִים וְאָז תֵּדְעוּ אֶת כָּל הַדְּבָרִים בַּתּוֹרָה.

5. I will take the seed that I will find on the ground and then I will send the seed to the mother of David.

א. לָקַחְתִּי אֶת הַזֶּרַע אֲשֶׁר מָצָאתִי עַל הָאֲדָמָה וְאָז שָׁלַחְתִּי אֶת הַזֶּרַע אֶל אֵם דָּוִד. ב. יִקַּח אֶת הַזֶּרַע אֲשֶׁר יִמְצָא עַל הָאֲדָמָה וְאָז יִשְׁלַח אֶת הַזֶּרַע אֶל אֵם דָּוִד. ג. לָקַח אֶת הַזֶּרַע אֲשֶׁר מָצָא עַל הָאֲדָמָה וְאָז שָׁלַח אֶת הַזֶּרַע אֶל אֵם דָּוִד. ד. נִקַּח אֶת הַזֶּרַע אֲשֶׁר נִמְצָא עַל הָאֲדָמָה וְאָז נִשְׁלַח אֶת הַזֶּרַע אֶל אֵם דָּוִד. ה. לְקַחְנוּ אֶת הַזֶּרַע אֲשֶׁר מָצָאנוּ עַל הָאֲדָמָה וְאָז שָׁלַחְנוּ אֶת הַזֶּרַע אֶל אֵם דָּוִד. ו. לְקְחוּ אֶת הַזֶּרַע אֲשֶׁר מָצְאוּ עַל הָאֲדָמָה וְאָז שָׁלְחוּ אֶת הַזֶּרַע אֶל אֵם דָּוִד. ז. יִקְחוּ אֶת הַזֶּרַע אֲשֶׁר יִמְצְאוּ עַל הָאֲדָמָה וְאָז יִשְׁלְחוּ אֶת הַזֶּרַע אֶל אֵם דָּוִד.

6. There is not a person today in the heavens and in the land who crossed over the desert, stood in front of the mountain, and also made peace.

א. אֵין מִשְׁפָּחָה הַיּוֹם בַּשָּׁמַיִם וּבָאָרֶץ אֲשֶׁר עָבְרָה אֶת הַמִּדְבָּר, עָמְדָה לִפְנֵי הָהָר, וְגַם עָשְׂתָה שָׁלוֹם. ב. אֵין עַמִּים הַיּוֹם בַּשָּׁמַיִם וּבָאָרֶץ אֲשֶׁר עָבְרוּ אֶת הַמִּדְבָּר, עָמְדוּ לִפְנֵי הָהָר, וְגַם עָשׂוּ שָׁלוֹם. ג. אֵין נָשִׁים הַיּוֹם בַּשָּׁמַיִם וּבָאָרֶץ אֲשֶׁר עָבְרוּ אֶת הַמִּדְבָּר, עָמְדוּ לִפְנֵי הָהָר, וְגַם עָשׂוּ שָׁלוֹם. ד. אֵין אִישׁ הַיּוֹם בַּשָּׁמַיִם וּבָאָרֶץ אֲשֶׁר עָבַר אֶת הַמִּדְבָּר, עָמַד לִפְנֵי הָהָר, וְגַם עָשָׂה שָׁלוֹם.

A TALL TALE: This is the House That

This is the house that Jacob made.

This is the woman who sat in the house that Jacob made.

These are the daughters who are in the family of the woman who sat in the house that Jacob made.

These are the young men who took the daughters who are in the family of the woman who sat in the house that Jacob made.

These are the chiefs who guarded the young men who took the daughters who are in the family of the woman who sat in the house that Jacob made.

This is the war which killed the chiefs who guarded the young men who took the daughters who are in the family of the woman who sat in the house that Jacob made.

This is the people who remembered the war which killed the chiefs who guarded the young men who took the daughters who are in the family of the woman who sat in the house that Jacob made.

Chapter 14

Oral Review

1. Before day there is night. Before day there was night. Before day there will be night. 2. Between the mountains and the sea there is no desert. Between the sea and the city there was no desert. Between the trees and the gates there will not be a desert. 3. What are the names of the children of David? These are the names of the children of David: Abraham and Sarah. Who is the father of Abraham and Sarah? David is the father. 4. The wind is on the face of the earth tonight. There is no wind on the face of the sea tonight. There will be no wind on the face of the sea today. 5. David is a king in the land of Egypt. David ruled in Jerusalem. David will rule forever and ever. David ruled over the people. David was a king there. 6. This is the mother and this is the father. I was the daughter and you were the son. I will not be the woman and you will not be the man. 7. Here we are in Bethlehem in the night. Behold we sat and also we ate in Bethlehem in the night. Behold we will sit and behold we will eat in the night. 8. The voice of Moses is from the mountain. You heard the voice of Moses from the mountain. You will hear the voice of Moses from the law. 9. Who crossed over toward the mountain, walked toward the desert and then went up toward the heavens? The children of Israel crossed over toward the mountain, walked toward the desert and then did not go up to Jerusalem. 10. Who will remember the words, will know the judgement and also will guard the law? We will remember the words, we will know the judgement and also we will guard the law forever.

Exercise 1

1. a good father, or A father is good. a good mother, or A mother is good. good sons, or Sons are good. good daughters, or Daughters are good. 2. a big sea, or A sea is big. the big hand, the big tents, big eyes, or eyes are big. 3. the wise man, a wise young woman, the wise priests, wise faces 4. the mother of the old master, the house of old Naomi, the old servants, the old eyes of Joseph 5. much peace, much earth, the many people, many families 6. with the evil sword, in the evil soul, from evil blood, to the evil cities 7. one desert, one city, under the one tree, the great war

(Exercise 1 continued)

8. this voice, this road, these waters (this water), these cattle   9. that leader, that mother, those nights, those judgements

Exercise 2

1. אֹהֶל אֶחָד, אִם אַחַת   2. אֶרֶץ גְּדוֹלָה, הָאִשָּׁה הַגְּדוֹלָה, בְּהֵמוֹת גְּדוֹלוֹת, תַּחַת הַשַּׁעַר הַגָּדוֹל   3. רוּחַ חָכָם, בַּת חָכְמָה, הַבָּנִים הַחֲכָמִים, נְפָשׁוֹת חֲכָמוֹת   4. הַלֶּחֶם הַזֶּה, הַלַּיְלָה הַהוּא, הַכֵּלִים הָאֵלֶּה, הֶהָרִים הָהֵם   5. יוֹסֵף הַזָּקֵן, לְאָה הָרָעָה, עֵצִים רַבִּים, תַּחַת אָחִים הַזְּקֵנִים   6. הַזֶּרַע הָרָע, לֵב טוֹב or לְבַב טוֹב, עֲבָדִים רַבִּים, שָׁמַיִם טוֹבִים   7. כֶּסֶף רַב, מִשְׁפָּט טוֹב, עֵינַיִם רָעוֹת, הַמְּקוֹמוֹת הַטּוֹבִים הָאֵלֶּה

Exercise 3

1. This place is bigger than that place.   2. Leah is older than David and also she is the good one.   3. The priests of Egypt were wiser than the kings of Moab.   4. Joseph is better than all of the young men in the family.   5. I knew that Sarah was very bad and Ruth was worse than Sarah.   6. There is much peace in the land because there are many chiefs of the city around.

Exercise 4

1. מ.ל.ך – I ruled, שׁ.מ.ר – I will guard, ע.ב.ר – I crossed over, ל.ק.ח – I will take, א.כ.ל – I will eat, א.מ.ר – I said, ה.י.ה – I will be, ע.מ.ד – I stood   2. ה.ל.ך – you walked (m sg), ז.כ.ר – you will remember, ע.ל.ה – you went up, ע.שׂ.ה – you made, י.ד.ע – you will know, י.שׁ.ב – you sat, כ.ת.ב – you will write, ק.ר.א – you will call   3. שׁ.מ.ע – you heard (f sg), שׁ.ל.ח – you will send, ע.שׂ.ה – you made, מ.צ.א – you will find, ר.א.ה – you saw, פ.ת.ח – you will open, שׁ.מ.ר – you will guard, א.כ.ל – you ate   4. מ.צ.א – he will find, ע.מ.ד – he stood, ז.כ.ר – he will remember, שׁ.ל.ח – he sent, פ.ת.ח – he will open, א.כ.ל – he will eat, י.שׁ.ב – he sat, י.ד.ע – he will know   5. מ.ל.ך – she ruled, כ.ת.ב – she will write, שׁ.מ.ע – she will hear, ה.ל.ך – she walked, א.מ.ר – she will say, ע.ב.ר – she crossed over, ל.ק.ח – she will take, ר.א.ה – she saw   6. ק.ר.א – we called, כ.ת.ב – we will write, שׁ.מ.ר – we will guard, ה.ל.ך – we will walk, ע.שׂ.ה – we did, ע.ל.ה – we went up, שׁ.מ.ע – we will hear, ה.י.ה – we were   7. מ.ל.ך –

you will rule (m pl), ז.כ.ר – you remembered, שׁ.ל.ח – you sent, פ.ת.ח – you will open, ה.ל.ך – you walked, א.מ.ר – you will say, ע.ב.ר – you crossed over, א.כ.ל – you will eat   8. ז.כ.ר – they will remember, ע.מ.ד – they stood, י.ד.ע – they will know, י.ד.ע – they knew, י.שׁ.ב – they sat, י.שׁ.ב – they will sit, ל.ק.ח – they took, ל.ק.ח – they will take   9. א.מ.ר – they said, ז.כ.ר – I will remember, שׁ.מ.ר – they guarded, כ.ת.ב – he will write, ע.שׂ.ה – they made, ה.י.ה – he was, י.שׁ.ב – we sat, פ.ת.ח – he opened   10. מ.ל.ך – he will rule, שׁ.ל.ח – I sent, שׁ.מ.ע – I will hear, ה.ל.ך – you will go (m sg), א.כ.ל – we ate, ע.ב.ר – they crossed over, ה.י.ה – they will be, מ.צ.א – he will find

Exercise 5

1. הָרָע, The evil people will take all of the gold from the hands of the priest.   2. רַבִּים, The words of the children of Jacob are more numerous than all the words of the people of Moab.   3. חֲכָמִים, Wise servants made vessels of silver for the elders in the land.   4. אַחַת, One woman with the name of Sarah resided in Bethlehem in those days.   5. גְּדוֹלִים, We crossed over toward Jerusalem and we saw very large gates around.   6. זְקֵנָה, "I am very old," said Naomi. "And also all of the women of the house are old."

Exercise 6

1. The many women of Bethlehem are in the big tent because there are evil people around.   2. In the days of the kings David was in Jerusalem and then he was very old.   3. This is the good king and these are the many slaves who will take the evil ones from the city.   4. One day we saw that there was good bread in the house. We took the good bread to the field of Jacob. We sat under a big tree and then we ate and behold it was very good!   5. There is not a wise mother in the family and the father is old and in this house there are no judgements of the law and there is war among the children.

Exercise 7

1. One day I will find much gold under the ground round about and then I will know that everything will be good in the world.

א. יוֹם אֶחָד הוּא יִמְצָא זָהָב רַב תַּחַת הָאֲדָמָה סָבִיב וְאָז יֵדַע כִּי הַכֹּל טוֹב בָּעוֹלָם.   ב. יוֹם אֶחָד אַתָּה תִּמְצָא זָהָב רַב תַּחַת הָאֲדָמָה סָבִיב וְאָז תֵּדַע כִּי הַכֹּל

(Exercise 7 continued)

ג. יוֹם אֶחָד אֲנַחְנוּ נִמְצָא זָהָב רַב תַּחַת הָאֲדָמָה סָבִיב וְאָז נֵדַע כִּי הַכֹּל טוֹב בָּעוֹלָם. ד. יוֹם אֶחָד הֵמָּה יִמְצְאוּ זָהָב רַב תַּחַת הָאֲדָמָה סָבִיב וְאָז יֵדְעוּ כִּי הַכֹּל טוֹב בָּעוֹלָם. ה. יוֹם אֶחָד הִיא תִּמְצָא זָהָב רַב תַּחַת הָאֲדָמָה סָבִיב וְאָז תֵּדַע כִּי הַכֹּל טוֹב בָּעוֹלָם.

טוֹב בָּעוֹלָם.

2. Who wrote about these evil women who resided in the mountains around?

א. מִי כָּתַב עַל הָאִישׁ הָרַע הַזֶּה אֲשֶׁר יָשַׁב בֶּהָרִים סָבִיב? ב. מִי כָּתַב עַל הַבַּת הָרָעָה הַזֹּאת אֲשֶׁר יָשְׁבָה בֶּהָרִים סָבִיב? ג. מִי כָּתַב עַל הַשָּׂרִים הָרָעִים הָאֵלֶּה אֲשֶׁר יָשְׁבוּ בֶּהָרִים סָבִיב? ד. מִי כָּתַב עַל הַנֶּפֶשׁ הָרָעָה הַזֹּאת אֲשֶׁר יָשְׁבָה בֶּהָרִים סָבִיב?

3. The evil chiefs did not hear the great voice of the priests and they made war instead of peace.

א. רָחֵל הָרָעָה לֹא שָׁמְעָה אֶת קוֹל הַכֹּהֲנִים הַגָּדוֹל וְהִיא עָשְׂתָה מִלְחָמָה תַּחַת שָׁלוֹם. ב. יוֹסֵף הָרַע לֹא שָׁמַע אֶת קוֹל הַכֹּהֲנִים הַגָּדוֹל וְהוּא עָשָׂה מִלְחָמָה תַּחַת שָׁלוֹם. ג. הַנְּפָשׁוֹת הָרָעוֹת לֹא שָׁמְעוּ אֶת קוֹל הַכֹּהֲנִים הַגָּדוֹל וְהֵנָּה עָשׂוּ מִלְחָמָה תַּחַת שָׁלוֹם. ד. הַבָּנִים הָרָעִים לֹא שָׁמְעוּ אֶת קוֹל הַכֹּהֲנִים הַגָּדוֹל וְהֵם עָשׂוּ מִלְחָמָה תַּחַת שָׁלוֹם. ה. מִשְׁפָּחָה רָעָה לֹא שָׁמְעָה אֶת קוֹל הַכֹּהֲנִים הַגָּדוֹל וְהִיא עָשְׂתָה מִלְחָמָה תַּחַת שָׁלוֹם.

4. We will go toward the mountain to a very big city and there we will eat many animals, say very many bad things and then we will take the people of the place for (as) slaves.

א. אָנֹכִי אֵלֵךְ הָהָרָה אֶל עִיר גְּדוֹלָה מְאֹד וְשָׁם אֹכַל בִּבְהֵמוֹת רַבּוֹת, אֹמַר דְּבָרִים רָעִים מְאֹד וְאָז אֶקַּח אֶת אַנְשֵׁי הַמָּקוֹם לַעֲבָדִים. ב. מֹשֶׁה יֵלֵךְ הָהָרָה אֶל עִיר גְּדוֹלָה מְאֹד וְשָׁם יֹאכַל בִּבְהֵמוֹת רַבּוֹת, יֹאמַר דְּבָרִים רָעִים מְאֹד וְאָז יִקַּח אֶת אַנְשֵׁי הַמָּקוֹם לַעֲבָדִים. ג. אַתֶּם תֵּלְכוּ הָהָרָה אֶל עִיר גְּדוֹלָה מְאֹד וְשָׁם תֹּאכְלוּ בִּבְהֵמוֹת רַבּוֹת, תֹּאמְרוּ דְּבָרִים רָעִים מְאֹד וְאָז תִּקְחוּ אֶת אַנְשֵׁי הַמָּקוֹם לַעֲבָדִים. ד. הִיא תֵּלֵךְ הָהָרָה אֶל עִיר גְּדוֹלָה מְאֹד וְשָׁם תֹּאכַל בִּבְהֵמוֹת רַבּוֹת, תֹּאמַר דְּבָרִים רָעִים מְאֹד וְאָז תִּקַּח אֶת אַנְשֵׁי הַמָּקוֹם לַעֲבָדִים. ה. הֵם יֵלְכוּ הָהָרָה אֶל עִיר גְּדוֹלָה מְאֹד

וְשָׁם יֹאכְלוּ בִּבְהֵמוֹת רַבּוֹת, יֹאמְרוּ דְּבָרִים רָעִים מְאֹד וְאָז יִקְחוּ אֶת אַנְשֵׁי הַמָּקוֹם לַעֲבָדִים. ו. אַתָּה תֵּלֵךְ הָהָרָה אֶל עִיר גְּדוֹלָה מְאֹד וְשָׁם תֹּאכַל בִּבְהֵמוֹת רַבּוֹת, תֹּאמַר דְּבָרִים רָעִים מְאֹד וְאָז תִּקַּח אֶת אַנְשֵׁי הַמָּקוֹם לַעֲבָדִים.

5. Joseph is the good one in the land and he is also bigger than all the people around.

א. לֵאָה הַטּוֹבָה בָּאָרֶץ וְהִיא גַּם גְּדוֹלָה מִכָּל הַנָּשִׁים סָבִיב. ב. אֲנַחְנוּ הַטּוֹבִים בָּאָרֶץ וַאֲנַחְנוּ גַּם גְּדוֹלִים מִכָּל הָאֲנָשִׁים סָבִיב. ג. הַנָּשִׁים הַטּוֹבוֹת בָּאָרֶץ וְהֵנָּה גַּם גְּדוֹלוֹת מִכָּל הַנָּשִׁים סָבִיב. ד. הָעֲבָדִים הַטּוֹבִים בָּאָרֶץ וְהֵם גַּם גְּדוֹלִים מִכָּל הָעֲבָדִים סָבִיב. ה. אַתָּה הַטּוֹב בָּאָרֶץ וְאַתָּה גַּם גָּדוֹל מִכָּל הָאֲנָשִׁים סָבִיב.

A TALL TALE: The Boy of Bread

In those days (once upon a time) there was a little house in the city. In the house there lived a little old woman and a little old man. There were no sons and there were no daughters in that house. Every day the little old woman made bread.

One day the little old woman made bread in the shape of a little boy. The old woman took the Gingerbread Boy in hand. And she said: "Now there is a little boy in this house."

But the Gingerbread Boy went from the hand of the little old woman. He ran away from the little old woman and also from the little old man. He ran away from the house and from the city.

The Gingerbread Boy ran away on the road toward the sea. On the road he saw a great king. This king was greater than all the kings on the face of the earth. The great king said: "Gingerbread Boy, from what have you run away?"
The Gingerbread Boy said: "I ran away from the little old woman and also I ran away from the little old man. I ran away from the house and from the city and also I will run away from this great king. I will run away! I will run away!..."

And the Gingerbread Boy ran away again toward the sea.

Then the Gingerbread Boy saw a priest that was sitting on the road under a tree. This priest was the best of all priests on the face of the earth.
The good priest said: "Gingerbread Boy, from what have you run away?"
The Gingerbread Boy said: "I have run away from the little old woman and also I have run away from the little old man. I have run away from the house and from the city. Then I ran away from the great king

(A TALL TALE continued)

and also I will run away also from this good priest. I will run away! I will run away!..."

And the Gingerbread Boy ran away again toward the sea.

Then the Gingerbread boy saw an evil beast on the road. This beast was the worst beast of all the beasts on the face of the earth.
The evil beast said: "Gingerbread Boy, from what have you run away?"

The Gingerbread Boy said: "I have run away from the little old woman and also I have run away from the little old man. I have run away from the house and from the city. I have run away from the great king and the good priest and I will also run away from this evil beast. I will run away! I will run away!"
The beast said: "I also will run away from all of these people."
And the Gingerbread Boy ran away again with the evil beast.

The Gingerbread Boy and the evil beast stood in front of the sea.
They said: "Here is the sea!"
The evil beast said: "If you will sit on the head of this evil beast you will not be in the sea."
The Gingerbread Boy said: "No! If I will sit there, you will eat this Gingerbread Boy."
The evil beast said: "Oh no! I will not ever eat the Gingerbread Boy. I will guard this Gingerbread Boy from the water."

The Gingerbread Boy was not wise and he went up on the head of the evil beast. The Gingerbread Boy sat on the head of the evil beast.
He said in a big voice: "How smart am I! Behold I have run away from the little old woman and also I have run away from the little old man. I have run away from the house and from the city. I have run away from the great king and the good priest and I will also run away from this evil beast."

But the evil beast said: "No! You will not run away from this evil beast."
Then the evil beast opened her mouth and she ate the Gingerbread Boy.
The evil beast said: "Oh! The Gingerbread Boy is the best bread of all the bread on the face of the earth!"

Chapter 15

Oral Review

1. This is a good land in the eyes of the wise priests.
2. This is the big field which is between those many mountains and that good land. 3. These are the very old people who sat around in the big field. 4. Here is the one road which passed the big city. 5. This servant is older than the servants of evil Egypt. 6. The servants of Egypt are greater than all of the servants under the heavens. 7. Joseph is good and Leah is better than Joseph because she obeyed a wise mother. 8. This family is bigger than that family. 9. There are many tents in the big desert and the evil ones will reside there. 10. There is no good land in that desert and the wise ones will go (away) from there. 11. There was one good one in all of the evil city and he went. 12. The wise ones (women) in Moab found good men instead of evil men. 13. If I will eat all of the good bread then you will eat bad bread. 14. If Joseph will open the big gates we will walk toward the city. 15. If the chiefs of Jerusalem will sit under the trees there will not be war around. 16. If you will walk to the big sea than you will find good earth. 17. This wise man is very evil. 18. This old woman is very good.

Exercise 1

1. my hand, my heart, my soul, my father, my name, my master, my brother, my road 2. your servant (*m sg*), your people, your name, your law, your land, your wife, your house, your judgement 3. your father (*f sg*), your head, your soul, your king, your son, your hand, your word, your tent 4. his daughter, his hand, his heart, his people, his servant, his place, his law, his father 5. her head, her people, her soul, her man, her house, her road, her brother, her earth 6. our king, our land, our son, our father, our bread, our heart, our people, our name 7. your soul (*m pl*), your eye, your father, your ground, your road, your head, your daughter, your flock 8. their land, their road, their descendent, their silver, their bread, their father, their brother, their judgement

Exercise 2

1. S 2. H 3. B 4. F 5. E 6. A 7. D 8. C 9. G 10. U 11. I 12. R 13. T 14. J 15. Q 16. M 17. N 18. L 19. P 20. O 21. K

Exercise 3

1. Jacob went out toward Jerusalem with meat of his cattle as an offering. 2. I made this gift for my mother for the Day of the Mother. 3. People of my city will judge between my flock and your flock. 4. I loved meat with my bread but I did not eat meat every day. 5. We sent our silver to our king for his throne. 6. That king was great and we guarded the honor of his name. 7. Their blood is on our land forever.

Exercise 4

1. כִּסְאוֹ, I went up on my throne and he went up on his throne. 2. מֵאַרְצְךָ, A man went out from his land and you went out from your land. 3. מַלְכָּם, Abraham will guard the honor of his king and the chiefs will guard the honor of their king. 4. לְמִנְחָתָךְ, They took the gold for their offering and you took the silver for your

(Exercise 4 continued)

offering. 5. אִשְׁתִּי, Jacob loved his wife and I loved my wife. 6. מִשְׁפָּטָהּ, Moses will write his judgement and Naomi will write her judgement. 7. אׇהֳלֶךָ, I stood in front of my tent in the night and you stood in front of your tent. 8. בְּנֵנוּ, The priest went out with his son from Egypt but we did not go out with our son.

Exercise 5

1. בֵּיתִי עׇמַד עַל יַד בֵּיתְךָ בְּתוֹךְ הַשָּׂדֶה. 2. נִשְׁמֹר אֶת צֹאנֵנוּ אֲשֶׁר תִּהְיֶה עַל אַרְצֵנוּ סָבִיב. 3. מֹשֶׁה יִשְׁפֹּט עַמּוֹ לִפְנֵי שַׁעֲרֵי הָעִיר. 4. שָׁמָּה נׇעֳמִי וְהִיא לׇקְחָה מִנְחָה לְאִמָּהּ אַךְ לֹא לׇקְחָה דָּבָר לְאׇבִיהָ. 5. דָּוִד אָהַב אֶת כְּבוֹדוֹ וְאֶת כַּסְפּוֹ אַךְ לֹא אָהַב אֶת אִשְׁתּוֹ. 6. בְּנֵנוּ יׇצָא מִגְּבוּל אַרְצֵנוּ עִם אִמּוֹ, אׇבִיו, אׇחִיו קׇטׇן, צֹאנוֹ, וּבְהֶמְתּוֹ. 7. הַנַּעַר הַזֶּה זׇכַר אֶת פְּנֵי בֵּיתוֹ לְעוֹלָם וָעֶד. 8. מַלְכֵּנוּ יׇדַע הַכֹּל עַל כְּלֵי הַזָּהָב.

Exercise 6

1. What is your name? My name is Sarah and the name of my brother is Moses. 2. Who will judge between my border and your border? His father will judge. 3. Who called to our small daughter? We called to your small daughter. 4. Who went out from the midst of my land toward the mountain? I went out with my flock from your land as far as the border of the mountains. 5. Who did you love with all of your heart and with all of your soul? I loved my son and my daughter with all of my heart and with all of my soul. 6. What did you see from the gates of your house? We saw your brother and his blood and his sword in his hand. 7. What will you eat under the tree near the water of the sea? I will eat meat of my flock and bread of my people. 8. Who will rule over your slave in the days of the war? Our father will rule over the slaves in these days.

Exercise 7

1. The chiefs went out on their way from their place in Egypt, and they crossed over the border.

א. אֲנִי יׇצָאתִי בְּדַרְכִּי מִמְּקוֹמִי בְּמִצְרַיִם, וַאֲנִי עׇבַרְתִּי אֶת הַגְּבוּל. ב. יוֹסֵף יׇצָא בְּדַרְכּוֹ מִמְּקוֹמוֹ בְּמִצְרַיִם, וְהוּא עׇבַר אֶת הַגְּבוּל. ג. אַתָּה יׇצָאתָ בְּדַרְכְּךָ מִמְּקוֹמְךָ בְּמִצְרַיִם, וְאַתָּה עׇבַרְתָּ אֶת הַגְּבוּל. ד. אֲנַחְנוּ יׇצָאנוּ בְּדַרְכֵּנוּ מִמְּקוֹמֵנוּ בְּמִצְרַיִם, וַאֲנַחְנוּ עׇבַרְנוּ אֶת הַגְּבוּל. ה. שָׂרָה יׇצְאָה בְּדַרְכָּהּ מִמְּקוֹמָהּ בְּמִצְרַיִם, וְהִיא עׇבְרָה אֶת הַגְּבוּל. ו. אַתֶּם יְצָאתֶם בְּדַרְכְּכֶם מִמְּקוֹמְכֶם בְּמִצְרַיִם, וְאַתֶּם עֲבַרְתֶּם אֶת הַגְּבוּל.

2. I guarded the honor of my father because I loved his soul with all of my heart.

א. אַתָּה שָׁמַרְתָּ אֶת כְּבוֹד אׇבִיךָ כִּי אׇהַבְתָּ אֶת נַפְשׁוֹ בְּכָל לְבׇבְךָ. ב. אַתֶּם שְׁמַרְתֶּם אֶת כְּבוֹד אֲבִיכֶם כִּי אֲהַבְתֶּם אֶת נַפְשׁוֹ בְּכָל לְבַבְכֶם. ג. נׇעֳמִי שׇמְרָה אֶת כְּבוֹד אׇבִיהָ כִּי אׇהֲבָה אֶת נַפְשׁוֹ בְּכָל לְבׇבָהּ. ד. אׇחִיךָ שׇמַר אֶת כְּבוֹד אׇבִיךָ כִּי אׇהַב אֶת נַפְשׁוֹ בְּכָל לְבָבוֹ. ה. הַבָּנִים שׇמְרוּ אֶת כְּבוֹד אֲבִיהֶם כִּי אׇהֲבוּ אֶת נַפְשׁוֹ בְּכָל לְבָבָם.

3. I loved my honor, and my name, and my voice, and my soul but I did not do a thing for my country.

א. הוּא אׇהַב אֶת כְּבוֹדוֹ, וְאֶת שְׁמוֹ, וְאֶת קוֹלוֹ, וְאֶת נַפְשׁוֹ אַךְ לֹא עׇשָׂה דָּבָר לְאַרְצוֹ. ב. אַתָּה אׇהַבְתָּ אֶת כְּבוֹדְךָ, וְאֶת שְׁמְךָ, וְאֶת קוֹלְךָ, וְאֶת נַפְשְׁךָ אַךְ לֹא עׇשִׂיתָ דָּבָר לְאַרְצְךָ. ג. אַתֶּם אֲהַבְתֶּם אֶת כְּבוֹדְכֶם, וְאֶת שְׁמְכֶם, וְאֶת קוֹלְכֶם, וְאֶת נַפְשְׁכֶם אַךְ לֹא עֲשִׂיתֶם דָּבָר לְאַרְצְכֶם. ד. הִיא אׇהֲבָה אֶת כְּבוֹדָהּ, וְאֶת שְׁמָהּ, וְאֶת קוֹלָהּ, וְאֶת נַפְשָׁהּ אַךְ לֹא עׇשְׂתָה דָּבָר לְאַרְצָהּ. ה. אַתְּ אׇהַבְתְּ אֶת כְּבוֹדְךְ, וְאֶת שְׁמֵךְ, וְאֶת קוֹלֵךְ, וְאֶת נַפְשֵׁךְ אַךְ לֹא עׇשִׂית דָּבָר לְאַרְצֵךְ.

4. Abraham will send his cattle to his land and he will guard his cattle from his evil king.

א. רוּת תִּשְׁלַח אֶת בְּהֶמְתָּהּ אֶל אַרְצָהּ וְהִיא תִּשְׁמֹר אֶת בְּהֶמְתָּהּ מִמַּלְכָּהּ הָרָע. ב. הֵם יִשְׁלְחוּ אֶת בְּהֶמְתָּם אֶל אַרְצָם וְהֵם יִשְׁמְרוּ אֶת בְּהֶמְתָּם מִמַּלְכָּם הָרָע. ג. אַתֶּם תִּשְׁלְחוּ אֶת בְּהֶמְתְּכֶם אֶל אַרְצְכֶם וְאַתֶּם תִּשְׁמְרוּ אֶת בְּהֶמְתְּכֶם מִמַּלְכְּכֶם הָרָע. ד. אַתָּה תִּשְׁלַח אֶת בְּהֶמְתְּךָ אֶל אַרְצְךָ וְאַתָּה תִּשְׁמֹר אֶת בְּהֶמְתְּךָ מִמַּלְכְּךָ הָרָע. ה. אֲנַחְנוּ נִשְׁלַח אֶת בְּהֶמְתֵּנוּ אֶל אַרְצֵנוּ וַאֲנַחְנוּ נִשְׁמֹר אֶת בְּהֶמְתֵּנוּ מִמַּלְכֵּנוּ הָרָע.

5. My place is in the seat of my father that is in my small house that is on my land that is in my country that is within my border.

א. מְקוֹמְךָ בְּכִסֵּא אׇבִיךָ אֲשֶׁר בְּבֵיתְךָ הַקָּטָן אֲשֶׁר עַל אַדְמׇתְךָ אֲשֶׁר בְּאַרְצְךָ אֲשֶׁר בְּתוֹךְ גְּבוּלְךָ. ב. מְקוֹמוֹ בְּכִסֵּא אׇבִיו אֲשֶׁר בְּבֵיתוֹ הַקָּטָן אֲשֶׁר עַל אַדְמׇתוֹ אֲשֶׁר

27

(Exercise 7 continued)

בְּאַרְצוֹ אֲשֶׁר בְּתוֹךְ גְּבוּלוֹ.   ג. מְקוֹמָהּ בְּכִסֵּא אָבִיהָ
אֲשֶׁר בְּבֵיתָהּ הַקָּטָן אֲשֶׁר עַל אַדְמָתָהּ אֲשֶׁר בְּאַרְצָהּ
אֲשֶׁר בְּתוֹךְ גְּבוּלָהּ.   ד. מְקוֹמְכֶם בְּכִסֵּא אֲבִיכֶם אֲשֶׁר
בְּבֵיתְכֶם הַקָּטָן אֲשֶׁר עַל אַדְמַתְכֶם אֲשֶׁר בְּאַרְצְכֶם
אֲשֶׁר בְּתוֹךְ גְּבוּלְכֶם.   ה. מְקוֹמָם בְּכִסֵּא אֲבִיהֶם אֲשֶׁר
בְּבֵיתָם הַקָּטָן אֲשֶׁר עַל אַדְמָתָם אֲשֶׁר בְּאַרְצָם אֲשֶׁר
בְּתוֹךְ גְּבוּלָם.

6. I will judge the meat of my flock and if it is good, I
will take the meat as a gift for my king.

א. יִשְׁפֹּט אֶת בְּשַׂר צֹאנוֹ וְאִם טוֹב, יִקַּח אֶת הַבָּשָׂר
כְּמִנְחָה לְמַלְכּוֹ.   ב. נִשְׁפֹּט אֶת בְּשַׂר צֹאנֵנוּ וְאִם טוֹב,
נִקַּח אֶת הַבָּשָׂר כְּמִנְחָה לְמַלְכֵּנוּ.   ג. תִּשְׁפֹּט (you, *msg*)
אֶת בְּשַׂר צֹאנְךָ וְאִם טוֹב, תִּקַּח אֶת הַבָּשָׂר כְּמִנְחָה
לְמַלְכְּךָ.   ד. יִשְׁפְּטוּ אֶת בְּשַׂר צֹאנָם וְאִם טוֹב, יִקְחוּ
אֶת הַבָּשָׂר כְּמִנְחָה לְמַלְכָּם.   ה. תִּשְׁפְּטוּ אֶת בְּשַׂר
צֹאנְכֶם וְאִם טוֹב, תִּקְחוּ אֶת הַבָּשָׂר כְּמִנְחָה לְמַלְכְּכֶם.

7. I went out from my border toward Jerusalem for the
honor of my people with bread and meat in my hand.

א. אַתָּה יָצָאתָ מִגְּבוּלְךָ יְרוּשָׁלַמָה לִכְבוֹד עַמְּךָ עִם
לֶחֶם וּבָשָׂר בְּיָדְךָ.   ב. רָחֵל יָצְאָה מִגְּבוּלָהּ יְרוּשָׁלַמָה
לִכְבוֹד עַמָּהּ עִם לֶחֶם וּבָשָׂר בְּיָדָהּ.   ג. בְּנֵי יִשְׂרָאֵל
יָצְאוּ מִגְּבוּלָם יְרוּשָׁלַמָה לִכְבוֹד עַמָּם עִם לֶחֶם וּבָשָׂר
בְּיָדָם.   ד. יוֹסֵף יָצָא מִגְּבוּלוֹ יְרוּשָׁלַמָה לִכְבוֹד עַמּוֹ
עִם לֶחֶם וּבָשָׂר בְּיָדוֹ.   ה. אֲנַחְנוּ יָצָאנוּ מִגְּבוּלֵנוּ
יְרוּשָׁלַמָה לִכְבוֹד עַמֵּנוּ עִם לֶחֶם וּבָשָׂר בְּיָדֵנוּ.   ו. אַתְּ
יָצָאת מִגְּבוּלֵךְ יְרוּשָׁלַמָה לִכְבוֹד עַמֵּךְ עִם לֶחֶם וּבָשָׂר
בְּיָדֵךְ.

Exercise 8

1. There is none like (as) our God. There is none like
our Lord. There is none like our King. There is none
like our Savior. 2. Who is like our God? Who is like
our Lord? Who is like our King? Who is like our
Savior? 3. Blessed is our God. Blessed is our Lord.
Blessed is our King. Blessed is our Savior. 4. You are
our God. You are our Lord. You are our King. You are
our Savior.

A TALL TALE

Within their small house resided David, and his old
father, and his old mother, and his good wife, and his
son and his daughter. Every day his father sat in his
chair and his mother sat in her chair. His wife made
their bread. His son and his daughter called out the
words of the law in their loud (big) voice(s). And David
made all of the utensils of his house from his place
within their small house. David loved all of the people
of his house but there was no peace because there was
no place for all of the people in their house. It was very
bad.

One day David went out as far as the border of his city
to the wise man.

Thus David said to the wise man: "My lord, our house
is very small and there are many people in that small
house. There is no room and there is no peace.
Everything is very bad!"

The wise man said: "Who are the people of your house?"

David said: "There is in my house my old father, and
my old mother, and my good wife, and my son, and my
daughter."

The wise man said: "Is there an animal near your
house?"

David said: "My lord, there is a large animal in the
field next to my house."

The wise man said: "Then you will take the animal from
the midst of the field to your house."

David went to his house and then he did what the wise
man said. He took his large animal from the midst of
the field to his house. And then there lived David and
his old father, and his old mother, and his good wife,
and his son and his daughter and also his large animal
within their small house. There was no peace because
there was no room and it was still very bad.

David went out again as far as the border of his city to
the wise man.

Thus David said: "My lord, there is in my house my old
father, and my old mother, and my good wife, and my
son, and my daughter, and also the large animal.
There is no peace because there is no room in our
house. And it is still very bad!"

The wise man said: "Do you have a flock of sheep?"

David said: "My lord, there is a flock of sheep in the
field."

The wise man said: "You will take one sheep from the
flock from the midst of the field to your house."

David went to the house and he did what the wise man
said. David took the sheep from the field to his small
house. Then David and his old father, and his old
mother, and his good wife, and his son, and his
daughter, and his large animal and also one sheep
resided within his small house. There was no peace
in their house. It was bad. It was very bad!

(A TALL TALE continued)

And again David went out as far as the border of his city to the wise man.

Thus David said: "My lord, there is in my house my old father, and my old mother, and my good wife, and my son, and my daughter, and my large animal, and also a sheep. There is no peace in our house. It is bad in our house. It is very bad!"

Then the wise man said: "You will take your large animal and the one sheep from within your house. You will take your animal and the sheep to the fields around."

David went to the house and he did what the wise man said. He took his large animal and the one sheep from within his house. Behold there was much peace in his house. There was a place for all the people in his house. Behold it was very good.

Then in the house there lived David and his old father, and his old mother, and his good wife, and his son, and his daughter. And behold there was peace in his house. It was good. It was very good!

David said: "Our lord is the wisest one, he is the wisest one of all the men under the heavens."

Chapter 16

Oral Review

1. I loved my father and my mother. Joseph loved his seat which was in the middle his house. You loved the honor of your king and the honor of your country. We loved our flock of sheep but we did not love our cattle. 2. They went out from the border of our country and there they judged all of our people. Leah will go out from within her small house and then she will eat her meat and her bread. My flock went out from within our place in front of the eyes of all our people. Abraham will go out from his land with a gift for his wife. 3. I will judge the offering of your flock before your eyes. Joseph judged between his brother and his father. You will judge who is the smallest of your flock. The priest will judge from his place in the seat of honor. 4. You saw the honor of the house of your father within Jerusalem. Your mother heard your voice and your word. We saw the meat of his animal which he took to Jerusalem as his offering. The chiefs heard your voice and they saw your land. 5. My son will remember my name forever. You will remember the soul of your father and the spirit of your mother. You remembered all of your money which is under your ground. You remembered with all of your heart and with all of your soul all of the words of your law.

Exercise 1

1. me, in me, to me, with me, from me, to me, upon me, after me   2. you (*m sg*), with you, to you, in you, before you, from you, upon you, after you   3. you (*f sg*), after you, in you, before you, to you, with you, upon you, to you   4. him, from him, to him, after him, in him, to him, upon him, before him   5. her, upon her, in her, before her, with her, to her, from her, after her   6. us, before us, in us, after us, to us, upon us, with us, from us   7. you (*m pl*), in you, to you, with you, before you, to you, from you, after you   8. them (*m pl*), after them, before them, to them, with them, upon them, to them, from them

Exercise 2

1. I will eat the bread and also you will eat it.
2. Joseph said the words and Leah heard them.   3. You will send your gift to Jerusalem and then you will send it to the priest.   4. He loved my brother and he also loved me.   5. You knew our father but you did not remember us.   6. We saw your mother and then we saw you.   7. Naomi will find your house and then she will find you.   8. Who opened the gates of the city? Who opened them?   9. Moses will take you and he will take your cattle.

Exercise 3

1. to us   2. with him   3. in me   4. me   5. to you (*m sg*)
6. before us   7. from me   8. them (*m pl*)   9. among us
10. in you (*m pl*)   11. upon him   12. after you (*f sg*)
13. between me   14. like you (*m sg*)   15. to him
16. after you (*m sg*)   17. in us   18. from you (*m pl*)
19. her   20. upon us   21. with her   22. to you (*f sg*)
23. in them   24. to you (*m pl*)   25. from you (*m sg*)
26. before him   27. after her   28. you (*m pl*)   29. instead of you (*m sg*)   30. us   31. within me   32. to him   33. before you (*m sg*)   34. from us, or from him   35. with me

Exercise 4

1. I have vessels of gold and he has vessels of silver.
2. Sarah does not have water but she has a seed.
3. The women of Bethlehem have many men but we do not have a man.   4. Joseph has a large family. He has many sons but he does not have one daughter.   5. I had an old woman. She had large eyes within a small face.
6. The chiefs of the desert have big heart(s) but they have sword(s) in their hand(s).   7. Jacob has wise women and many children but he did not have bread in his house.   8. We do not have justice because there is blood and war in our land. 9. Moses said to the priests: "Peace upon you!"

Exercise 5

1. עִמִּי, Jacob went out with me from the border of our place.   2. אַחֲרֵיכֶם, We did not cross over after you

(Exercise 5 continued)

and we did not find our way. 3. לִי ,לִי, I have sons and also daughters and I do not have a house. 4. עָלָיו, The servants made the throne of the king and the king sat on it. 5. לְפָנֶיהָ ,לָנוּ, Rachel called to us from among the mountains before her but we did not hear her. 6. לְפָנֶיךָ, We stood before you and also we wrote on the gate of the city. 7. כָּמוֹהָ, There is not a woman like her in this big world. 8. בֵּינֵיהֶם ,בָּהֶם, There is good and evil in them and there is a war between them. 9. מִמֶּנָּה, Sarah will take Jacob from her if she will not guard him. 10. תַּחְתָּיו, They sent Abraham instead of him to the war in Egypt. 11. אוֹתְךָ ,לְךָ, I saw you and also I called to you. 12. אוֹתוֹ ,עִמּוֹ, The father loved him but did not sit with him. 13. בֵּינְךָ ,בֵּינִי, The priest will judge between me and you.

Exercise 6

1. אוֹתָם, The man will guard them from the water of the sea. 2. אוֹתוֹ, The bread was good because I made it. 3. אוֹתָהּ, The children will take her toward the desert. 4. אֶתְכֶם, Within that city there will be wise ones and they will judge you. 5. אוֹתְךָ, They found you within your tent. 6. אוֹתִי, This is my lord and he loved me with all of his heart. 7. אוֹתָנוּ, In those days they remembered us as people of peace.

Exercise 7

1. I will not go after you to your place because I heard bad things about you.

א. לֹא אֵלֵךְ אַחֲרָיו אֶל מְקוֹמוֹ כִּי דְּבָרִים רָעִים שָׁמַעְתִּי עָלָיו. ב. לֹא אֵלֵךְ אַחֲרֵיכֶם אֶל מְקוֹמְכֶם כִּי דְּבָרִים רָעִים שָׁמַעְתִּי עֲלֵיכֶם. ג. לֹא אֵלֵךְ אַחֲרַיִךְ אֶל מְקוֹמָהּ כִּי דְּבָרִים רָעִים שָׁמַעְתִּי עָלַיִךְ. ד. לֹא אֵלֵךְ אַחֲרֵיהֶם אֶל מְקוֹמָם כִּי דְּבָרִים רָעִים שָׁמַעְתִּי עֲלֵיהֶם.

2. The people went out to their road, their flock in front of them, the city behind them and the gold and silver in their hand.

א. יָצָא אַבְרָהָם לְדַרְכּוֹ, צֹאנוֹ לְפָנָיו, הָעִיר אַחֲרָיו וְהַזָּהָב וְהַכֶּסֶף בְּיָדוֹ. ב. יָצָאנוּ אֲנַחְנוּ לְדַרְכֵּנוּ, צֹאנֵנוּ לְפָנֵינוּ, הָעִיר אַחֲרֵינוּ וְהַזָּהָב וְהַכֶּסֶף בְּיָדֵנוּ. ג. יָצָאתָ אַתָּה לְדַרְכֶּךָ, צֹאנְךָ לְפָנֶיךָ, הָעִיר אַחֲרֶיךָ וְהַזָּהָב

וְהַכֶּסֶף בְּיָדֶךָ. ד. יָצָאתִי אָנֹכִי לְדַרְכִּי, צֹאנִי לְפָנַי, הָעִיר אַחֲרַי וְהַזָּהָב וְהַכֶּסֶף בְּיָדִי. ה. יְצָאתֶם אַתֶּם לְדַרְכְּכֶם, צֹאנְכֶם לִפְנֵיכֶם, הָעִיר אַחֲרֵיכֶם וְהַזָּהָב וְהַכֶּסֶף בְּיֶדְכֶם.

3. My soul went out to you and your name I remembered because I loved you.

א. נַפְשִׁי יָצְאָה אֵלָיו וְאֶת שְׁמוֹ זָכַרְתִּי כִּי אוֹתוֹ אָהַבְתִּי. ב. נַפְשִׁי יָצְאָה אֲלֵיכֶם וְאֶת שְׁמְכֶם זָכַרְתִּי כִּי אֶתְכֶם אָהַבְתִּי. ג. נַפְשִׁי יָצְאָה אֵלַיִךְ וְאֶת שְׁמָהּ זָכַרְתִּי כִּי אוֹתָהּ אָהַבְתִּי. ד. נַפְשִׁי יָצְאָה אֵלַיִךְ וְאֶת שְׁמֵךְ זָכַרְתִּי כִּי אוֹתָךְ אָהַבְתִּי. ה. נַפְשִׁי יָצְאָה אֲלֵיהֶם וְאֶת שְׁמָם זָכַרְתִּי כִּי אוֹתָם אָהַבְתִּי. ו. נַפְשִׁי יָצְאָה אֵלֶיךָ וְאֶת שְׁמֶךָ זָכַרְתִּי כִּי אוֹתְךָ אָהַבְתִּי.

4. David is a wise young man, there was not a man as wise as him in the Torah and there is not a son better than him.

א. לֵאָה נַעֲרָה חֲכָמָה, לֹא הָיְתָה אִשָּׁה חֲכָמָה כָּמוֹהָ בַּתּוֹרָה וְאֵין בַּת טוֹבָה מִמֶּנָּה. ב. אָנֹכִי נַעַר חָכָם, לֹא הָיָה אִישׁ חָכָם כָּמוֹנִי בַּתּוֹרָה וְאֵין בֵּן טוֹב מִמֶּנִּי. OR אָנֹכִי נַעֲרָה חֲכָמָה, לֹא הָיְתָה אִשָּׁה חֲכָמָה כָּמוֹנִי בַּתּוֹרָה וְאֵין בַּת טוֹבָה מִמֶּנִּי. ג. אֲנַחְנוּ נְעָרִים חֲכָמִים, לֹא הָיוּ אֲנָשִׁים חֲכָמִים כָּמוֹנוּ בַּתּוֹרָה וְאֵין בָּנִים טוֹבִים מִמֶּנּוּ. ד. הֵם נְעָרִים חֲכָמִים, לֹא הָיוּ אֲנָשִׁים חֲכָמִים כָּמוֹהֶם בַּתּוֹרָה וְאֵין בָּנִים טוֹבִים מֵהֶם. ה. אַתֶּם נְעָרִים חֲכָמִים, לֹא הָיוּ אֲנָשִׁים חֲכָמִים כָּמוֹכֶם בַּתּוֹרָה וְאֵין בָּנִים טוֹבִים מִכֶּם.

5. We went up toward the mountain, we stood on (with) the ground under us, we saw the fields in front of us, and the trees behind us, and a good wind was with us.

א. אָנֹכִי עָלִיתִי הָהָרָה, עָמַדְתִּי עַל הָאֲדָמָה תַּחְתַּי, רָאִיתִי אֶת הַשָּׂדוֹת לְפָנַי, וְאֶת הָעֵצִים אַחֲרַי, וְרוּחַ טוֹב עִמִּי. ב. הוּא עָלָה הָהָרָה, עָמַד עַל הָאֲדָמָה תַּחְתָּיו, רָאָה אֶת הַשָּׂדוֹת לְפָנָיו, וְאֶת הָעֵצִים אַחֲרָיו, וְרוּחַ טוֹב עִמּוֹ. ג. אַתָּה עָלִיתָ הָהָרָה, עָמַדְתָּ עַל הָאֲדָמָה תַּחְתֶּיךָ, רָאִיתָ אֶת הַשָּׂדוֹת לְפָנֶיךָ, וְאֶת הָעֵצִים אַחֲרֶיךָ, וְרוּחַ טוֹב עִמְּךָ. ד. הֵם עָלוּ הָהָרָה, עָמְדוּ עַל הָאֲדָמָה תַּחְתָּם, רָאוּ אֶת הַשָּׂדוֹת לִפְנֵיהֶם, וְאֶת הָעֵצִים אַחֲרֵיהֶם, וְרוּחַ טוֹב עִמָּם. ה. אַתֶּם עֲלִיתֶם הָהָרָה, עֲמַדְתֶּם עַל הָאֲדָמָה תַּחְתֵּיכֶם, רְאִיתֶם אֶת הַשָּׂדוֹת לִפְנֵיכֶם, וְאֶת הָעֵצִים אַחֲרֵיכֶם, וְרוּחַ טוֹב עִמָּכֶם.

(Exercise 7 continued)

ו. הִיא עָלְתָה הָהָרָה, עָמְדָה עַל הָאֲדָמָה תַּחְתֶּיהָ,
רָאֲתָה אֶת הַשָּׂדוֹת לְפָנֶיהָ, וְאֶת הָעֵצִים אַחֲרֶיהָ, וְרוּחַ
טוֹב עִמָּהּ.

6. I am the son, and I have many servants who will find a good heart in me forever and ever.

א. הוּא הַבֵּן, וְיֵשׁ לוֹ עֲבָדִים רַבִּים אֲשֶׁר יִמְצְאוּ בּוֹ לֵב
טוֹב לְעוֹלָם וָעֶד. ב. אֲנַחְנוּ הַבָּנִים, וְיֵשׁ לָנוּ עֲבָדִים
רַבִּים אֲשֶׁר יִמְצְאוּ בָּנוּ לֵב טוֹב לְעוֹלָם וָעֶד. ג. אַתָּה
הַבֵּן, וְיֵשׁ לְךָ עֲבָדִים רַבִּים אֲשֶׁר יִמְצְאוּ בְּךָ לֵב טוֹב
לְעוֹלָם וָעֶד. ד. הִיא הַבַּת, וְיֵשׁ לָהּ עֲבָדִים רַבִּים
אֲשֶׁר יִמְצְאוּ בָּהּ לֵב טוֹב לְעוֹלָם וָעֶד. ה. הֵמָּה
הַבָּנִים, וְיֵשׁ לָהֶם עֲבָדִים רַבִּים אֲשֶׁר יִמְצְאוּ בָּהֶם לֵב
טוֹב לְעוֹלָם וָעֶד. ו. אַתֶּם הַבָּנִים, וְיֵשׁ לָכֶם עֲבָדִים
רַבִּים אֲשֶׁר יִמְצְאוּ בָּכֶם לֵב טוֹב לְעוֹלָם וָעֶד.

7. She found him in the desert, she took the gold from him but she sent the water with him.

א. הִיא מָצְאָה אוֹתִי בַּמִּדְבָּר, לָקְחָה אֶת הַזָּהָב מִמֶּנִּי
אַךְ אֶת הַמַּיִם שָׁלְחָה עִמִּי. ב. הִיא מָצְאָה אוֹתְךָ
בַּמִּדְבָּר, לָקְחָה אֶת הַזָּהָב מִמְּךָ אַךְ אֶת הַמַּיִם שָׁלְחָה
עִמְּךָ. ג. הִיא מָצְאָה אוֹתָהּ בַּמִּדְבָּר, לָקְחָה אֶת הַזָּהָב
מִמֶּנָּה אַךְ אֶת הַמַּיִם שָׁלְחָה עִמָּהּ. ד. הִיא מָצְאָה
אוֹתָנוּ בַּמִּדְבָּר, לָקְחָה אֶת הַזָּהָב מִמֶּנּוּ אַךְ אֶת הַמַּיִם
שָׁלְחָה עִמָּנוּ. ה. הִיא מָצְאָה אֶתְכֶם בַּמִּדְבָּר, לָקְחָה
אֶת הַזָּהָב מִכֶּם אַךְ אֶת הַמַּיִם שָׁלְחָה עִמָּכֶם. ו. הִיא
מָצְאָה אוֹתָם בַּמִּדְבָּר, לָקְחָה אֶת הַזָּהָב מֵהֶם אַךְ אֶת
הַמַּיִם שָׁלְחָה עִמָּם.

A TALL TALE: Little Red Riding Hood

In those days (once upon a time) there was a small young woman and her name was Little Red Riding Hood. She lived with her mother and her father in their big house near the border of the forest. In the midst of the forest the mother of her mother lived and her name was The Old One.

One day her mother said to Little Red Riding Hood: "The Old One is sick. It will be good if you go to her and you will take bread and meat with you."

Little Red Riding Hood said: "I will go with a good spirit and I will take the things for The Old One."

Her mother said to her: "Good, my daughter, but you will remember that there is a big and bad wolf in the middle of the forest. You will only go on the big road where many people have gone. And you will not say a word to man or to beast."

Little Red Riding Hood said: "My mother, I will remember your word. I will obey you, I will remember that there is a big and bad wolf within the forest. I will walk only on the big road where many people have walked. And I will not say a word to man or to beast and also I will guard the bread and the meat. I will take them to The Old One."

Then her mother said to her: "Good, my daughter, may you go in peace!"

Little Red Riding Hood took the bread and the meat and she went out on (to) her way.

She said in her heart: "I will remember, I will remember everything."

Little Red Riding Hood walked in the forest on the big road to the house of The Old One. She walked and she walked. And behold she saw a big and bad wolf near the road.

The wolf said to Little Red Riding Hood: "Who are you, little girl (young woman), and what have you been doing in the midst of this forest?"

Little Red Riding Hood did not remember the words of her mother and she said: "My name is Little Red Riding Hood and I am on my way to the house of The Old One who is sick."

The wolf said: "And what is in your hand?"

Little Red Riding Hood said: "I have bread and meat which I will guard and I will also take to the house of The Old One who is sick."

The wolf said to her: "You are a good girl. May you go in peace."

Then the wolf went on his way.

He said in his heart: "I will also go to the house of The Old One. I will eat the bread and the meat and The Old One and I will also eat Little Red Riding Hood. I have not eaten for many days."

The wolf was wiser than Little Red Riding Hood and he knew all of the small paths among the forest. He did not go on the big road but he went on a small path to the house of The Old One. Little Red Riding Hood went on the big road but the wolf was in the house of The Old One before her.

The wolf opened the gates of her house, he saw The Old One who sat inside it and then he ate her. The wolf sat on the chair of The Old One.

(A TALL TALE continued)

After these things Little Red Riding Hood walked until (she came to) the house of The Old One. She saw the gates of the house of The Old One and she heard a voice from within the house.

The voice said: "Who is there?"

She said: "This is me, Little Red Riding Hood."

And in her heart she knew that this voice was bigger than the voice of The Old One which she remembered.

She said: "How big your voice is! Who are you? Are you The Old One?"

The voice said: "I am The Old One, mother of your mother. I am very sick."

Then Little Red Riding Hood opened the gates of the house and she walked to the chair of The Old One.

She said: "How big your eyes are!"

The wolf said: "It is good (the better) for me to see you."

She said: "How big your hands are!"

The wolf said: "It is good (the better) for me to take you."

And again she said: "How big your mouth is!"

The wolf said: "It is good (the better) for me to eat you."

Then the wolf went out from his chair, he ate her and also her bread and also her meat. And then he was very sick.

Thus the wolf said: "It is not good for me to eat The Old One, and the girl and the bread and the meat on one day. I am sick. I am very sick. It is bad for me. It is very bad for me."

Behold the wolf opened his big mouth. The meat came out. The bread came out. Little Red Riding Hood came out and also The Old One came out. The wolf was not sick any more. And he went on his way. In the house of The Old One everything was good until this day.

Chapter 17

Oral Review

1. You wrote the words on the gate. You wrote them on it. 2. We will take the animal to the mountains. We will take her to them. 3. You heard David within the tent. You heard him within it. 4. The priest will judge between the commander and the children of Israel. The priest will judge between him and them. 5. The woman stood in front of the sea and she called to her son. The woman stood in front of it and she called to him. 6. David will rule in Jerusalem after that king. David will rule in it after him. 7. The children of Israel went out from Egypt like slaves. The children of Israel went out from it like them. 8. If you will go with this man you will find gold under the land. If you will go with him you will find gold under it. 9. The king loved silver instead of good judgements. The king loved it instead of them.

Exercise 1

1. I will see, I will do, I will answer, I will go, I will cross over, I will go up, I will remember, I will stand 2. you will do (m sg), you will stand, you will cross over, you will guard, you will see, you will answer, you will go up, you will know 3. you will cross over (f sg), you will rule, you will see, you will do, you will stand, you will go up, you will answer, you will send 4. he will go up, he will stand, he will go out, he will see, he will do, he will answer, he will open, he will cross over 5. she will stand, she will answer, she will eat, she will do, she will see, she will be, she will go up, she will cross over 6. we will do, we will call, we will answer, we will cross over, we will go up, we will stand, we will see, we will take 7. you will go up (m pl), you will see, you will write, you will do, you will cross over, you will stand, you will say, you will answer 8. they will answer (m pl), they will cross over, they will do, they will see, they will stand, they will find, they will go up, they will hear

Exercise 2

1. you loved (m sg) – and you will love 2. he judged – and he will judge 3. we ate – and we will eat 4. I guarded – and I will guard 5. she said – and she will say 6. you heard (f sg) – and you will hear 7. you were (m pl) – and you will be 8. they answer – and they will answer 9. he walked – and he will walk 10. I will remember – and I remembered 11. he will send – and he sent 12. they will know – and they knew 13. he will see – and he saw 14. you (m sg)/she will go forth – and you/she went forth 15. we will sit – and we sat 16. you will open (f sg) – and you opened 17. he made – and he will make 18. you will cross over (m pl) – and you crossed over 19. and he called – and he will call 20. and I stood – and I will stand 21. and you will write (m sg) – and you/she wrote 22. and we guarded – and we will guard 23. and they will find – and they found 24. and he will rule – and he ruled 25. and you (m sg) you took – and you will take 26. and you answer (m pl) – and you answered 27. and they went up – and they will go up

Exercise 3

1. Moses said to the children of Israel at that time: "This is the mountain of holiness." And Moses will say to the children of Israel at that time: "This is the mountain of holiness." And Moses said to the children of Israel at that time: "This is the mountain of holiness." Moses will say to the children of Israel at that time:

(Exercise 3 continued)

"This is the mountain of holiness."   2. After a hundred years the man was old. And the man will be old after a hundred years. After a hundred years the man will be old. And the man was old after a hundred years.   3. I will now stand before you with my heart in my hand. And I stood before you with my heart in my hand. And I will now stand before you with my heart in my hand. Then I stood before you with my heart in my hand. 4. He answered the messenger of the king with many words. He will answer the messenger of the king with many words. And he will answer the messenger of the king with many words. And he answered the messenger of the king with many words.   5. The priests saw the altar of his holiness. And the priests saw the altar of his holiness. The priests will see the altar of his holiness. And the priests will see the altar of his holiness.

Exercise 4

1. Thus Joseph said to Leah: "What did you love in Bethlehem?" Thus Leah answered: "I loved living water, small trees and also the face of the man of my heart." 2. And the lord of Moab said: "Who will stand near the Holy of Holies now?" And the priest answered: "In every time and in every year the priests will stand near the Holy of Holies." 3. And David called to Moses: "Who will judge the meat which is on the altar?" And Moses answered: "The old priest will judge the meat before the offering of the day." 4. Leah said to Naomi: "Who is the wise one who sat on the seat of honor in front of the altar?" Naomi answered: "This is the chief of the people who sat on the seat of honor in front of the altar."

Exercise 5

1. And the messenger of David said: "You will not take my chair from me." אָמַר   2. And it came to pass in that time a hundred messengers ate all of the meat in the tent. הָיָה   3. And Joseph will go on his way, and he will see the altar of holiness, and he will open his mouth, and he will say: "What is this?" יִרְאֶה ,יֵלֵךְ, יֹאמַר ,יִפְתַּח   4. And we stood with our king and we crossed over our border and we saw our land in a time of peace. רָאִינוּ ,עָבַרְנוּ ,עָמַדְנוּ   5. I called to Abraham at that time and Abraham answered afterwards. עָנָה   6. The messenger opened his mouth and he said to the hundred people around: "Peace." אָמַר ,פָּתַח   7. And it came to pass in that year a hundred fathers of the people stood before the altar and made an animal of gold. עָשׂוּ ,עָמְדוּ ,הָיָה

Exercise 6

1. And said Joseph to the children of Israel: "I will hear your voice and I will answer you."

א. וַיֹּאמֶר יוֹסֵף אֶל בְּנֵי יִשְׂרָאֵל: "נִשְׁמַע אֶת קוֹלְכֶם וְעָנִינוּ אֶתְכֶם."   ב. וַיֹּאמֶר יוֹסֵף אֶל בְּנֵי יִשְׂרָאֵל: "יִשְׁמְעוּ אֶת קוֹלְכֶם וְעָנוּ אֶתְכֶם."   ג. וַיֹּאמֶר יוֹסֵף אֶל בְּנֵי יִשְׂרָאֵל: "הִיא תִּשְׁמַע אֶת קוֹלְכֶם וְעָנְתָה אֶתְכֶם."   ד. וַיֹּאמֶר יוֹסֵף אֶל בְּנֵי יִשְׂרָאֵל: "יִשְׁמַע אֶת קוֹלְכֶם וְעָנָה אֶתְכֶם."

2. And the messenger stood there and he opened his mouth and he said words of holiness to them.

א. עָמַדְתִּי שָׁם וָאֶפְתַּח אֶת פִּי וָאֹמַר דִּבְרֵי קֹדֶשׁ אֲלֵיהֶם.   ב. וְעָמְדוּ אֲחֵי רוּת שָׁם וַיִּפְתְּחוּ אֶת פִּיהֶם וַיֹּאמְרוּ דִּבְרֵי קֹדֶשׁ אֲלֵיהֶם.   ג. וַתַּעֲמֹד שָׁם וַתִּפְתַּח אֶת פִּיךְ וַתֹּאמֶר דִּבְרֵי קֹדֶשׁ אֲלֵיהֶם.   ד. וַנַּעֲמֹד שָׁם וַנִּפְתַּח אֶת פִּינוּ וַנֹּאמֶר דִּבְרֵי קֹדֶשׁ אֲלֵיהֶם.

3. In the time of the war Jacob sent a hundred men to his king and also he took bread for every person who was still in life (alive).

א. בְּעֵת הַמִּלְחָמָה שָׁלַחְתִּי מֵאָה אִישׁ לְמַלְכִּי וְגַם לָקַחְתִּי לֶחֶם לְכֹל נֶפֶשׁ אֲשֶׁר עוֹד בַּחַיִּים.   ב. בְּעֵת הַמִּלְחָמָה שָׁלַחְנוּ מֵאָה אִישׁ לְמַלְכֵּנוּ וְגַם לָקַחְנוּ לֶחֶם לְכֹל נֶפֶשׁ אֲשֶׁר עוֹד בַּחַיִּים.   ג. בְּעֵת הַמִּלְחָמָה שָׁלְחוּ הַמַּלְאָכִים מֵאָה אִישׁ לְמַלְכָּם וְגַם לָקְחוּ לֶחֶם לְכֹל נֶפֶשׁ אֲשֶׁר עוֹד בַּחַיִּים.   ד. בְּעֵת הַמִּלְחָמָה שָׁלַחְתָּ מֵאָה אִישׁ לְמַלְכְּךָ וְגַם לָקַחְתָּ לֶחֶם לְכֹל נֶפֶשׁ אֲשֶׁר עוֹד בַּחַיִּים.   ה. בְּעֵת הַמִּלְחָמָה שְׁלַחְתֶּם מֵאָה אִישׁ לְמַלְכְּכֶם וְגַם לְקַחְתֶּם לֶחֶם לְכֹל נֶפֶשׁ אֲשֶׁר עוֹד בַּחַיִּים.

4 The king is still alive and he will guard his mouth, his hand, and his head but he will not guard his heart.

א. אֲנִי עוֹד חַי וְשָׁמַרְתִּי אֶת פִּי, אֶת יָדִי, וְאֶת רֹאשִׁי אַךְ לֹא אֶשְׁמֹר אֶת לִבִּי.   ב. אַתָּה עוֹד חַי וְשָׁמַרְתָּ אֶת פִּיךָ, אֶת יָדְךָ, וְאֶת רֹאשְׁךָ אַךְ לֹא תִּשְׁמֹר אֶת לִבְּךָ.   ג. אַתֶּם עוֹד חַיִּים וּשְׁמַרְתֶּם אֶת פִּיכֶם, אֶת יְדֵכֶם, וְאֶת רֹאשְׁכֶם אַךְ לֹא תִּשְׁמְרוּ אֶת לִבְּכֶם.   ד. הַמַּלְאָכִים עוֹד חַיִּים וְשָׁמְרוּ אֶת פִּיהֶם, אֶת יָדָם, וְאֶת רֹאשָׁם אַךְ

33

(Exercise 6 continued)

ה.אֲנַחְנוּ עוֹד חַיִּים וְשָׁמַרְנוּ אֶת לֹא יִשְׁמְרוּ אֶת לִבָּם.
פִּינוּ, אֶת יָדֵנוּ, וְאֶת רֹאשֵׁנוּ אַךְ לֹא נִשְׁמֹר אֶת לִבֵּנוּ.

5. If my father is still alive I will take him now with me to my house and will make for him a hundred things of gold.

א.אִם אָבִיךָ עוֹד חַי אַתָּה תִּקַּח אוֹתוֹ עַתָּה עִמְּךָ
לְבֵיתְךָ וְעָשִׂיתָ לוֹ מֵאָה דִּבְרֵי זָהָב.   ב.אִם אָבִיהָ
עוֹד חַי רָחֵל תִּקַּח אוֹתוֹ עַתָּה עִמָּה לְבֵיתָהּ וְעָשְׂתָה לוֹ
מֵאָה דִּבְרֵי זָהָב.   ג.אִם אָבִיו עוֹד חַי יוֹסֵף יִקַּח
אוֹתוֹ עַתָּה עִמּוֹ לְבֵיתוֹ וְעָשָׂה לוֹ מֵאָה דִּבְרֵי זָהָב.
ד.אִם אָבִינוּ עוֹד חַי אֲנַחְנוּ נִקַּח אוֹתוֹ עַתָּה עִמָּנוּ
לְבֵיתֵנוּ וְעָשִׂינוּ לוֹ מֵאָה דִּבְרֵי זָהָב.   ה.אִם אֲבִיכֶם
עוֹד חַי אַתֶּם תִּקְחוּ אוֹתוֹ עַתָּה עִמָּכֶם לְבֵיתְכֶם
וַעֲשִׂיתֶם לוֹ מֵאָה דִּבְרֵי זָהָב.

6. And the children of Israel will hear the judgements of Abraham and thus they will do them.

א.וְשָׁמַעְתָּ אַתָּה אֶת מִשְׁפְּטֵי אַבְרָהָם וְכֵן תַּעֲשֶׂה אוֹתָם.
ב.וְשָׁמְעָה שָׂרָה אֶת מִשְׁפְּטֵי אַבְרָהָם וְכֵן תַּעֲשֶׂה אוֹתָם.
ג.וְשָׁמַע הוּא אֶת מִשְׁפְּטֵי אַבְרָהָם וְכֵן יַעֲשֶׂה אוֹתָם.
ד.וְשָׁמַעְנוּ אֲנַחְנוּ אֶת מִשְׁפְּטֵי אַבְרָהָם וְכֵן נַעֲשֶׂה אוֹתָם.
ה.וּשְׁמַעְתֶּם אַתֶּם אֶת מִשְׁפְּטֵי אַבְרָהָם וְכֵן תַּעֲשׂוּ אוֹתָם.

7. And he went to his city and he saw there many women and he knew afterward that they were also evil women.

א.וָאֵלֵךְ לְעִירִי וָאֶרְאֶה שָׁם נָשִׁים רַבּוֹת וָאֵדַע אַחֲרֵי
כֵן כִּי הֵנָּה גַּם נָשִׁים רָעוֹת.   ב.וַתֵּלֶךְ נָעֳמִי לְעִירָהּ
וַתֵּרְאֶה שָׁם נָשִׁים רַבּוֹת וַתֵּדַע אַחֲרֵי כֵן כִּי הֵנָּה גַּם
נָשִׁים רָעוֹת.   ג.וַיֵּלֶךְ יוֹסֵף לְעִירוֹ וַיַּרְא שָׁם נָשִׁים
רַבּוֹת וַיֵּדַע אַחֲרֵי כֵן כִּי הֵנָּה גַּם נָשִׁים רָעוֹת.

8. The master of war will stand with his sword in his hand and with honor in his heart forever and ever.

א.אֶעֱמֹד עִם חַרְבִּי בְּיָדִי וְעִם כָּבוֹד בִּלְבָבִי לְעוֹלָם
וָעֶד.   ב.תַּעֲמֹד עִם חַרְבְּךָ בְּיָדְךָ וְעִם כָּבוֹד בִּלְבָבְךָ
לְעוֹלָם וָעֶד.   ג.תַּעַמְדוּ עִם חַרְבְּכֶם בְּיֶדְכֶם וְעִם
כָּבוֹד בִּלְבַבְכֶם לְעוֹלָם וָעֶד.   ד.הֵמָּה יַעַמְדוּ עִם
חַרְבָּם בְּיָדָם וְעִם כָּבוֹד בִּלְבָבָם לְעוֹלָם וָעֶד.

Exercise 7

1. And said Moses to the children of Israel: "This is the law." אֲלֵיהֶם, Moses said to them: "This is the law."
2. There was the vessel of holiness on the altar. עָלָיו, And there was the vessel of holiness on it.   3. And the man stood in front of the gates of holiness. לִפְנֵיהֶם, The man stood in front of them.   4. And we will go out from the desert and we will stand behind the mountains. אַחֲרֵיהֶם, מִמֶּנּוּ, We will go out from it and then we will stand behind them.   5. Every year he answered his father in words of peace. אוֹתוֹ, And he answered him and he said words of peace.   6. And he saw that the life was good with sons. עִמָּם, He saw that the life was good with them.

A TALL TALE: Cinderella

And it came to pass many years ago there was a good man in the land and he had a good and very beautiful wife. They had one beautiful and good daughter like her mother and her name was Cinderella. And it came to pass afterward that the mother of Cinderella died. And her father took an evil and not beautiful (ugly) new wife. This woman had evil and ugly daughters.

The new wife and the daughters did not love Cinderella because she was more beautiful and better than them. They made life bad for her. And Cinderella was like a slave in the house.

And it came to pass in those days a great king ruled over all of this land and he had a wise and good son. The son of the king did not have a wife because he did not love all (any) of the young women whom he had seen until now.

The king had a great banquet for his son. He sent messengers to all of the land around from border to border. The messengers called out to all of the beautiful people in the land and to all of the young women.

They said in the name of the king: "Peace upon you! Behold there will be a great banquet in the house of the king in another hundred days. At the time of the banquet the son of the king will take the young woman who is the most beautiful for his wife."

And the family of Cinderella heard the words of the messengers of the king. The evil daughters said in their heart(s) that they were the most beautiful of all the young women of the land. And they knew that they would go to the banquet of the king.

Cinderella also heard the words of the messengers of the king.

(A TALL TALE continued)

And Cinderella said in her heart: "I will forever not (never) go to the banquet of the king because I do not have good clothing. And now it is very bad for me."

The day of the banquet came to pass.

The new wife and the evil daughters said: "Tonight we will go to the banquet of the king with the good clothing and then we will be the most beautiful of all the young women!"

And thus they did.

Cinderella did not go to the banquet with the new wife and the daughters. And Cinderella sat in the house and she listened afterward to the sound of the banquet from the house of the king. And it was very bad for her.

And it came to pass at that time the spirit of her mother who died stood before her .

The spirit of her mother said to her: "You are still in the house? All of the young women of the land are now in the banquet of the king."

Cinderella answered: "I do not have good clothing. The new wife took them from me. Therefore I did not go to the banquet."

The spirit of her mother said to her: "Here are clothes of silver and clothes of gold and also shoes of gold for you."

Cinderella answered the spirit of her mother: "How good it is for me! These clothes are beautiful on me. Now I will go to the banquet."

The spirit of her mother said to her: "And so you will go! But you will go out from the banquet before midnight. After midnight all of these beautiful clothes will not be yours."

And Cinderella went to the banquet of the king.

She said in her heart: "I will remember all of the words of the spirit of my mother."

There were beautiful people at the banquet and they saw Cinderella.

And the people said: "Who is this beautiful young woman?"

The son of the king saw Cinderella and his heart went up. And the son of the king went to Cinderella and he took her hand in his hand. And they were together all the night him with her.

And behold it was midnight!

Cinderella remembered the words of the spirit of her mother and she went out from the house of the king toward home. And she did not say a thing to the son of the king.

And the son of the king walked (around) but he did not see Cinderella in the house of the king. He also did not find her near the house of the king. He saw and behold he found one shoe of gold on the road. The son of the king took the shoe of gold in his hand and he remembered that beautiful young woman.

The son of the king said: "I will guard this shoe until I find the most beautiful young woman of all the young women of the land. I will go after her every day and every year until I find her."

The son of the king went out after the banquet to all of the land, from city to city and from border to border to every place. And he went to every house where there was a young woman.

The son of the king said to the young women in each house: "Is there another shoe of gold like this shoe in your house?" And thus he did every day.

And it came to pass after many days the son of the king went as far as the house of Cinderella. The new wife and the evil daughters were in the house.

The son of the king said: "Is there another shoe of gold like this shoe in your house?"

And the new wife answered him: "We do not have a shoe of gold like this but we have many beautiful shoes!"

Cinderella heard the voice of the son of the king and she took the shoe of gold in her hand and she said: "I, I have a shoe of gold like this shoe. Here it is in my hand."

The son of the king said to her: "I remembered that at the banquet you had beautiful clothing and you were very beautiful also. Now you do not have beautiful clothing but you are the most beautiful of all."

And the son of the king took Cinderella for his wife.

And Cinderella and the son of the king lived together for many years. And they had a good life.

Chapter 18

Oral Review

1. There was at that time much meat in Jerusalem. There was at that time much meat in Jerusalem.
2. You will love the face of David and the money of Abraham. You loved the face of David and the money of Abraham.   3. And the old man saw the flock in the field. The old man will see the flock in the field.

(Oral Review continued)

4. We will remember now all of the names of the brothers of Joseph. We will remember now all of the names of the brothers of Joseph.   5. The priests judged from the Holy of Holies all year. The priests will judge from the Holy of Holies all year.   6. The sons will make vessels of holiness for the altar. The sons made vessels of holiness for the altar.   7. The messenger opened his mouth and he answered the voice of the heavens. The messenger opened his mouth and he answered the voice of the heavens.   8. We will go up toward the land and there we will see small young men with big heads. We will go up toward the land and we will see small young men with large heads.   9. I will cross over toward the desert and I will sit within your tent. I crossed over toward the desert and I sat within your tent.   10. His father and his mother stood in his house and they guarded it. His father and his mother stood in his house and they guarded it.

Exercise 1

1. I gave, I built, I drank, I went down, I will give, I will build, I will drink, I will go down   2. you built (*m sg*), you you gave, you went down, you drank, you will go down, you will drink, you will build, you will give   3. you will go down (*f sg*), you will give, you will drink, you will build, you drank, you built, you went down, you gave   4. he drank, he built, he gave, he went down, he will go down, he will give, he will build, he will drink   5. she will give, she went down, she will go down, she gave, she built, she drank, she will build, she will drink   6. we built, we will give, we will go down, we drank, we will build, we gave, we will drink, we went down   7. you will go down (*m pl*), you gave, you built, you will drink, you went down, you drank, you will build, you will give   8. they drank (*m pl*), they will give, they built, they went down, they will drink, they will build, they gave, they will go down

Exercise 2

1. N   2. B   3. P   4. M   5. K   6. J   7. H   8. F   9. E   10. I   11. G   12. L   13. O   14. C   15. A   16. D

Exercise 3

1. He is building a house from stones. The builders built the camp.   2. Rebecca is a doer of evil deeds. The man who is doing good, he is righteous.   3. A large nation is going down toward Egypt. The ones who are going down went when they said.   4. Aaron is giving a present to his mother. The one who is giving the money resides among us.   5. These tribes are drinking a lot of water. The drinking man is also eating.

Exercise 4

1.נָתַתִּי אַבְנֵי כֶּסֶף לְשָׂרָה.   2.תִּתֵּן מִנְחָה לִי עַתָּה.

3.הַצַּדִּיק נָתַן לֶחֶם לַמַּחֲנֶה.   4.כַּאֲשֶׁר רִבְקָה תִּתֵּן

מַיִם לַבְּהֵמָה, הַבְּהֵמָה תִּשְׁתֶּה.   5.מַעֲשֵׂי הַגּוֹיִם

כְּתוּבִים בָּרוּחַ.   6.וְנָתְנוּ שָׁלוֹם לַגּוֹיִם אַחַר הַמִּלְחָמָה.

7.יַעֲקֹב יִתֵּן חֶרֶב לְעֶבֶד כַּאֲשֶׁר יֵרֵד מֵאַרְצוֹ.   8.נָתְנוּ

כָּל לִבֵּנוּ (לְבָבֵנוּ) לָהֶם כַּאֲשֶׁר בָּנוּ לָנוּ בָּתִּים.

Exercise 5

1. The righteous one is residing in the camp. The tribe which is residing in the camp will build an altar. The residents built camps. The residents of the camp are from the tribe of Aaron.   2. He is going down with the family towards Egypt. The family who is going down resided in Egypt. Families are going down to Egypt. The ones who go down are from the family of David.   3. The law is written. The deed of Rebecca is written in the law. The deeds of Aaron are written in the law. The deeds are done and are written in the law.   4. He is seeing the stone with open eyes. The one who sees took the stone. The eyes are not seeing the stone. The eyes of the man are seeing the stone.   5. The righteous man is giving water to the builder. The water is given to the builder. The givers of the water are righteous. The vessel is given to the builder.   6. The judge is judging with a foot in his mouth. The judges have big feet. The judge is standing on one foot. The judge of the tribe wrote with his foot.

Exercise 6

1. יָרַד ,יֵרֵד, A man who was knowing went down/will go down from the mountain with a righteous tribe.   2. אֶתֵּן ,נָתַתִּי, I gave/will give a stone of gold to Rachel, my wife.   3. יִשְׁתּוּ ,שָׁתוּ, The ones going down drank/will drink all of the water in the camps of these nations.   4. תִּבְנֶה ,בָּנִיתָ, You built/will build the altar with legs standing under it.   5. יִשְׁפֹּט ,שָׁפַט, The old priest judged/will judge the deeds of the guards in the night.   6. יֵצְאוּ ,יָצְאוּ, The slaves who were given to the king went out/will go out before him.   7. שָׁפְטוּ, יִשְׁפְּטוּ, The righteous judges judged/will judge the evil tribe.   8. יִקַּח ,לָקַח, The descendent of Jacob took/will take a seat made from gold.

Exercise 7

1. The guards of the place walked within the city, saw that everything was good and also they did great deeds.

א.שׁוֹמֵר הַמָּקוֹם הָלַךְ בְּתוֹךְ הָעִיר, רָאָה כִּי הַכֹּל טוֹב

וְגַם עָשָׂה מַעֲשִׂים גְּדוֹלִים.   ב.יוֹשֶׁבֶת הָעִיר הָלְכָה

בְּתוֹךְ הָעִיר, רָאֲתָה כִּי הַכֹּל טוֹב וְגַם עָשְׂתָה מַעֲשִׂים

גְּדוֹלִים.   ג.אַתָּה הָלַכְתָּ בְּתוֹךְ הָעִיר, רָאִיתָ כִּי הַכֹּל

(Exercise 7 continued)

ד.אַתֶּם הֲלַכְתֶּם   טוֹב וְגַם עֲשִׂיתָ מַעֲשִׂים גְּדוֹלִים.
בְּתוֹךְ הָעִיר, רְאִיתֶם כִּי הַכֹּל טוֹב וְגַם עֲשִׂיתֶם מַעֲשִׂים
גְּדוֹלִים.   ה.אֲנַחְנוּ הָלַכְנוּ בְּתוֹךְ הָעִיר, רָאִינוּ כִּי
הַכֹּל טוֹב וְגַם עָשִׂינוּ מַעֲשִׂים גְּדוֹלִים.

2. He built an altar from stones of gold and then he went down from the camp, ate bread and also drank water.

א.בָּנִיתָ מִזְבֵּחַ מֵאַבְנֵי זָהָב וְאָז יָרַדְתָּ מִן הַמַּחֲנֶה,
אָכַלְתָּ לֶחֶם וְגַם שָׁתִיתָ מָיִם.   ב.הוּא יִבְנֶה מִזְבֵּחַ
מֵאַבְנֵי זָהָב וְאָז יֵרֵד מִן הַמַּחֲנֶה, יֹאכַל לֶחֶם וְגַם יִשְׁתֶּה
מַיִם.   ג.נִבְנֶה מִזְבֵּחַ מֵאַבְנֵי זָהָב וְאָז נֵרֵד מִן הַמַּחֲנֶה,
נֹאכַל לֶחֶם וְגַם נִשְׁתֶּה מַיִם.   ד.הֵם בָּנוּ מִזְבֵּחַ מֵאַבְנֵי
זָהָב וְאָז יָרְדוּ מִן הַמַּחֲנֶה, אָכְלוּ לֶחֶם וְגַם שָׁתוּ
מַיִם.   ה.בָּנִיתִי מִזְבֵּחַ מֵאַבְנֵי זָהָב וְאָז יָרַדְתִּי מִן
הַמַּחֲנֶה, אָכַלְתִּי לֶחֶם וְגַם שָׁתִיתִי מַיִם.   ו.אֶבְנֶה
מִזְבֵּחַ מֵאַבְנֵי זָהָב וְאָז אֵרֵד מִן הַמַּחֲנֶה, אֹכַל לֶחֶם וְגַם
אֶשְׁתֶּה מַיִם.

3. And my father will sit under the tree standing in the field and he will see his flock that is walking around.

א.וְיָשַׁבְתִּי אָנֹכִי תַּחַת הָעֵץ הָעוֹמֵד בַּשָּׂדֶה וְרָאִיתִי אֶת
צֹאנִי הַהֹלֶכֶת סָבִיב.   ב.וְיָשַׁבְתָּ אַתָּה תַּחַת הָעֵץ
הָעוֹמֵד בַּשָּׂדֶה וְרָאִיתָ אֶת צֹאנְךָ הַהֹלֶכֶת סָבִיב.
ג.וְיָשַׁבְנוּ אֲנַחְנוּ תַּחַת הָעֵץ הָעוֹמֵד בַּשָּׂדֶה וְרָאִינוּ
אֶת צֹאנֵנוּ הַהֹלֶכֶת סָבִיב.   ד.וִישַׁבְתֶּם אַתֶּם תַּחַת
הָעֵץ הָעוֹמֵד בַּשָּׂדֶה וּרְאִיתֶם אֶת צֹאנְכֶם הַהֹלֶכֶת
סָבִיב.   ה.וְיָשְׁבוּ מַלְאָכִים צַדִּיקִים תַּחַת הָעֵץ
הָעוֹמֵד בַּשָּׂדֶה וְרָאוּ אֶת צֹאנָם הַהֹלֶכֶת סָבִיב.

4. Aaron went down in front of the camps of the tribe and he saw the nation doing evil deeds and he called it (them) bad names.

א.הַכֹּהֲנִים יָרְדוּ לִפְנֵי מַחֲנוֹת הַמַּטֶּה וַיִּרְאוּ אֶת הַגּוֹי
הָעֹשֶׂה מַעֲשִׂים רָעִים וַיִּקְרְאוּ אֹתוֹ שֵׁמוֹת רָעִים.
ב.אֲנַחְנוּ יָרַדְנוּ לִפְנֵי מַחֲנוֹת הַמַּטֶּה וַנִּרְאֶה אֶת הַגּוֹי
הָעֹשֶׂה מַעֲשִׂים רָעִים וַנִּקְרָא אֹתוֹ שֵׁמוֹת רָעִים.
ג.אַתֶּם יְרַדְתֶּם לִפְנֵי מַחֲנוֹת הַמַּטֶּה וַתִּרְאוּ אֶת הַגּוֹי
הָעֹשֶׂה מַעֲשִׂים רָעִים וַתִּקְרְאוּ אֹתוֹ שֵׁמוֹת רָעִים.
ד.אֲנִי יָרַדְתִּי לִפְנֵי מַחֲנוֹת הַמַּטֶּה וָאֶרְאֶה אֶת הַגּוֹי
הָעֹשֶׂה מַעֲשִׂים רָעִים וָאֶקְרָא אֹתוֹ שֵׁמוֹת רָעִים.

5. If you know good from bad you will judge the lives of the children of Israel and also you will write it for them.

א.אִם אִישׁ חָכָם יוֹדֵעַ טוֹב מֵרַע יִשְׁפֹּט אֶת חַיֵּי בְּנֵי
יִשְׂרָאֵל וְגַם יִכְתֹּב לָהֶם אֹתוֹ.   ב.אִם אֲנַחְנוּ יוֹדְעִים
טוֹב מֵרַע נִשְׁפֹּט אֶת חַיֵּי בְּנֵי יִשְׂרָאֵל וְגַם נִכְתֹּב לָהֶם
אֹתוֹ.   ג.אִם כֹּהֲנִים יוֹדְעִים טוֹב מֵרַע יִשְׁפְּטוּ אֶת חַיֵּי
בְּנֵי יִשְׂרָאֵל וְגַם יִכְתְּבוּ לָהֶם אֹתוֹ.   ד.אִם אַתֶּם
יוֹדְעִים טוֹב מֵרַע תִּשְׁפְּטוּ אֶת חַיֵּי בְּנֵי יִשְׂרָאֵל וְגַם
תִּכְתְּבוּ לָהֶם אֹתוֹ.

6. When Rebecca saw what was written on the ground she found her way.

א.כַּאֲשֶׁר רָאָה הַמַּלְאָךְ מֶה הָיָה כָּתוּב עַל הָאֲדָמָה
הוּא מָצָא אֶת דַּרְכּוֹ.   ב.כַּאֲשֶׁר רָאוּ הַשָּׂרִים מֶה הָיָה
כָּתוּב עַל הָאֲדָמָה הֵם מָצְאוּ אֶת דַּרְכָּם.   ג.כַּאֲשֶׁר
רָאִיתִי אֲנִי מֶה הָיָה כָּתוּב עַל הָאֲדָמָה אֲנִי מָצָאתִי אֶת
דַּרְכִּי.   ד.כַּאֲשֶׁר רָאִיתָ אַתָּה מֶה הָיָה כָּתוּב עַל
הָאֲדָמָה אַתָּה מָצָאתָ אֶת דַּרְכְּךָ.

7. And Joseph went down to the sea with a vessel in his hand and he sat there and gave water to his people and it (they) drank.

א.וַיֵּרְדוּ הַשָּׂרִים אֶל הַיָּם עִם כְּלִי בְּיָדָם וַיֵּשְׁבוּ שָׁם
וַיִּתְּנוּ מַיִם לְעַמָּם וַיֵּשְׁתְּ.   ב.וַנֵּרֶד אֲנַחְנוּ אֶל הַיָּם עִם
כְּלִי בְּיָדֵנוּ וַנֵּשֶׁב שָׁם וַנִּתֵּן מַיִם לְעַמֵּנוּ וַיֵּשְׁתְּ.   ג.וַתֵּרֶד
אַתָּה אֶל הַיָּם עִם כְּלִי בְּיָדְךָ וַתֵּשֶׁב שָׁם וַתִּתֵּן מַיִם
לְעַמְּךָ וַיֵּשְׁתְּ.   ד.וַתֵּרְדוּ אַתֶּם אֶל הַיָּם עִם כְּלִי
בְּיֶדְכֶם וַתֵּשְׁבוּ שָׁם וַתִּתְּנוּ מַיִם לְעַמְּכֶם וַיֵּשְׁתְּ.

8. There is no honor in his house because the blood of his brother is on his hand and therefore the commander did not send a thing to him.

א.אֵין כָּבוֹד בְּבֵיתִי כִּי דַּם אָחִי עַל יָדִי וְעַל כֵּן הַשָּׂר
לֹא שָׁלַח דָּבָר אֵלַי.   ב.אֵין כָּבוֹד בְּבֵיתְךָ כִּי דַּם
אָחִיךָ עַל יָדְךָ וְעַל כֵּן הַשָּׂר לֹא שָׁלַח דָּבָר אֵלֶיךָ.
ג.אֵין כָּבוֹד בְּבֵיתָהּ כִּי דַּם אָחִיהָ עַל יָדָהּ וְעַל כֵּן
הַשָּׂר לֹא שָׁלַח דָּבָר אֵלֶיהָ.   ד.אֵין כָּבוֹד בְּבֵיתְךָ כִּי
דַּם אָחִיךָ עַל יָדֶךָ וְעַל כֵּן הַשָּׂר לֹא שָׁלַח דָּבָר אֵלֶיךָ.

A TALL TALE:
Goldilocks and the Righteous Bears

And it came to pass in those days righteous Bears lived in their house near the forest. And there was in the family Papa Bear, Mama Bear, and Sonny Bear.

37

(A TALL TALE continued)

These bears were doing good deeds and giving things to all of the animals of the forest. Therefore all of the animals knew that the doors of the house of the bears are open when they go out. There is no one alive who would take from them.

Every day Mama Bear makes bread and gives it to the family. She makes a very big bread for Papa Bear, she makes a big bread for her(self) and she makes a small bread for her son.

One day Mama Bear made a bread and she said: "We will go down to the forest because today is very beautiful. I will give you your bread afterwards."

And thus they did. And the righteous bears went down to the forest and the doors of their house were open.

And it came to pass on this beautiful day Goldilocks was also going down to the forest. She sees the beautiful trees around and she hears the sound of the small animals. Goldilocks walked and saw and behold there was a small house and the doors were open.

Goldilocks walked up to the house. She crossed over between the open doors to the house of the bears and she found the bread that had been made for the family.

Goldilocks ate from the bread of Papa Bear and she said: "Oh, this is (too) much bread for me."

She also ate from the bread of Mama Bear and she said: "This bread is still (too) much for me."

Goldilocks ate from the bread of Sonny Bear and she said: "This bread is small and it is good for me. And now I will eat all (of it)." And thus she did.

And it came to pass after these things Goldilocks found the chairs standing in the house.

She sat on the seat of Papa Bear and she said: "Oh, this seat is very big for me.

She sat on the chair of Mama Bear and she said: "This chair is still (too) big for me."

She sat on the chair of Sonny Bear and she said: "Oh, this chair is little and it is good for me."

Goldilocks broke the little chair as she was sitting on it. And behold the chair was broken.

After that she found the beds standing in the house.

She lay down on the bed of Papa Bear and she said: "Oh, this bed is very big for me."

She lay down on the bed of Mama Bear and she said: "This bed is still (too) big for me."

And she lay down on the bed of Sonny Bear and she said: "This bed is little and it is good for me. I will lie down on this good little bed forever."

At that time the righteous Bears went up to their house.

Papa Bear said in his very big voice: "Who was eating my bread?"

Mama Bear said in her big voice: "Who was eating my bread?"

Sonny Bear said in his small voice: "Who ate my bread and there is no bread for me anymore?"

Papa Bear saw his chair standing in its place.

He said in his very big voice: "Who was sitting in my chair?"

Mama Bear saw her chair standing in its place and she said in her big voice: "Who was sitting in my chair?"

Sonny Bear saw the place of his chair but his chair was not standing in its place.

Sonny Bear said: "Who sat in my chair and now it is broken?"

Papa Bear saw his bed standing in its place and he said in his very big voice: "Who was lying in my bed?"

Mama Bear saw her bed standing in its place and she said in her big voice: "Who was lying in my bed?"

Sonny Bear saw his bed standing in its place and a young woman (girl) was in it.

Sonny Bear said in his small voice: "Who was lying in my bed and still is lying there?"

Goldilocks heard the voices of the righteous bears and she opened her eyes and she saw the bears standing next to her.

Thus Papa Bear said in his big voice: "What are you doing in our house?"

Goldilocks said in a small voice: "Forgive me! I knew that this was your house but your house is very beautiful and your bread is very plentiful and your chair and your bed are very good. I love your place. I will live with you forever and ever."

And thus she did.

Chapter 19

Oral Review: Name that Tune!

1. The man in the field, the man in the field,
Hi Ho the Dario, the man in the field.
The man takes a wife, the man takes a wife,
Hi Ho the Dario, the man takes a wife.

2. Brother Jacob, brother Jacob,
You are sitting, you are sitting.
A sound is calling now, a sound is calling now.
Ding ding dong, Ding ding dong.

3. Old McDonald had a field, E-I-E-I-O.
And in the field he had a flock, E-I-E-I-O.
With a baa, baa there, and a baa, baa there
Here a baa, and there a baa, in every place a baa, baa.

4. Jack (Jacob) and Jill went up (on) the mountain
And took a dish of water.
Jack went down and his head was not good
And Jill was after him.

5. This land is your land.
This land is my land...

6. She loves you – Yeah, yeah, yeah.
She loves you – Yeah, yeah, yeah.

7. This little animal goes to the city.
This little animal sits in the house.
This little animal eats meat.
This little animal doesn't eat a thing.
This little animal calls "E-E-E" all the way home(wards).

Exercise 1

1. you will remember (*m sg*), you will stand, you will say, you will be, you will know, you will go out, you will eat, you will sit   2. remember! (*m sg*), stand!, speak!, be!, know!, go out!, eat!, sit!   3. you will do (*f sg*), you will see, you will take, you will listen, you will go down, you will know, you will go up, you will sit   4. do! (*f sg*), see!, take!, listen!, go down!, know!, go up!, sit!   5. you will go (*m pl*), you will write, you will drink, you will guard, you will cross over, you will do, you will see, you will send   6. go! (*m pl*), stand!, drink!, guard!, cross over!, do!, see!, send!   7. Do not speak! (*m sg*), Do not go!, Do not take!, You shall not do! (Thou shall not do!), You shall not go up! (Thou shall not go up!)

Exercise 2

1. three people   2. one mouth   3. eight nations   4. six flocks   5. two women   6. the four nights   7. seven days   8. five families   9. one war   10. ten nations   11. seven legs   12. nine fields   13. a thousand seeds   14. six young men   15. the two altars   16 the six vessels   17. the one Holy of Holies   18. the three tents

19. two eyes   20. four commanders   21. three little words

Exercise 3

1. one + one = two   2. two + two = four   3. nine + three = twelve   4. eight + nine = seventeen   5. two + twelve = fourteen   6. eleven - five = six   7. sixteen - two = fourteen   8. thirteen + five = eighteen   9. ten + ten = twenty   10. twenty - seven = thirteen   11. five + six = eleven   12. twelve - eight = four   13. nine + five = fourteen

Exercise 4

1. Take (*m sg*) three animals and nine flocks! Take (*m pl*) three animals and four flocks! Take (*f sg*) three animals and fifteen flocks! Do not take (*m sg*) three animals and fourteen flocks! 2. Go (*m sg*) toward the house (home) with one young man! Go (*f sg*) home with the seven young men! Go (*m pl*) home with twenty young men! Do not go (*f sg*) home with young men! 3. See (*f sg*) David the king between the two camps! See (*m sg*) six kings within the camps! See (*m pl*) the four kings near the camps! Do not see (*m pl*) the seven kings!   4. Go up (*m sg*) as far as the top of the one mountain in the desert! Go up (*f sg*) as far as the eight mountains with the offering! Go up (*m pl*) as far as the mountain with a thousand people! Do not go up (*m sg*) to the mountain!   5. Say (*f sg*) this word to one mother! Say (*m sg*) this word to twelve slaves! Say (*m pl*) this word to the five chiefs! Do not say (*m sg*) this word! 6. Make (*m pl*) for you (yourself) ten altars! Make (*m sg*) for yourself altars on (in) five places! Make (*f sg*) the ten altars from stones! You shall not make (*m pl*) altars in Egypt!   7. Obey (*f sg*) (the voice of) the six angels! Obey (*m sg*) the three women! Harken (*m pl*) to the voice of the people! Do not obey (*m pl*) them!

Exercise 5

1.A. You will go up to the mountain and from there you will see the thousand guards.

‏.B אַל תַּעֲלֶה אֶל הָהָר וּמִשָּׁם אַל תִּרְאֶה אֶת אֶלֶף הַשּׁוֹמְרִים!

Do not go up to the mountain and from there you will not see the thousand guards!

‏.C עֲלֵה אֶל הָהָר וּמִשָּׁם רְאֵה אֶת אֶלֶף הַשּׁוֹמְרִים!

Go up to the mountain and from there see the thousand guards!

2.A. You will go to the six judges living in the city.

‏.B אַל תֵּלְכוּ אֶל שֵׁשֶׁת הַשֹּׁפְטִים הַיּוֹשְׁבִים בָּעִיר!

Do not go to the six judges living in the city!

(Exercise 5 continued)

C.‏ לְכוּ אֶל שֵׁשֶׁת הַשּׁוֹפְטִים הַיּוֹשְׁבִים בָּעִיר!

Go to the six judges living in the city!

3.A. You will hear the voice going up from the desert.

B.‏ אַל תִּשְׁמְעוּ אֶת הַקּוֹל הָעוֹלֶה מִן הַמִּדְבָּר!

Do not listen to the voice going up from the desert!

C.‏ שִׁמְעוּ אֶת הַקּוֹל הָעוֹלֶה מִן הַמִּדְבָּר!

Hear the voice going up from the desert!

4.A. You will call to the people who know the law.

B.‏ אַל תִּקְרְאִי אֶל הָאֲנָשִׁים הַיּוֹדְעִים אֶת הַתּוֹרָה!

Do not call to the people who know the law!

C.‏ קִרְאִי אֶל הָאֲנָשִׁים הַיּוֹדְעִים אֶת הַתּוֹרָה!

Call to the people who know the law!

5.A. You will take four priests with you to the city.

B.‏ אַל תִּקַּח אַרְבָּעָה כֹּהֲנִים עִמְּךָ לָעִיר!

Do not take four priests with you to the city!

C.‏ קַח אַרְבָּעָה כֹּהֲנִים עִמְּךָ לָעִיר!

Take four priests with you to the city!

6.A. You will do seven bad deeds in front of seven good women.

B.‏ אַל תַּעֲשׂוּ שִׁבְעָה מַעֲשִׂים רָעִים לִפְנֵי שֶׁבַע נָשִׁים טוֹבוֹת!

Do not do seven bad deeds in front of seven good women!

C.‏ עֲשׂוּ שִׁבְעָה מַעֲשִׂים רָעִים לִפְנֵי שֶׁבַע נָשִׁים טוֹבוֹת!

Do seven bad deeds in front of seven good women!

Exercise 6

1. I took three stones in my hand and I went up to my land and I made five vessels from them.

א.‏ קַח שָׁלֹשׁ אֲבָנִים בְּיָדְךָ וַעֲלֵה לְאַדְמָתְךָ וַעֲשֵׂה חֲמִשָּׁה כֵּלִים מֵהֶם.‏ ב.‏ אַל תִּקַּח שָׁלֹשׁ אֲבָנִים בְּיָדְךָ וְאַל

תַּעֲלֶה לְאַדְמָתְךָ וְאַל תַּעֲשֶׂה חֲמִשָּׁה כֵּלִים מֵהֶם.‏ ג.‏ קְחוּ שָׁלֹשׁ אֲבָנִים בְּיֶדְכֶם וְעֲלוּ לְאַדְמַתְכֶם וְעֲשׂוּ חֲמִשָּׁה כֵּלִים מֵהֶם.‏ ד.‏ וַיִּקַּח שָׁלֹשׁ אֲבָנִים בְּיָדוֹ וַיַּעַל לְאַדְמָתוֹ וַיַּעַשׂ חֲמִשָּׁה כֵּלִים מֵהֶם.‏

2. When Abraham the righteous one saw the evil deeds of the tribes of Israel, he went down to the camp, took the swords from them, built a house of law and then he judged them.

א.‏ כַּאֲשֶׁר הַשָּׂרִים הַצַּדִּיקִים רָאוּ אֶת מַעֲשֵׂי יִשְׂרָאֵל הָרָעִים, הֵם יָרְדוּ אֶל הַמַּחֲנֶה, לָקְחוּ אֶת הַחֶרֶב מֵהֶם, בָּנוּ בֵּית מִשְׁפָּט וְאָז שָׁפְטוּ אוֹתָם.‏ ב.‏ כַּאֲשֶׁר הָאֵם הַצַּדִּיקָה רָאֲתָה אֶת מַעֲשֵׂי יִשְׂרָאֵל הָרָעִים, הִיא יָרְדָה אֶל הַמַּחֲנֶה, לָקְחָה אֶת הַחֶרֶב מֵהֶם, בָּנְתָה בֵּית מִשְׁפָּט וְאָז שָׁפְטָה אוֹתָם.‏ ג.‏ כַּאֲשֶׁר אַתָּה הַצַּדִּיק רָאִיתָ אֶת מַעֲשֵׂי יִשְׂרָאֵל הָרָעִים, יָרַדְתָּ אֶל הַמַּחֲנֶה, לָקַחְתָּ אֶת הַחֶרֶב מֵהֶם, בָּנִיתָ בֵּית מִשְׁפָּט וְאָז שָׁפַטְתָּ אוֹתָם.‏ ד.‏ כַּאֲשֶׁר אֲנַחְנוּ הַצַּדִּיקִים רָאִינוּ אֶת מַעֲשֵׂי יִשְׂרָאֵל הָרָעִים, יָרַדְנוּ אֶל הַמַּחֲנֶה, לָקַחְנוּ אֶת הַחֶרֶב מֵהֶם, בָּנִינוּ בֵּית מִשְׁפָּט וְאָז שָׁפַטְנוּ אוֹתָם.‏ ה.‏ כַּאֲשֶׁר אָנֹכִי הַצַּדִּיק רָאִיתִי אֶת מַעֲשֵׂי יִשְׂרָאֵל הָרָעִים, יָרַדְתִּי אֶל הַמַּחֲנֶה, לָקַחְתִּי אֶת הַחֶרֶב מֵהֶם, בָּנִיתִי בֵּית מִשְׁפָּט וְאָז שָׁפַטְתִּי אוֹתָם.‏ ו.‏ כַּאֲשֶׁר אַתֶּם הַצַּדִּיקִים רְאִיתֶם אֶת מַעֲשֵׂי יִשְׂרָאֵל הָרָעִים, יָרַדְתֶּם אֶל הַמַּחֲנֶה, לָקַחְתֶּם אֶת הַחֶרֶב מֵהֶם, בְּנִיתֶם בֵּית מִשְׁפָּט וְאָז שָׁפַטְתֶּם אוֹתָם.‏

3. And you will say to him: "You will go toward the desert and you will go up toward the mountain, and you will see stones and you will take them to the altar and you will hear the voice of the heavens, and you will make an offering there."

א.‏ וְאָמַרְתָּ אֵלָיו: "לֵךְ מִדְבָּרָה וַעֲלֵה הָהָרָה, וּרְאֵה אֲבָנִים וְקַח אוֹתָם לַמִּזְבֵּחַ וּשְׁמַע אֶת קוֹל הַשָּׁמַיִם, וַעֲשֵׂה מִנְחָה שָׁם!" ב.‏ וְאָמַרְתָּ אֵלֶיהָ: "לְכִי מִדְבָּרָה וַעֲלִי הָהָרָה, וּרְאִי אֲבָנִים וּקְחִי אוֹתָם לַמִּזְבֵּחַ וְשִׁמְעִי אֶת קוֹל הַשָּׁמַיִם, וַעֲשִׂי מִנְחָה שָׁם!" ג.‏ וְאָמַרְתָּ אֲלֵיהֶם: "לְכוּ מִדְבָּרָה וַעֲלוּ הָהָרָה, וּרְאוּ אֲבָנִים וּקְחוּ אוֹתָם לַמִּזְבֵּחַ וְשִׁמְעוּ אֶת קוֹל הַשָּׁמַיִם, וַעֲשׂוּ מִנְחָה שָׁם!" ד.‏ וְאָמַרְתָּ אֲלֵיהֶם: "אַל תֵּלְכוּ מִדְבָּרָה וְאַל תַּעֲלוּ הָהָרָה, וְאַל תִּרְאוּ אֲבָנִים וְאַל תִּקְחוּ אוֹתָם לַמִּזְבֵּחַ וְאַל תִּשְׁמְעוּ אֶת קוֹל הַשָּׁמַיִם, וְאַל תַּעֲשׂוּ מִנְחָה שָׁם!"

40

(Exercise 6 continued)

4. And he sent him seven flocks (of sheep), and five chairs of silver and he gave him everything as a gift.

א.הוּא שָׁלַח אֵלָיו שֶׁבַע צֹאן, וַחֲמִשָּׁה כִּסְאֵי כֶּסֶף וְתֵן לוֹ הַכֹּל כְּמִנְחָה! ב.וְשָׁלְחוּ אֵלָיו שֶׁבַע צֹאן, וַחֲמִשָּׁה כִּסְאֵי כֶּסֶף וְנָתְנוּ לוֹ הַכֹּל כְּמִנְחָה! ג.וַתִּשְׁלְחוּ אֵלָיו שֶׁבַע צֹאן, וַחֲמִשָּׁה כִּסְאֵי כֶּסֶף וַתִּתְנוּ לוֹ הַכֹּל כְּמִנְחָה! ד.וְשָׁלַחְתִּי אֵלָיו שֶׁבַע צֹאן, וַחֲמִשָּׁה כִּסְאֵי כֶּסֶף וְנָתַתִּי לוֹ הַכֹּל כְּמִנְחָה! ה.וְשָׁלַחְתְּ אֵלָיו שֶׁבַע צֹאן, וַחֲמִשָּׁה כִּסְאֵי כֶּסֶף וְנָתַתְּ לוֹ הַכֹּל כְּמִנְחָה! ו.שָׁלְחוּ אֵלָיו שֶׁבַע צֹאן, וַחֲמִשָּׁה כִּסְאֵי כֶּסֶף תְּנוּ לוֹ הַכֹּל כְּמִנְחָה!

5. Know everything that is written about Moses and listen to the words written about his brother Aaron!

א.תֵּדְעוּ אֶת הַכֹּל אֲשֶׁר כָּתוּב עַל מֹשֶׁה וּשְׁמַעְתֶּם אֶת הַדְּבָרִים הַכְּתָבִים עַל אָחִיו אַהֲרֹן. ב.דְּעִי אֶת הַכֹּל אֲשֶׁר כָּתוּב עַל מֹשֶׁה וְשִׁמְעִי אֶת הַדְּבָרִים הַכְּתָבִים עַל אָחִיו אַהֲרֹן! ג.אַל תֵּדַע אֶת הַכֹּל אֲשֶׁר כָּתוּב עַל מֹשֶׁה וְאַל תִּשְׁמַע אֶת הַדְּבָרִים הַכְּתָבִים עַל אָחִיו אַהֲרֹן. ד.דְּעוּ אֶת הַכֹּל אֲשֶׁר כָּתוּב עַל מֹשֶׁה וְשִׁמְעוּ אֶת הַדְּבָרִים הַכְּתָבִים עַל אָחִיו אַהֲרֹן!

6. If Leah will open the gate, who will she find there and what will she answer to the lord of her house?

א.אִם דָּוִד יִפְתַּח אֶת הַשַּׁעַר, אֶת מִי יִמְצָא שָׁם וּמָה יַעֲנֶה לָאָדוֹן בֵּיתוֹ? ב.אִם הַכֹּהֲנִים יִפְתְּחוּ אֶת הַשַּׁעַר, אֶת מִי יִמְצְאוּ שָׁם וּמָה יַעֲנוּ לָאָדוֹן בֵּיתָם? ג.אִם אַתָּה תִּפְתַּח אֶת הַשַּׁעַר, אֶת מִי תִּמְצָא שָׁם וּמָה תַּעֲנֶה לָאָדוֹן בֵּיתְךָ? ד.אִם אֲנִי אֶפְתַּח אֶת הַשַּׁעַר, אֶת מִי אֶמְצָא שָׁם וּמָה אֶעֱנֶה לָאָדוֹן בֵּיתִי? ה.אִם אֲנַחְנוּ נִפְתַּח אֶת הַשַּׁעַר, אֶת מִי נִמְצָא שָׁם וּמָה נַעֲנֶה לָאָדוֹן בֵּיתֵנוּ?

7. Say the words to your son and then I will see if he will listen to your voice and if he will do everything!

א.אִמְרִי אֶת הַדְּבָרִים לִבְנֵךְ וְאָז אֶרְאֶה אִם יִשְׁמַע לְקוֹלֵךְ וְאִם יַעֲשֶׂה אֶת הַכֹּל! ב.אִמְרוּ אֶת הַדְּבָרִים לִבְנֵכֶם וְאָז אֶרְאֶה אִם יִשְׁמַע לְקוֹלְכֶם וְאִם יַעֲשֶׂה אֶת הַכֹּל! ג.תִּקְרְאִי אֶת הַדְּבָרִים לִבְנֵךְ וְאָז אֶרְאֶה אִם יִשְׁמַע לְקוֹלֵךְ וְאִם יַעֲשֶׂה אֶת הַכֹּל! ד.קִרְאוּ אֶת

הַדְּבָרִים לִבְנֵכֶם וְאָז אֶרְאֶה אִם יִשְׁמַע לְקוֹלְכֶם וְאִם יַעֲשֶׂה אֶת הַכֹּל!

A TALL TALE: The Sleeping Princess

And it came to pass in those days, a king and his wife lived in their large house within their land. They had silver and gold, many utensils and good servants, but they did not have sons and daughters. And it came to pass after ten years, the wife of the king gave birth to a little daughter. And they loved her very much. The king made a great feast for his small daughter. The king sent messengers who would call out to all the people within their border.

And they said in the name of the king: "Behold, the king has a daughter. In five more days there will be a great feast in the house of the king. Go to the feast and give a gift to the princess!"

The messengers also called out to the seven good spirits, but they did not call out to the one evil spirit who lived in the land.

And it was the day of the feast, and all the people of the land were standing in the house of the king.

The king was sitting on the throne of honor and he said to his wife: "See all of the people from our land and all of the presents for our little daughter."

The seven good spirits are also at the feast. Each one has a blessing as a gift for the princess.

Spirit one proclaimed: "May you be good."

Spirit two proclaimed: "May you be beautiful."

Spirit three proclaimed: "May you be wise."

Spirit four proclaimed: "May you be righteous."

Spirit five proclaimed: "May you have silver and gold."

Spirit six proclaimed: "May you have Torah (Jewish law), a marriage canopy, and good deeds."

The one evil spirit came to the feast and said: "You did not call me to this feast. But I also have a blessing for the princess. I will give her an evil blessing and here it is: 'When you will be sixteen years old, you will see an old woman within the house of the king. This woman will give you a sword of gold. When you take the sword, blood will flow from your hand and you will die!'"

After these words, the evil spirit went out from the feast.

Spirit seven proclaimed: "This is a very evil blessing but I have not yet given a blessing. I also have a blessing for the princess. I will give her a good blessing and here it is: The blessing of life! You will not die but you will sleep a hundred years and all of the people of the house of the king will sleep with you. And

(A TALL TALE continued)

after a hundred years, a prince will stand before you. He will take your hand and then you will rise to life. And all of the people of the house of the king will also rise to life with you."

It was after the day of the feast, and the king said to the servants: "Go from border to border and take all swords which are in our land and guard them in the place which no person would know!" And thus they did.

And behold, it came to pass after sixteen years, the princess was big (grown up) and beautiful, wise and good. Her father and her mother loved her very much. The king and his wife made a feast for the princess.

An old woman came to the feast and in her hand was a sword of gold.

She saw the princess and she said to her: "Peace to you, beautiful princess. I have a sword of gold. Take it as a present!"

The princess said: "I have never seen a thing (anything) like this!"

The princess took the sword of gold in her hand and blood came out of her hand. And she lay down on the ground and she slept. And all of the people of the house of the king slept with her.

After these things, there were large trees all around near the house of the king. All seven good spirits watched over the house of the king (for) a hundred years.

And it came to pass after a hundred years in that land, there was a good and wise prince who was twenty years old. He heard about the princess who was lying down and sleeping in the house of the king among large trees.

And he said in his heart: "I will find this young woman. I heard from my father that this princess is beautiful, good, wise, and righteous, and she also has a lot of silver and gold."

He knew that he would find her.

And the prince walked many days and many nights. He did not eat bread and he did not drink water. But he remembered the words of his father about the princess, and he went after her with all of his heart.

And it came to pass after twenty days and twenty nights on the road, the prince saw a large field, and in the midst of it there were large trees, and in the middle of them there was a house. And he crossed over to the trees and he found the gate of the house and he opened it. And the prince saw within the house many people sleeping Then he knew that there he would also find the princess. And behold, he saw she was lying on the ground and she was still very beautiful.

The prince saw the sword and the blood. And he stood in front of the princess. He took her hand in his hand and he kissed her. And the beautiful princess arose to life. And all of the people of the house of the king arose to life with her.

The seven good spirits came and they said: "A hundred years have passed, the evil blessing has also passed. This is the time for good blessings!" And thus it was.

And it came to pass, this prince and this princess had Torah (Jewish law), a wedding canopy and good deeds.

Chapter 20

Oral Review

1. Say all the law to the five sons! Do not say one good word to the three evil nations! You said to the ten commanders of the war: "Give us peace!" 2. You went to the two large cities but you settled in one small city. Go to nine countries but do not live there! Do not go to the four tribes in that place. 3. Take sixteen instruments of gold to the great priest in the Holy of Holies! Do not take sixteen people with you to the desert! You took twenty thousand animals to the fields of your father. 4. Hear the voice(s) of (from) a thousand men! You heard the sound of four spirits in the night. Hear the sound of the blood of your brother from the ground! 5. Go up to Jerusalem with seven men and eight women! Do not go up to the camps of Israel with seven sword(s) in your hand! You went up to the brothers of Jacob with eight flocks (of sheep) as a gift. 6. Make an altar from six stones in this place! Do not do an evil deed to a woman a hundred years old! You made these ten tents standing on the road. 7. See the three messengers of the king in front of his throne! See our land and a thousand trees on it! We saw seventeen small houses on the border round about.

Exercise 1

1. I lay down, I gave birth, I was able, I inherited, I will lie down, I will give birth, I will be able, I will inherit 2. you were able (m sg), you inherited, you lay down, lie down!, do not lie down!, you will be able, you will inherit 3. you inherited (f sg), you will inherit, lie down!, do not lie down!, you are giving birth, you were able, you will be able 4. he was able, he has inherited, he lay down, he begot, he will be able, he will inherit, he will beget, he will lay down 5. she will lie down, she was able, she will inherit, she will give birth, she inherited, she lay down, she will be able, she gave birth 6. we inherited, we lay down, we were able, we will inherit, we will be able, we will lie down, we gave birth, we gave 7. you will inherit (m pl), you will be able, you inherited, you were able, you lay down, you will lie down, you will judge 8. they were able, they lay down, they will be able, they will lie down, they inherited, they will inherit, they begat, they will beget

42

Exercise 2

1. F 2. J 3. N 4. P 5. C 6. H 7. D 8. M 9. Q
10. L 11. A 12. G 13. I 14. R 15. B 16. O 17. E
18. K

Exercise 3

כ.ת.ב, – perfect כָּתַבְתִּי, כָּתַבְתָּ, כָּתַבְתְּ, כָּתַב, כָּתְבָה,
כָּתַבְנוּ, כְּתַבְתֶּם, כְּתַבְתֶּן, כָּתְבוּ, כָּתְבוּ

כ.ת.ב, – imperfect אֶכְתֹּב, תִּכְתֹּב, תִּכְתְּבִי, יִכְתֹּב,
תִּכְתֹּב, נִכְתֹּב, תִּכְתְּבוּ, תִּכְתֹּבְנָה, יִכְתְּבוּ, תִּכְתֹּבְנָה

כ.ת.ב, – participle כּוֹתֵב, כּוֹתֶבֶת, כּוֹתְבִים, כּוֹתְבוֹת

כ.ת.ב, – passive participle כָּתוּב, כְּתוּבָה, כְּתוּבִים,
כְּתוּבוֹת

The following forms are never used in the Bible, but we
have included them here for completeness.

כ.ת.ב, – command כְּתֹב, כִּתְבִי, כִּתְבוּ, כְּתֹבְנָה

כ.ת.ב, – emphasis (לִ)כְתֹב, regular: infinitive, כָּתוֹב

Exercise 4

1. You went to see only him. 2. I will be able to give
(to) him his sword or my sword. 3. Please go to build
this city! 4. The army went down to take the property
of David or the property of Joseph. 5. Please go up to
take possession of the land of your father. 6. A woman
of strength will send her son to watch over the people.
7. We were guarding the bread to eat it. 8. The
strength of the army went out to make war. 9. Please
go to my house to eat, and to drink, and to see all of the
family! 10. And Isaac said to his brother saying:
"Don't go to drink!"

Exercise 5

1.A. Men of strength took possession of the land.

B. אַנְשֵׁי חַיִל יָכְלוּ לָרֶשֶׁת אֶת הָאָרֶץ.

Men of strength were able to take possession of the
land.

2.A. The army of Egypt went to the war.

B. צְבָא מִצְרַיִם יָכֹל לָלֶכֶת לַמִּלְחָמָה.

The army of Egypt was able to go to the war.

3.A. Sarah gave birth to Isaac.

B. שָׂרָה יָכְלָה לָלֶדֶת אֶת יִצְחָק.

Sarah was able to give birth to Isaac.

4.A. The descendent(s) of Abraham will take possession
of their inheritance.

B. זֶרַע אַבְרָהָם יוּכְלוּ לָרֶשֶׁת אֶת נַחֲלָתָם.

The descendent(s) of Abraham will be able to take
possession of their inheritance.

5.A. Seven armies stood on the border of Bethlehem.

B. שִׁבְעָה צְבָאוֹת יָכְלוּ לַעֲמֹד עַל גְּבוּל בֵּית לֶחֶם.

Seven armies were able to stand on the border of
Bethlehem.

6.A. I ate bread and meat in the night.

B. יָכֹלְתִּי לֶאֱכֹל לֶחֶם וּבָשָׂר בַּלַּיְלָה.

I was able to eat bread and meat in the night.

7.A. You will give me all of my inheritance now.

B. תּוּכְלוּ לָתֵת לִי אֶת כָּל נַחֲלָתִי עַתָּה.

You will be able to give all of my inheritance now.

8.A. We heard the words of Moses.

B. יָכֹלְנוּ לִשְׁמֹעַ אֶת דִּבְרֵי מֹשֶׁה.

We were able to hear the words of Moses.

9.A. You saw the tribes of Moab in the mountains all
around.

B. יָכֹלְתָּ לִרְאוֹת אֶת מַטּוֹת מוֹאָב בֶּהָרִים סָבִיב.

You were able to see the tribes of Moab in the
mountains all around.

10.A. You will lie down only in your place.

B. תּוּכַל לִשְׁכַּב רַק בִּמְקוֹמֶךָ.

You will be able to lie down only in your place.

Exercise 6

1. צְבָא מִצְרַיִם לֹא יָכֹל לָרֶדֶת לִפְנֵיהֶם. 2. יִירְשׁוּ אֶת
חֵיל מוֹאָב רַק אַחֲרֵי מֵאָה שָׁנָה. 3. תִּשְׁכַּב בְּבֵית
הַמֶּלֶךְ, וְיָלְדָה בֵּן. 4. כֹּה אָמַר יִצְחָק אֶל כָּל הָעָם
לֵאמֹר: "לְכוּ לִשְׁמֹעַ אֶת קוֹל מֹשֶׁה בֵּין שַׁעֲרֵי
יְרוּשָׁלַם." 5. בָּנִים, זִכְרוּ נָא לִשְׁמֹר אֶת הַתּוֹרָה!

(Exercise 6 continued)

6.תּוּכַל לָתֵת לְאָחִיךָ בְּהֵמָה אוֹ צֹאן אוֹ בָּשָׂר רַב מִן נַחֲלָתֶךָ.

Exercise 7

1. If you will only really obey me and you will guard my inheritance, I will give Naomi to you.   2. We will surely do everything for the children of Isaac because thus it was written in the law.   3. The mother said to her son, saying: "If you will really eat all of your bread, you will be big."   4. Behold I knew that you would surely rule over us.   5. You will surely give all of your force(s) to the army on the border of your property.   6. David will surely go in place of his servent to see the laws written in the stone.

Exercise 8

1. Rachel will go down from the mountains to see the face of Joseph and the eyes of Joseph and then she will cross over the field to listen to the words of his mouth but she will not go out to give him her hand and she will not lie down next to his feet.

א.אֲנִי אֵרֵד מֵהֶהָרִים לִרְאוֹת אֶת פְּנֵי יוֹסֵף וְאֶת עֵינֵי יוֹסֵף וְאָז אֶעֱבֹר אֶת הַשָּׂדֶה לִשְׁמֹעַ אֶת דִּבְרֵי פִּיו אַךְ לֹא אֵצֵא לָתֵת לוֹ אֶת יָדִי וְלֹא אֶשְׁכַּב עַל יַד רַגְלוֹ. ב.אֲנַחְנוּ נֵרֵד מֵהֶהָרִים לִרְאוֹת אֶת פְּנֵי יוֹסֵף וְאֶת עֵינֵי יוֹסֵף וְאָז נַעֲבֹר אֶת הַשָּׂדֶה לִשְׁמֹעַ אֶת דִּבְרֵי פִּיו אַךְ לֹא נֵצֵא לָתֵת לוֹ אֶת יָדֵנוּ וְלֹא נִשְׁכַּב עַל יַד רַגְלוֹ. ג.הֵמָּה יֵרְדוּ מֵהֶהָרִים לִרְאוֹת אֶת פְּנֵי יוֹסֵף וְאֶת עֵינֵי יוֹסֵף וְאָז יַעַבְרוּ אֶת הַשָּׂדֶה לִשְׁמֹעַ אֶת דִּבְרֵי פִּיו אַךְ לֹא יֵצְאוּ לָתֵת לוֹ אֶת יָדָם וְלֹא יִשְׁכְּבוּ עַל יַד רַגְלוֹ. ד.אַתְּ תֵּרְדִי מֵהֶהָרִים לִרְאוֹת אֶת פְּנֵי יוֹסֵף וְאֶת עֵינֵי יוֹסֵף וְאָז תַּעַבְרִי אֶת הַשָּׂדֶה לִשְׁמֹעַ אֶת דִּבְרֵי פִּיו אַךְ לֹא תֵּצְאִי לָתֵת לוֹ אֶת יָדֵךְ וְלֹא תִּשְׁכְּבִי עַל יַד רַגְלוֹ.

2. Old Aaron ruled over his land with justice and he built gates of silver, and he opened them and he called to all of the righteous to guard over them.

א.לֵאָה הַזְּקֵנָה מָלְכָה עַל אַרְצָהּ בְּמִשְׁפָּט וְהִיא בָּנְתָה שַׁעֲרֵי כֶסֶף, וַתִּפְתַּח אֹתָם וַתִּקְרָא לְכָל הַצַּדִּיקִים לִשְׁמֹר עֲלֵיהֶם.   ב.אָנֹכִי הַזָּקֵן (הַזְּקֵנָה) מָלַכְתִּי עַל אַרְצִי בְּמִשְׁפָּט וַאֲנִי בָּנִיתִי שַׁעֲרֵי כֶסֶף, וָאֶפְתַּח אֹתָם וָאֶקְרָא לְכָל הַצַּדִּיקִים לִשְׁמֹר עֲלֵיהֶם.   ג.אַתָּה הַזָּקֵן מָלַכְתָּ עַל אַרְצְךָ בְּמִשְׁפָּט וְאַתָּה בָּנִיתָ שַׁעֲרֵי כֶסֶף, וַתִּפְתַּח אֹתָם וַתִּקְרָא לְכָל הַצַּדִּיקִים לִשְׁמֹר עֲלֵיהֶם.

ד.הַשָּׂרִים הַחֲכָמִים הַזְּקֵנִים מָלְכוּ עַל אַרְצָם בְּמִשְׁפָּט וְהֵמָּה בָּנוּ שַׁעֲרֵי כֶסֶף, וַיִּפְתְּחוּ אֹתָם וַיִּקְרְאוּ לְכָל הַצַּדִּיקִים לִשְׁמֹר עֲלֵיהֶם.

3. If you will really drink all of the water from the open vessel and if you will really eat all of the meat of the altar then you will really hear the voice of the priest who will not be able to eat or drink.

א.אִם שָׁתֹה אֶשְׁתֶּה אֶת כָּל הַמַּיִם מִן הַכְּלִי הַפָּתוּחַ וְאִם אָכוֹל אֹכַל אֶת כָּל בְּשַׂר הַמִּזְבֵּחַ אָז שָׁמוֹעַ אֶשְׁמַע אֶת קוֹל הַכֹּהֵן אֲשֶׁר לֹא יוּכַל לֶאֱכֹל אוֹ לִשְׁתּוֹת. ב.אִם שָׁתֹה תִּשְׁתּוּ אֶת כָּל הַמַּיִם מִן הַכְּלִי הַפָּתוּחַ וְאִם אָכוֹל תֹּאכְלוּ אֶת כָּל בְּשַׂר הַמִּזְבֵּחַ אָז שָׁמוֹעַ תִּשְׁמְעוּ אֶת קוֹל הַכֹּהֵן אֲשֶׁר לֹא יוּכַל לֶאֱכֹל אוֹ לִשְׁתּוֹת. ג.אִם שָׁתֹה יִשְׁתֶּה אֶת כָּל הַמַּיִם מִן הַכְּלִי הַפָּתוּחַ וְאִם אָכוֹל יֹאכַל אֶת כָּל בְּשַׂר הַמִּזְבֵּחַ אָז שָׁמוֹעַ יִשְׁמַע אֶת קוֹל הַכֹּהֵן אֲשֶׁר לֹא יוּכַל לֶאֱכֹל אוֹ לִשְׁתּוֹת.   ד.אִם שָׁתֹה יִשְׁתּוּ אֶת כָּל הַמַּיִם מִן הַכְּלִי הַפָּתוּחַ וְאִם אָכוֹל יֹאכְלוּ אֶת כָּל בְּשַׂר הַמִּזְבֵּחַ אָז שָׁמוֹעַ יִשְׁמְעוּ אֶת קוֹל הַכֹּהֵן אֲשֶׁר לֹא יוּכַל לֶאֱכֹל אוֹ לִשְׁתּוֹת.   ה.אִם שָׁתֹה נִשְׁתֶּה אֶת כָּל הַמַּיִם מִן הַכְּלִי הַפָּתוּחַ וְאִם אָכוֹל נֹאכַל אֶת כָּל בְּשַׂר הַמִּזְבֵּחַ אָז שָׁמוֹעַ נִשְׁמַע אֶת קוֹל הַכֹּהֵן אֲשֶׁר לֹא יוּכַל לֶאֱכֹל אוֹ לִשְׁתּוֹת.

4. He was able to lie down in peace on all (of) the nights because his inheritance was large (numerous) and his strength was great and his son was wise and the army was guarding on his border.

א.אֲנִי יָכֹלְתִּי לִשְׁכַּב בְּשָׁלוֹם בְּכָל הַלֵּילוֹת כִּי נַחֲלָתִי רַבָּה וְחֵילִי גָּדוֹל וּבְנִי חָכָם וְהַצָּבָא שׁוֹמֵר עַל גְּבוּלִי. ב.אַתָּה יָכֹלְתָּ לִשְׁכַּב בְּשָׁלוֹם בְּכָל הַלֵּילוֹת כִּי נַחֲלָתְךָ רַבָּה וְחֵילְךָ גָּדוֹל וּבִנְךָ חָכָם וְהַצָּבָא שׁוֹמֵר עַל גְּבוּלֶךָ. ג.הֵם יָכְלוּ לִשְׁכַּב בְּשָׁלוֹם בְּכָל הַלֵּילוֹת כִּי נַחֲלָתָם רַבָּה וְחֵילָם גָּדוֹל וּבְנָם חָכָם וְהַצָּבָא שׁוֹמֵר עַל גְּבוּלָם.

5. Thus the mother said in those days, saying: "Sit in the house of justice, say only words of holiness, do good, see everything, and give honor to the law."

א.כֹּה אָמְרָה הָאֵם בַּיָּמִים הָהֵם לֵאמֹר: "שְׁבִי בְּבֵית הַמִּשְׁפָּט, אִמְרִי רַק דִּבְרֵי קֹדֶשׁ, עֲשִׂי טוֹב, רְאִי אֶת הַכֹּל, וּתְנִי כָּבוֹד לַתּוֹרָה!"   ב.כֹּה אָמְרָה הָאֵם בַּיָּמִים הָהֵם לֵאמֹר: "שֵׁב בְּבֵית הַמִּשְׁפָּט, אֱמֹר רַק דִּבְרֵי קֹדֶשׁ, עֲשֵׂה טוֹב, רְאֵה אֶת הַכֹּל, וְתֵן כָּבוֹד לַתּוֹרָה!"   ג.כֹּה אָמְרָה הָאֵם בַּיָּמִים הָהֵם לֵאמֹר: "תֵּשֵׁב בְּבֵית

44

(Exercise 8 continued)

הַמִּשְׁפָּט, תֹאמַר רַק דִּבְרֵי קֹדֶשׁ, תַּעֲשֶׂה טוֹב, תִּרְאֶה אֶת הַכֹּל, וְנָתַתָּ כָּבוֹד לַתּוֹרָה!" ד. כֹּה אָמְרָה הָאֵם בַּיָּמִים הָהֵם לֵאמֹר: "אַל תֵּשְׁבִי בְּבֵית הַמִּשְׁפָּט, אַל תֹאמְרִי רַק דִּבְרֵי קֹדֶשׁ, אַל תַּעֲשֶׂה טוֹב, אַל תִּרְאִי אֶת הַכֹּל, וְאַל תִּתְּנִי כָּבוֹד לַתּוֹרָה!"

A TALL TALE: Love at First Sight

And it came to pass in those days a king (יָשַׁב) lived in the land and he had a lot of power and a lot of property. The wife of the king (יָלְדָה) gave birth to only one daughter and her name was Rebecca. All of the people of the land will surely know that one day Rebecca (תִּירַשׁ) will inherit all of the property of her father. Therefore when Rebecca was seventeen years old, all of the young men around (יָצְאוּ) went out after her. They (הָלְכוּ) went every day (לִרְאוֹת) to see her and she did not (נָתְנָה) give her heart to them.

Rebecca said to them, saying: "Please (צְאוּ) go! Go away from me and (רְדוּ) go down home (towards the house)." They (שָׁמְעוּ) obeyed her and (הָלְכוּ) they went away from (from before) her.

And it came to pass there was one man by the name of Isaac, and he did not have an inheritance from his father. And one day he (מָצָא) found his way to her. On his seeing (when he saw) Rebecca (אָהַב) he loved her.

And he (קָרָא) called to her, saying: "I (אוֹהֵב) love you with all of my heart. (אֶתֵּן) I will give you everything that (אוּכַל) I will be able (לָתֵת) to give. I do not have an inheritance from my father but I have two good hands and a good head, and I (אוּכַל) will be able (לַעֲשׂוֹת) to make you a good life."

Rebecca (עָנְתָה) answered him, saying: "On my seeing (when I saw) you I also (אוֹהֶבֶת) love you very much. But I will not (אוּכַל) be able (לָקַחַת) to take a man (husband) until (אֶהְיֶה) I will be twenty years old."

Isaac (עָנָה) answered her, saying: "I will really give you all of my heart and all of my soul. And when (תִּהְיִי) you will be twenty (אֶקַּח) I will take you for my wife.

And in (during) these years I (אֵלֵךְ) will go (לִבְנוֹת) to build a house for us."

Rebecca said to him, saying: "Please (זְכֹר) remember me every day and every time in your walking (when you walk) on the road, in your sitting (when you sit) in the house which you (תִּבְנֶה) will build, and also in your lying down (when you lie down) on all of the nights (every night) in (during) all three years."

Then Isaac (לָקַח) took her hand within his hand and he (אָמַר) said: "(אֶרְאֶה) I will see you in three more years."

And he (יָצָא) went out from there and (וְיִבֶן) he built her a house.

After three years Isaac (לָקַח) took Rebecca for his wife and Rebecca (לָקְחָה) took Isaac for her husband and they (הָלְכוּ) went (לָשֶׁבֶת) to live in their house which Isaac (בָּנָה) built.

And (וַיִּהְיוּ) they had a good life forever.

Chapter 21

Oral Review

1. Go to the open gate! You went to my tent to see them. I will not go to the city because he lives there. Who was able to go in the desert? Rebecca will be able to find water for the feet of the walkers. 2. In my seeing Sarah (when I saw Sarah) I also loved her. I saw the written judgements in the law. The messenger will see the righteous one only after seven years. See your strength and all your inheritance! The seeing man (the man who sees) is a wise man. 3. He took bread in an open dish and sat under a little tree and ate his bread. Take your son whom you love to Bethlehem! The chiefs took all of the men of Moab for the army. I will go out to take silver and gold to the king. Only the man that takes a wife will beget sons. 4. Moses said to the children of Israel saying: "Give honor to the law!" Rebecca said to Sarah: "I will give you my man if you will give me your man." Please say to your brothers saying: "Give a gift to our father!" The one who says words of peace is not giving his soul to the wars. He said in his heart (to himself): "The law given to me will stand forever." 5. Aaron will hear the voice of his people and will build an animal of gold for it (them, the people). Listen to the words of the priest every day and every night!

Exercise 1

1. I put, I got up, I turned aside, I returned, I will return, I will put, I will come, I will die 2. you got up

(Exercise 1 continued)

(*m sg*), you returned, you put, you came, you will come, you will die, you will turn aside, arise! 3. you put (*f sg*), you returned, you came, you got up, return!, you will put, you returned, you will return, you will come 4. he returned, he got up, he will return, he will die, he died, he put, he will turn aside, he will come, he will put 5. she will put, she came, she returned, she died, she will die, she will get up, she will return, she put 6. we returned, we will return, we will put, we arose, we came, we will come, we will die, we put 7. you put (*m pl*), you came, you will return, you will arise, you will turn aside, you died, return! 8. they will come, they will die, they will arise, they will turn aside, they put, they came, they returned, they arose

Exercise 2

קָמְתִּי, קַמְתָּ, קַמְתְּ, קָם, קָמָה, קַמְנוּ, קַמְתֶּם, — perfect
קַמְתֶּן, קָמוּ, קָמוּ; — imperfect אָקוּם, תָּקוּם, תָּקוּמִי,
יָקוּם, תָּקוּם, נָקוּם, תָּקוּמוּ, תָּקֹמְנָה, יָקוּמוּ, תָּקֹמְנָה;
קָם, קָמָה, קָמִים, קָמוֹת; — participle
קוּם, קוּמִי, קוּמוּ; — command
קוּם (לְ)קוּם, emphasis — regular :infinitives קוּם

Exercise 3

1. In those days a prophet arose and he knew the sins of the people. The prophet arises and stands before the people. 2. David ate bad fruit and then died. Behold he is dying in front of us with a sword in his heart. 3. The army of Pharaoh will come to take the camps of Moab. The army of Egypt came after Pharaoh but it did not find him. 4. Wicked people turn aside from the commandments. Good people turned aside (away) from wicked sins. 5. The tribe returned from the desert because it had no wine or fruit. Return, my people, to guard the rams in (on) my land all around. 6. The prophets put all of the wine in front of the Holy of Holies. Rebecca puts her mouth on the dish and drinks wine from it.

Exercise 4

1. בִּנְךָ יָבוֹא לִרְאוֹת אֶת הָאֵילִים אֲשֶׁר שָׁבוּ לִשְׂדֵי
מוֹאָב. 2. פַּרְעֹה קָרָא אֶל עַמּוֹ לֵאמֹר: "קוּם וְסוּר מִן
הַנָּבִיא הָרָשָׁע." 3. אַבְרָהָם שָׁם אֶת הַיַּיִן בִּכְלִי פָּתוּחַ
וְאָז שָׁתָה אוֹתוֹ. 4. הַבֵּן אָמַר לְאָבִיו לֵאמֹר: "לֹא
אֶשְׁמֹר אֶת הַמִּצְוֹת. רַק אֶעֱשֶׂה עֲוֹנוֹת." 5. הָעֶבֶד
אָכַל אֶת הַפְּרִי וְאָז מֵת. 6. כֹּה כָּתְבָה בִּתִּי אַחַר
הַמִּלְחָמָה: "עֶשְׂרִים נְפָשׁוֹת יָלְדוּ."

Exercise 5

1. You put two rams on the altar. Did you put two rams on the altar? 2. The wicked Pharaoh will not return from Egypt. Will not the wicked Pharaoh return from Egypt? 3. Three prophets turned aside from the commandments of the law. Did three prophets turn aside from the commandments of the law? 4. You will arise to drink wine made from the fruit of the tree. Will you rise up to drink wine made from the fruit of the tree? 5. Did the evil one come to see the flock? The evil one came to see the flock. 6. Will you die if you will not return to the commandments? You will surely die if you do not return to the commandments.

Exercise 6

1. The ten sons (אָהֲבוּ) loved (לִרְאוֹת) to see the six daughters when they (שָׁתוּ) drank wine. The ten sons (אָהֲבוּ) loved (לִרְאוֹת) to see the six daughters when (יִשְׁתּוּ) they might drink wine. 2. You (זְכַרְתֶּם) remembered (לָקוּם) to get up when the nine prophets (בָּאוּ) came. You (תִּזְכְּרוּ) will remember (לָקוּם) to get up when the nine prophets (יָבוֹאוּ) will come. 3. My father (מֵת) died on his seeing (when he saw) my mother (מֵתָה) die. My father (יָמוּת) will die on seeing (when he sees) my mother (תָּמוּת) will die. 4. My sin (הָיָה) was (לֶאֱכֹל) to eat from the fruit of the tree and not (לָתֵת) to give a fruit to my brother. My sin (יִהְיֶה) will be (לֶאֱכֹל) to eat from the fruit of the tree and not (לָתֵת) to give a fruit to my brother. 5. (תָּבוֹא) You will come to the camp because the rams (יָשׁוּבוּ) will return to our land. (בָּאתָ) You came to the camp because the rams (שָׁבוּ) returned to our land. (בֹּא) Come to the camp because the rams (שָׁבִים) are returning to our land. 6. I did not (שַׂמְתִּי) put all of the wine in the camp and (שָׁתֹה שָׁתִיתִי) I really drank it only with my wife. I will not (אָשִׂים) put all of the wine in the camp and (אֶשְׁתֶּה שָׁתֹה) I will really drink it only with my wife. 7. The priests (סָרוּ) turned aside from the evil ways and (שָׁבוּ) returned to the commandments. The priests (יָסוּרוּ) will turn aside from the evil ways and (יָשׁוּבוּ) will return to the commandments. 8. Did you not (זָכַרְתָּ) remember the sins of Pharaoh all the days of your life? Will you not (תִּזְכֹּר) remember the sins of Pharaoh all the days of your life? 9. Do not (תִּשְׁלְחִי, תִּשְׁלַח, תִּשְׁלְחוּ) send Leah to the tribes of the people round about.

46

Exercise 7

1. And it came to pass at that time Pharaoh ruled in the land. – הוּא הָיָה   2. And he answered and he said: "The rams are near the border." – הוּא עָנָה   3. And he built an altar from a thousand stones. – הוּא בָּנָה   4. And he got up and he turned aside from the eight evil prophets. – הוּא קָם וְהוּא סָר   5. And he saw the strength of the army and he went up toward the mountain. – הוּא רָאָה/הוּא עָלָה   6. And he made very good wine and he drank it with the prophet. – הוּא עָשָׂה/הוּא שָׁתָה   7. And Isaac returned to his father, and he put his sword in him, and his father died. – הוּא שָׂם/הוּא מֵת/הוּא שָׁב

Exercise 8

1. I turned aside from my father and also I did my sin and therefore I did not inherit my property.

א. אַתָּה סַרְתָּ מֵאָבִיךָ וְגַם עָשִׂיתָ אֶת עֲוֹנְךָ וְעַל כֵּן לֹא יָרַשְׁתָּ אֶת נַחֲלָתֶךָ.   ב. יִצְחָק סָר מֵאָבִיו וְגַם עָשָׂה אֶת עֲוֹנוֹ וְעַל כֵּן לֹא יָרַשׁ אֶת נַחֲלָתוֹ.   ג. אֲנַחְנוּ סַרְנוּ מֵאָבִינוּ וְגַם עָשִׂינוּ אֶת עֲוֹנֵנוּ וְעַל כֵּן לֹא יָרַשְׁנוּ אֶת נַחֲלָתֵנוּ.   ד. הַכֹּהֲנִים סָרוּ מֵאֲבִיהֶם וְגַם עָשׂוּ אֶת עֲוֹנָם וְעַל כֵּן לֹא יָרְשׁוּ אֶת נַחֲלָתָם.

2. The rams of the mountains crossed over to the field and they ate all of the fruit of the ground and they died.

א. אַתָּה עָבַרְתָּ אֶל הַשָּׂדֶה וַתֹּאכַל אֶת כָּל פְּרִי הָאֲדָמָה וַתָּמוּת.   ב. אַתֶּם עֲבַרְתֶּם אֶל הַשָּׂדֶה וַתֹּאכְלוּ אֶת כָּל פְּרִי הָאֲדָמָה וַתָּמוּתוּ.   ג. אֲנַחְנוּ עָבַרְנוּ אֶל הַשָּׂדֶה וַנֹּאכַל אֶת כָּל פְּרִי הָאֲדָמָה וַנָּמוּתוּ.   ד. אָנֹכִי עָבַרְתִּי אֶל הַשָּׂדֶה וָאֹכַל אֶת כָּל פְּרִי הָאֲדָמָה וָאָמוּת.

3. You really remembered all the commandments of the prophet but you really did many sins and you will not be able to stand in the Holy of Holies in the coming days.

א. זָכֹר זָכַרְתָּ אֶת כָּל מִצְוֹת הַנָּבִיא אַךְ עָשֹׂה עָשִׂיתָ עֲוֹנוֹת רַבּוֹת וְלֹא אוּכַל לַעֲמֹד בְּקֹדֶשׁ הַקֳּדָשִׁים בַּיָּמִים הַבָּאִים.   ב. זָכֹר יִזְכֹּר אֶת כָּל מִצְוֹת הַנָּבִיא אַךְ עָשֹׂה יַעֲשֶׂה עֲוֹנוֹת רַבּוֹת וְלֹא יוּכַל לַעֲמֹד בְּקֹדֶשׁ הַקֳּדָשִׁים בַּיָּמִים הַבָּאִים.   ג. זָכֹר תִּזְכְּרוּ אֶת כָּל מִצְוֹת הַנָּבִיא אַךְ עָשֹׂה תַּעֲשׂוּ עֲוֹנוֹת רַבּוֹת וְלֹא תוּכְלוּ לַעֲמֹד בְּקֹדֶשׁ הַקֳּדָשִׁים בַּיָּמִים הַבָּאִים.   ד. זָכֹר יִזְכְּרוּ אֶת כָּל מִצְוֹת הַנָּבִיא אַךְ עָשֹׂה יַעֲשׂוּ עֲוֹנוֹת רַבּוֹת וְלֹא יוּכְלוּ לַעֲמֹד בְּקֹדֶשׁ הַקֳּדָשִׁים בַּיָּמִים הַבָּאִים.   ה. זָכֹר זָכְרוּ אֶת כָּל מִצְוֹת הַנָּבִיא אַךְ עָשֹׂה עָשׂוּ עֲוֹנוֹת רַבּוֹת וְלֹא יוּכְלוּ לַעֲמֹד בְּקֹדֶשׁ הַקֳּדָשִׁים בַּיָּמִים הַבָּאִים.

4. Moses the prophet returned to us and stood before us and judged between me and you.

א. אִשְׁתִּי שָׁבָה אֵלֵינוּ וַתַּעֲמֹד לְפָנֵינוּ וַתִּשְׁפֹּט בֵּינִי וּבֵינֶךְ.   ב. הַכֹּהֲנִים שָׁבוּ אֵלֵינוּ וַיַּעַמְדוּ לְפָנֵינוּ וַיִּשְׁפְּטוּ בֵּינִי וּבֵינֶךְ.   ג. אַתָּה שַׁבְתָּ אֵלֵינוּ וַתַּעֲמֹד וַתִּשְׁפֹּט בֵּינִי וּבֵינֶךְ.   ד. אַתֶּם שַׁבְתֶּם אֵלֵינוּ וַתַּעַמְדוּ לְפָנֵינוּ וַתִּשְׁפְּטוּ בֵּינִי וּבֵינֶךְ.

5. You will come to your house and then you will put your money in your place and then you will eat your bread and your meat but you will not drink (from) the wine of your brother.

א. אֲנִי אָבֹא לְבֵיתִי וְאָז אָשִׂים אֶת כַּסְפִּי בִּמְקוֹמִי וְאָז אֹכַל אֶת לַחְמִי וְאֶת בְּשָׂרִי אַךְ לֹא אֶשְׁתֶּה מִיֵּין אָחִי.   ב. יוֹסֵף יָבוֹא לְבֵיתוֹ וְאָז יָשִׂים אֶת כַּסְפּוֹ בִּמְקוֹמוֹ וְאָז יֹאכַל אֶת לַחְמוֹ וְאֶת בְּשָׂרוֹ אַךְ לֹא יִשְׁתֶּה מִיֵּין אָחִיו.   ג. אֲנַחְנוּ נָבוֹא לְבֵיתֵנוּ וְאָז נָשִׂים אֶת כַּסְפֵּנוּ בִּמְקוֹמֵנוּ וְאָז נֹאכַל אֶת לַחְמֵנוּ וְאֶת בְּשָׂרֵנוּ אַךְ לֹא נִשְׁתֶּה מִיֵּין אָחִינוּ.   ד. אַתֶּם תָּבוֹאוּ לְבֵיתְכֶם וְאָז תָּשִׂימוּ אֶת כַּסְפְּכֶם בִּמְקוֹמְכֶם וְאָז תֹּאכְלוּ אֶת לַחְמְכֶם וְאֶת בְּשַׂרְכֶם אַךְ לֹא תִּשְׁתּוּ מִיֵּין אֲחִיכֶם.   ה. הֵמָּה יָבוֹאוּ לְבֵיתָם וְאָז יָשִׂימוּ אֶת כַּסְפָּם בִּמְקוֹמָם וְאָז יֹאכְלוּ אֶת לַחְמָם וְאֶת בְּשָׂרָם אַךְ לֹא יִשְׁתּוּ מִיֵּין אֲחִיהֶם.

6. Joseph got up and he walked to the fields of his brother and he saw the sin of his brother and he turned from him.

א. וַיָּקוּמוּ הַנְּבִיאִים וַיֵּלְכוּ לִשְׂדֵי אֲחִיהֶם וַיִּרְאוּ אֶת עֲוֹן אֲחִיהֶם וַיָּסוּרוּ מִמֶּנּוּ.   ב. וָאָקוּם אֲנִי וָאֵלֵךְ לִשְׂדֵי אָחִי וָאֶרְאֶה אֶת עֲוֹן אָחִי וָאָסוּר מִמֶּנּוּ.   ג. וַתָּקוּם אַתָּה וַתֵּלֶךְ לִשְׂדֵי אָחִיךָ וַתִּרְאֶה אֶת עֲוֹן אָחִיךָ וַתָּסוּר מִמֶּנּוּ.   ד. וַנָּקוּם אֲנַחְנוּ וַנֵּלֶךְ לִשְׂדֵי אָחִינוּ וַנִּרְאֶה אֶת עֲוֹן אָחִינוּ וַנָּסוּר מִמֶּנּוּ.

A TALL TALE: Jacob and the Tall Tree

In those days there was a woman and she had one son and his name was Jacob. They did not have bread or fruit to eat and there was no wine to drink and there was also no money in their house. They only had one cow.

47

(A TALL TALE continued)

The mother said to Jacob her son, saying: "Take our cow to the city and sell her! And return home with the money in your hand!"
Jacob got up in the morning and went out on the road and he took the one cow with him.

He saw an old man when he was walking on the road. The old man said to him: "Peace to you Jacob!"
Jacob answered: "Peace to you."
Jacob said in his heart (to himself): "I have not seen this man until now but he knows my name. How wise he is!"

The old man said: "What are you going to do with that cow?"
Jacob answered and said: "I will take her to sell her in the city."
The old one said: "Turn aside from your way and please see this big seed in my hand. Give me the cow and then I will give you this seed."
And Jacob answered: "What good is a seed to me?"
The old one said: "If you will take this big seed, you will have a lot of gold and silver. If you will put the seed in the ground at night, in the morning there will be a tree taller than all the trees that you have seen until this (very) day! Give me your cow instead of (in exchange for) this big seed!"
And Jacob said to himself: "If silver and also gold will come from this big seed, it is good for me to take the seed and to give the cow to the old man."
Therefore Jacob took the seed in his hand and he gave his cow to the old man.
Jacob returned to his house.

When he came to his house, he saw his mother standing there.
She said to him: "I see that you sold the cow. Give me the money which they gave (to) you instead of (in exchange for) her!"
Jacob answered his mother, saying: "I did not sell the cow. But I gave her to a wise old man that I saw on the road. And he gave me this big seed which is in my hand."
His mother called in a big voice: "You are an evil young man! You did a big sin. Will we be able to eat or to drink a seed? Now, come in the house and lie down to sleep because there is no bread to eat!"

After these things, the mother turned aside from the face of her son and she took the big seed and she put it on the ground near the house. She went to the house and she lay down to sleep because she also did not have bread to eat.

It was night and it was morning and Jacob got up and he saw a very tall tree near their house and the tree was going up as far as the heavens. The tree was taller than all the trees which Jacob had seen until that (very) day. Jacob went up on the tree until he came to the gates of heaven. And he saw and behold there was

a road before him. He walked and he came to a very big house. At the gate of the house he saw a very big woman. He had not seen until that (very) day a big house like this and a big woman like this.

Jacob said to her: "Peace to you, good woman! Can you give me bread? Bread has not come to my mouth all day!"
But the big woman answered him: "Turn away from my house, young man! My husband is bigger than me, and his name is Goliath, and he very much loves to eat young men. If he will see you in our house, he will eat you!"

And Jacob was still standing there with the woman and they heard a big voice. The woman said: "Behold my husband is coming! Sit under the chair and Goliath will not see you!"

Goliath came to the middle of the house and he called (out) in a big voice, saying: "Did I not hear a voice of a young man when I was coming toward the house? Is there a young man who I will be able to eat? I will put the young man on the fire and then I will eat him!"
His wife said to him, saying: "Peace to you my husband. There is not a young man in our house but there is a ram on the fire and I will give it to you to eat. Please sit!"

Goliath sat and he ate the ram and he said to his wife: "And now give me the big bird which gives eggs of gold!"
Goliath said to the bird: "Bird, bird! Give me eggs of gold!"
The bird gave big eggs and they are eggs of gold! And when he saw many eggs, Goliath lay down to sleep.

Jacob saw everything from his place under the chair. Jacob said to himself: "Now Goliath lies down to sleep. I will take the bird with me and I will return to the house. We will be able to sell the eggs of gold and then we will have a lot of money."
Jacob took the bird.
The bird opened her mouth and she said in a big voice: "Goliath, get up! Get up!"
Goliath got up from his place and he saw the young man taking the bird.

Jacob went out with the bird in his hand from the house of Goliath and he returned to the big tree, and Goliath was behind him. Jacob went down on the big tree until he returned to his house.

Goliath said from the gates of heaven: "I will also go down on the big tree after him and I will take the bird from him."
But Goliath was bigger than Jacob and the tree fell from under him when he put his his foot on it, and Goliath died.

After these things, every day the bird gave many eggs of gold to Jacob and to his mother. And thus they had bread and fruit to eat and wine to drink and from that day life was good.

CHAPTER 22

Oral Review

1. Leah was able to give birth in her house and her mother was with her. We will be able to put all of our bread in front of you. My evil son was able to turn aside from me and from my property. The prophets were able to arise among us and in the midst of our land. 2. Please get up to come to the camp and to sit in it with us! Return to find the seven old ones walking after us! Turn aside from the rams standing in front of you and return to the flock behind you! Know the names of the twenty messengers and come in front of them! 3. It was night and David lay down and put his sword under him. Moses answered and said, saying: "Do not put your hand on her!" Joseph died and lay in the earth with a stone on (top of) him. Pharaoh returned to Egypt and all of the people returned with him. The prophet arose and he turned aside from the sins of the people around. 4. In our eating (when we were eating) our bread we saw animals in the field behind us. When you were sitting in your house you judged between me and my brother. As (when) I heard your voice from the mountain I went up on it. From my knowing (because I know) your name I will be able to return to your place. In your going (while you were going) on the road you returned to the commandments of your father. 5. I have seven dishes and I put bread and fruit in the midst (inside) of them. Seven prophets will arise among you. Behold a hundred wicked ones are doing sins in front of us.

Exercise 1

1. my fathers, my brothers, my feet, my daughters, my things, my mountain, my utensils, my hands, my prophets 2. your (*m sg*) days, your deeds, your judgements, your gates, your eyes, your face, your fathers, your houses 3. your (*f sg*) feet, your gates, your deeds, your hands, your ways, your sons, your daughters, your blood 4. his fathers, his stones, his tents, his brothers, his people, his women (wives), his generations, his chiefs 5. her feet, her cities, her eyes, her face, her hands, her sons, her daughters, her utensils 6. our priests, our kings, our sins, our eyes, our chiefs, our days, our lords, our generations 7. your (*m pl*) tents, your women, your daughters, your ways, your altars, your prophets 8. their hands, their feet, their heads, their faces, their eyes, their doings, their brothers

Exercise 2

1. עֵינֶיךָ, דְּבָרַי, אֲנָשָׁיו, נְבִיאֵיכֶם, מַעֲשֵׂיהֶם, בָּנֶיךָ

2. כֹּהֲנֵינוּ, בָּנֶיהָ, הָרַי, עֲוֹנוֹתֵיהֶם, רַגְלֶיךָ, יְדֵיכֶם

3. דּוֹרוֹתָיו, דָּמֶיךָ, כֵּלֶיהָ, יָמֵינוּ, אַחַי, אֹהָלָיו

4. עֵינֵינוּ, בָּתֵּיהֶם, יָמֶיךָ, אֶחָיו, יָדֶיהָ, מִזְבְּחוֹתֵיכֶם

5. רָאשֵׁיהֶם, רַגְלֶיךָ, מַעֲשֶׂיךָ, כֵּלַי, עֲווֹנוֹתֵינוּ, יָדָיו

6. בְּנוֹתֵיכֶם, אֲבוֹתַי, מִשְׁפָּטֶיךָ, פְּנֵיהֶם, דּוֹרוֹתֵינוּ

Exercise 3

1. He called to me in the light of the morning and he said: "Here I am." 2. Here you are breaking the Ark of Holiness. 3. Here I am seeing the light of the heavens. 4. Moses counted all of his people in this month. 5. Will all of us return to the service of the tent of meeting in the morning? 6. The children of the covenant are not coming to the Ark of Holiness. 7. Isaac is not in the midst of his families. 8. The light of truth is not in our generations. 9. Our generations turned aside from all of the commandments. 10. Abraham took their vessels and he broke all of them.

Exercise 4

1. שָׂם, יָשִׂימוּ, שָׂמוּ, In the light of the morning our priests put/will put/are putting the Ark of the Covenant in the tent of the meeting. 2. סָר or סָרָה, אָסוּר, סַרְתִּי, I have turned/will turn/am turning aside from my sins and I will return/have returned/am returning to the commandments in that month. 3. קָמִים, יָקוּמוּ, קָמוּ, Have his generations arisen/will his generations arise/do his generations rise up to do the work of the covenant? 4. מֵתִים, יָמוּתוּ, מֵתוּ, In this month in the evening all of our prophets died/will die/are dying in the midst of our people. 5. בָּאִים, נָבוֹא, בָּאנוּ, All of us came/will come/are coming to see the sea in the evening. 6. מוֹצֵא, תִּמְצָא, מָצָאתָ, You found/will find/are finding favor in my eyes in all of the time (all the time). 7. וַתְּקוּמוּ, וְקַמְתֶּם – שָׂמִים, תָּשִׂימוּ, שַׂמְתֶּם קָמִים, In its season you put/will put/are putting the Torah in the ark and you will arise/have arisen/are arising as one people to give it honor. 8. יִסְפְּרוּ, סָפְרוּ סוֹפְרִים, Did our chiefs count/will our chiefs count/are our chiefs counting the men in our armies? 9. שָׁבְרָה, סָרוֹת, תָּסֹרְנָה, סָרוּ – שׁוֹבֶרֶת, תִּשְׁבֹּר, Ruth broke/will break/breaks her hands when her eyes turned/will turn/turn aside (away) from the road.

Exercise 5

1. Did you go out in the morning or in the evening to guard the Ark of the Covenant?

יָצָאתִי בַּבֹּקֶר לִשְׁמֹר אֶת אֲרוֹן הַבְּרִית.

(Exercise 5 continued)

2. Did the tribe of Pharaoh cross over to Jerusalem with the spirit of peace or with the spirit of war?

עָבַר מַטֵּה פַּרְעֹה בְּרוּחַ הַמִּלְחָמָה.

3. What did you count near the ark of wood?

סָפַרְתִּי אֶת כְּלֵי הַזָּהָב עַל יַד אֲרוֹן הָעֵץ.

4. Are you not the blood of my blood and the flesh of my flesh?

אֲנִי דַם דָּמְךָ וּבְשַׂר בְּשָׂרְךָ כִּי אָנֹכִי אָבִיךָ.

5. Who is the righteous one who crossed over with you from Bethlehem?

יִצְחָק הוּא הָיָה הַצַּדִּיק אֲשֶׁר עָבַר עִמָּנוּ.

6. Might you not still find favor in the eyes of Leah?

אֶמְצָא חֵן בְּעֵינֵי לֵאָה בַּחֹדֶשׁ הַזֶּה.

7. Did Sarah break the chair in which she sat?

לֹא, שָׂרָה לֹא שָׁבְרָה אֶת הַכִּסֵּא, יִצְחָק שָׁבַר אֹתוֹ.

8. Did you count the many rams on our land?

לֹא, לֹא סָפַרְתִּי אֶת הָאֵילִים הָהֵם, אַךְ אֶסְפֹּר אוֹתָם עַתָּה.

Exercise 6

1. His generations inherited all of the law but they were not able to give it to their sons.

א.אָנֹכִי יָרַשְׁתִּי אֶת הַתּוֹרָה כֻּלָּהּ אַךְ לֹא יָכֹלְתִּי לָתֵת אוֹתָהּ לְבָנַי.   ב.הַנָּבִיא יָרַשׁ אֶת הַתּוֹרָה כֻּלָּהּ אַךְ לֹא יָכֹל לָתֵת אוֹתָהּ לְבָנָיו.   ג.אַתָּה יָרַשְׁתָּ אֶת הַתּוֹרָה כֻּלָּהּ אַךְ לֹא יָכֹלְתָּ לָתֵת אוֹתָהּ לְבָנֶיךָ.   ד.רָחֵל יָרְשָׁה אֶת הַתּוֹרָה כֻּלָּהּ אַךְ לֹא יָכְלָה לָתֵת אוֹתָהּ לְבָנֶיהָ.   ה.אַתֶּם יְרַשְׁתֶּם אֶת הַתּוֹרָה כֻּלָּהּ אַךְ לֹא יְכָלְתֶּם לָתֵת אוֹתָהּ לִבְנֵיכֶם.

2. In the light of the morning their families went down toward the desert and they took with them all of their money and there they built their cities and they lay down in them.

א.בְּאוֹר הַבֹּקֶר אֲנִי יָרַדְתִּי מִדְבָּרָה וָאֶקַּח עִמִּי אֶת כַּסְפִּי כֻּלּוֹ וָאֶבְנֶה שָׁם אֶת עָרַי וָאֶשְׁכַּב בָּן.   ב.בְּאוֹר הַבֹּקֶר אֲדוֹנִי יָרַד מִדְבָּרָה וַיִּקַּח עִמּוֹ אֶת כַּסְפּוֹ כֻּלּוֹ וַיִּבְנֶה שָׁם אֶת עָרָיו וַיִּשְׁכַּב בָּן.   ג.בְּאוֹר הַבֹּקֶר אַתֶּם יְרַדְתֶּם מִדְבָּרָה וַתִּקְחוּ עִמָּכֶם אֶת כַּסְפְּכֶם כֻּלּוֹ וַתִּבְנוּ שָׁם אֶת עָרֵיכֶם וַתִּשְׁכְּבוּ בָּן.   ד.בְּאוֹר הַבֹּקֶר אַתָּה יָרַדְתָּ מִדְבָּרָה וַתִּקַּח עִמְּךָ אֶת כַּסְפְּךָ כֻּלּוֹ וַתִּבְנֶה שָׁם אֶת עָרֶיךָ וַתִּשְׁכַּב בָּן.

3. We arose in the morning and then we came to the tent of meeting, and there we ate our bread and also drank the wine of our fathers with our daughters.

א.קַמְנוּ בַּבֹּקֶר וְאָז אָבוֹא אֶל אֹהֶל מוֹעֵד, וְשָׁם אֹכַל אֶת לַחְמִי וְגַם אֶשְׁתֶּה אֶת יֵין אֲבוֹתַי עִם בְּנוֹתַי.   ב.אַתָּה תָקוּם בַּבֹּקֶר וְאָז תָּבוֹא אֶל אֹהֶל מוֹעֵד, וְשָׁם תֹּאכַל אֶת לַחְמְךָ וְגַם תִּשְׁתֶּה אֶת יֵין אֲבוֹתֶיךָ עִם בְּנוֹתֶיךָ.   ג.קַמְתֶּם בַּבֹּקֶר וְאָז בָּאתֶם אֶל אֹהֶל מוֹעֵד, וְשָׁם אֲכַלְתֶּם אֶת לַחְמְכֶם וְגַם שְׁתִיתֶם אֶת יֵין אֲבוֹתֵיכֶם עִם בְּנוֹתֵיכֶם.   ד.קוּם בַּבֹּקֶר וְאָז בּוֹא אֶל אֹהֶל מוֹעֵד, וְשָׁם אֱכֹל לַחְמְךָ וְגַם שְׁתֵה אֶת יֵין אֲבוֹתֶיךָ עִם בְּנוֹתֶיךָ!   ה.יָקוּמוּ בַּבֹּקֶר וְאָז יָבוֹאוּ אֶל אֹהֶל מוֹעֵד, וְשָׁם יֹאכְלוּ לַחְמָם וְגַם יִשְׁתּוּ אֶת יֵין אֲבוֹתֵיהֶם עִם בְּנוֹתֵיהֶם.

4. The children of Israel did their work with their hands and thus they stood on their feet from morning until evening.

א.אֲנַחְנוּ עָשִׂינוּ אֶת עֲבוֹדָתֵנוּ בְּיָדֵינוּ וְכֵן עָמַדְנוּ עַל רַגְלֵינוּ מִבֹּקֶר עַד עֶרֶב.   ב.אַהֲרֹן עָשָׂה אֶת עֲבוֹדָתוֹ בְּיָדָיו וְכֵן עָמַד עַל רַגְלָיו מִבֹּקֶר עַד עֶרֶב.   ג.אֲנִי עָשִׂיתִי אֶת עֲבוֹדָתִי בְּיָדִי וְכֵן עָמַדְתִּי עַל רַגְלַי מִבֹּקֶר עַד עֶרֶב.   ד.אַתֶּם עֲשִׂיתֶם אֶת עֲבוֹדַתְכֶם בִּידֵיכֶם וְכֵן עֲמַדְתֶּם עַל רַגְלֵיכֶם מִבֹּקֶר עַד עֶרֶב.

5. My brothers will not remember my face until I come before them with my power and my possessions and my flock(s).

א.אֶחָיו לֹא יִזְכְּרוּ אֶת פָּנָיו עַד אֲשֶׁר יָבוֹא לִפְנֵיהֶם עִם חֵילוֹ וְנַחֲלָתוֹ וְצֹאנוֹ.   ב.אַחֶיךָ לֹא יִזְכְּרוּ אֶת פָּנֶיךָ עַד אֲשֶׁר תָּבוֹא לִפְנֵיהֶם עִם חֵילְךָ וְנַחֲלָתְךָ וְצֹאנְךָ.   ג.אֲחֵיהֶם לֹא יִזְכְּרוּ אֶת פְּנֵיהֶם עַד אֲשֶׁר יָבוֹאוּ לִפְנֵיהֶם עִם חֵילָם וְנַחֲלָתָם וְצֹאנָם.

(Exercise 6 continued)

6. You loved your mother with all of your heart and with all of your soul but afterward your face turned away from her and your eyes were on Rachel.

א. אָהַבְתִּי אֶת אִמִּי בְּכָל לְבָבִי וּבְכָל נַפְשִׁי אַךְ פָּנַי סָרוּ מִמֶּנָּה אַחֲרֵי כֵן וְעֵינַי עַל רָחֵל.   ב. אֲהַבְתֶּם אֶת אִמְּכֶם בְּכָל לְבַבְכֶם וּבְכָל נַפְשְׁכֶם אַךְ פְּנֵיכֶם סָרוּ מִמֶּנָּה אַחֲרֵי כֵן וְעֵינֵיכֶם עַל רָחֵל.   ג. אָהֲבוּ אֶת אִמָּם בְּכָל לְבָבָם וּבְכָל נַפְשָׁם אַךְ פְּנֵיהֶם סָרוּ מִמֶּנָּה אַחֲרֵי כֵן וְעֵינֵיהֶם עַל רָחֵל.   ד. אָהַב אֶת אִמּוֹ בְּכָל לְבָבוֹ וּבְכָל נַפְשׁוֹ אַךְ פָּנָיו סָרוּ מִמֶּנָּה אַחֲרֵי כֵן וְעֵינָיו עַל רָחֵל.

7. The messengers came to our house and they counted our sons and our daughters and they sent them from the midst of our people to be slaves for them.

א. וַתָּבוֹא לְבֵיתֵנוּ וַתִּסְפֹּר אֶת בָּנֵינוּ וְאֶת בְּנוֹתֵינוּ וַתִּשְׁלַח אוֹתָם מִקֶּרֶב עַמֵּנוּ לִהְיוֹת לָךְ עֲבָדִים.   ב. וַיָּבוֹא אַהֲרֹן לְבֵיתֵנוּ וַיִּסְפֹּר אֶת בָּנֵינוּ וְאֶת בְּנוֹתֵינוּ וַיִּשְׁלַח אוֹתָם מִקֶּרֶב עַמֵּנוּ לִהְיוֹת לוֹ עֲבָדִים.   ג. וַתָּבוֹאוּ לְבֵיתֵנוּ וַתִּסְפְּרוּ אֶת בָּנֵינוּ וְאֶת בְּנוֹתֵינוּ וַתִּשְׁלְחוּ אוֹתָם מִקֶּרֶב עַמֵּנוּ לִהְיוֹת לָכֶם עֲבָדִים.   ד. וַתָּבוֹא רִבְקָה לְבֵיתֵנוּ וַתִּסְפֹּר אֶת בָּנֵינוּ וְאֶת בְּנוֹתֵינוּ וַתִּשְׁלַח אוֹתָם מִקֶּרֶב עַמֵּנוּ לִהְיוֹת לָהּ עֲבָדִים.

8. Like his ancestors before him David loved his many wives, begat his many children, did sins (sinned), broke many hearts and also died as a king.

א. כַּאֲבוֹתֶיךָ לְפָנֶיךָ אָהַבְתָּ אֶת נָשֶׁיךָ הָרַבּוֹת, יָלַדְתָּ אֶת בָּנֶיךָ הָרַבִּים, עָשִׂיתָ עֲוֹנוֹת, שָׁבַרְתָּ לֵבָב רַב וְגַם מַתָּ כְּמֶלֶךְ.   ב. כַּאֲבוֹתֵינוּ לְפָנֵינוּ אָהַבְנוּ אֶת נָשֵׁינוּ הָרַבּוֹת, יָלַדְנוּ אֶת בָּנֵינוּ הָרַבִּים, עָשִׂינוּ עֲוֹנוֹת, שָׁבַרְנוּ לֵבָב רַב וְגַם מַתְנוּ כִּמְלָכִים.   ג. כַּאֲבוֹתֵיכֶם לִפְנֵיכֶם אֲהַבְתֶּם אֶת נְשֵׁיכֶם הָרַבּוֹת, יְלַדְתֶּם אֶת בְּנֵיכֶם הָרַבִּים, עֲשִׂיתֶם עֲוֹנוֹת, שָׁבַרְתֶּם לֵבָב רַב וְגַם מַתֶּם כִּמְלָכִים.   ד. כַּאֲבוֹתֵיהֶם לִפְנֵיהֶם הֵמָּה אָהֲבוּ אֶת נְשֵׁיהֶם הָרַבּוֹת, יָלְדוּ אֶת בְּנֵיהֶם הָרַבִּים, עָשׂוּ עֲוֹנוֹת, שָׁבְרוּ לֵבָב רַב וְגַם מֵתוּ כִּמְלָכִים.

A TALL TALE: The Daughter of the King (The Princess) and the Stone

It came to pass in those days before our generations, a king and a queen reigned over all of the land. The queen gave birth to only one son. When he was seventeen years old, all of the people in the land knew that the son of the king (the prince) would take a wife.

The queen loved her son with all of her heart. The queen said to all of the people of her household that only a young woman that would be in truth a daughter of a king (a true princess) would be able to be the wife of her son. The word went out to all of the land that a young woman who would not find favor in the eyes of the queen would not be the wife of the prince.

The people sent their daughters to the house of the king from all the lands around. When the queen heard that a young woman was coming, she put a little stone under the bed that the young woman would lie down in (in which the young woman would lie down), and she said in her heart (to herself): "Only a young woman who would be a real princess will know that there is a little stone under the bed."
One evening a young woman from the land of Moab came to the house of the king.
The queen said to her: "Good evening. Come, sit in our midst! We will eat bread and fruit and also we will drink wine and afterward you will go to lie down in the bed and in the morning I will judge you."
And thus they did.

All of them arose in the morning and they sat (down) to eat.

The queen said to the young woman from Moab, saying: "Good morning to you, were you able to sleep?"
The young woman answered: "The bed was very good. It was good for me all night."
The queen judged her in her heart (to herself): "She did not know that there is a stone under the bed. Therefore this one is not a true princess and she will not be the wife of my son. And also (besides) her eyes are the smallest eyes of the daughters of our land (she has the smallest eyes of all the daughters in our land)."
The queen stood up and said to the young woman: "Return to your land and to your people because you will not be the wife of my son!"
The young woman went out to her land.

After these things a young woman came from the land of Egypt to the house of the king.
The queen said to her: "Good evening. Come, sit in our midst! We will eat bread and fruit and also we will drink a lot of wine and afterward you will go to lie down in the bed and in the morning I will judge you."
And thus they did.

All of them got up in the morning and sat (down) to eat.
The queen said to the young woman from the land of Egypt, saying: "Good morning to you. Were you able to sleep?"
The young woman answered: "The bed found favor in my eyes (I liked the bed). This bed was better than the beds in Egypt."
The queen judged her in her heart (to herself): "She did not know that there is a stone under the bed. Therefore this one is not a true princess and will not be the wife of my son."

51

(A TALL TALE continued)

The queen stood and she said to the young woman: "You return to Egypt and turn away from my son because you will not be his wife!"
The young woman answered: "What did I do and what were my sins? Did I not find favor in your eyes? All of you found favor in my eyes."
The queen answered, saying: "You are a good young woman, but your hands are big and your feet are small and you are not a true princess. Go!"
And the young woman went out to her land.

And it came to pass every evening a young woman came to the house of the king, ate, drank, and lay down in the bed with the stone under it. And every morning that young woman arose and the queen judged her. And there was not one young woman who knew that there was a stone under the bed. And there was not one young woman who was a true princess. The queen could not count all of the young women who came.

And it came to pass after many months, a young woman came in the middle of the night to the house of the king. She did not know who was living in that house.
She called in a big voice: "Do you have water or bread in your house? I have been on the road many days and I cannot go anymore. Give me bread and water or I will die!"

All of the people of the house of the king heard the voice of the young woman and all of them arose and went to see who was calling. The queen went down to give her bread and water.
The queen said to her: "Come, sit in our midst! I will give you water to drink and bread to eat and you will not die and then you will be able to lie down in (the) bed."
And thus is was.

All of them arose in the morning and sat (down) to eat. The queen said to the young woman, saying: "Good morning to you. Were you able to sleep?"
The young woman answered: "I was not able to sleep all night. I was not able to find a good place in that bed and my eyes were open all night."

The queen said to all of those around: "Here is a princess, here is a true princess. You did not know that I put a little stone under the bed and also the young women did not know that a stone was under the bed. And only a young women who is a true princess would not be able to sleep with a little stone under the bed."

All of the people of the house of the king heard her words. All of them knew that there was a true princess in their midst.
The queen said: "I did not know if a true princess would come for my one (only) son and here you are in our midst. It is good for us, very good."

And it came to pass at its appointed time on the first of the month, they wrote the covenant between the son of the king and the true princess. They lived all of their days in the house of the king and they did not break the covenant forever.

CHAPTER 23

Oral Review

1. The king is not counting his money in front of his servants. Your servants counted all of your bread and then they ate it. Your good servant will not count your sins in front of you. The servants of the tent of meeting counted its vessels within the camp.   2. In our days we are not taking many women. In his days, Abraham took two of his wives and behold they gave birth to his sons. Sarah his wife did not inherit his property. Their wives did not find favor in their eyes every time.
3. With one hand I can break only one thing. With my hands and your hands we can break all of their things. If we break all of their things, the sin will be in our hands. Did you not do with your hands an evil sin?
4. The righteous man did not stand on his feet because he is old. Here they are getting up on their feet in front of the Ark of the Covenant. The army walked on its (their) feet from morning until evening. Here I am standing on the border, one foot in my land and one foot in your land.   5. The truth was as a light for our ancestors in their generations. The judgement was good in the eyes of his ancestors. Will you do the service of the law to honor your ancestors? And it came to pass your father saw the ark of holiness.

Exercise 1

1. I sought, I commanded, I spoke, I told, I will seek, I will command, I will speak I will recount   2. you smashed (m sg), you set free, you blessed, you sought, you will smash, you will set free, you will bless,. you will seek   3. you commanded (f sg), you spoke, you recounted, you smashed, you will command, you will speak, you will tell, you will smash   4. he spoke, he retold, he smashed, he sought, he set free, he blessed, he commanded, he made, he went down   5. he will speak, he will retell, he will smash, he will seek, he will set free, he will bless, he will command, he will be   6. she spoke, she retold, she smashed, she set free, she will speak, she will retell, she will smash, she will set free   7. we blessed, we sought, we commanded, we spoke, we will speak, we will command, we will seek, we will bless   8. you recounted (m pl), you smashed, you set free, you blessed, you will smash, you will set free, you will bless   9. they set free, they blessed, they told, they sought, they spoke, they commanded, they smashed, they built   10. they will smash, they will seek, they will speak, they will bless, they will retell, they will set free, they will command, they will know   11. I/you/he is commanding, I/you/he is blessing, I/you/she is speaking, I/you/she is speaking, I/you/she is commanding, we/you/they (m) are setting free, we/you/they (m) are seeking   12. set free! (m sg), bless!

(Exercise 1 continued)

(*f sg*), speak! (*m pl*), seek! (*m pl*), to bless, to retell, to seek, to speak

Exercise 2

בִּקַּשְׁתִּי, בִּקַּשְׁתָּ, בִּקַּשְׁתְּ, בִּקֵּשׁ, בִּקְשָׁה, – perfect
בִּקַּשְׁנוּ, בִּקַּשְׁתֶּם, בִּקַּשְׁתֶּן, בִּקְּשׁוּ, בִּקְּשׁוּ;

אֲבַקֵּשׁ, תְּבַקֵּשׁ, תְּבַקְּשִׁי, יְבַקֵּשׁ, תְּבַקֵּשׁ, – imperfect
נְבַקֵּשׁ, תְּבַקְּשׁוּ, תְּבַקֵּשְׁנָה, יְבַקְּשׁוּ, תְּבַקֵּשְׁנָה;

מְבַקֵּשׁ, מְבַקֶּשֶׁת, מְבַקְּשִׁים, מְבַקְּשׁוֹת; – participle

בַּקֵּשׁ, בַּקְּשׁוּ; – command   לְבַקֵּשׁ – infinitive

Exercise 3

1. Abraham set free the slaves but he did not send their clothes with them.   2. The daughter of Pharaoh broke his heart and also smashed all of his vessels.   3. We will seek (out) our ancestors in order that they will bless us.   4. Isaac will always speak to the children of Israel from the opening of the tent of meeting.   5. Jacob commanded his people to do the commandments.   6. Moses spoke to Aaron and his sons, saying: "Peace to you."   7. I counted the animals and then I told David that there are twenty animals.

Exercise 4

1. בֵּרֵךְ, יְבָרֵךְ, מְבָרֵךְ – וְשִׁלַּח, וַיְשַׁלַּח, וּמְשַׁלֵּחַ – לִמְצֹא   2. צִוָּה, יְצַוֶּה, מְצַוֶּה – לָשׁוּב   3. דִּבְּרוּ, יְדַבְּרוּ, מְדַבְּרִים – עָשׂוּ, יַעֲשׂוּ, עוֹשִׂים – בִּקְּשׁוּ, יְבַקְּשׁוּ, מְבַקְּשִׁים   4. שַׂמְתִּי, אָשִׂים, שָׂם, שָׂמָה – בֵּרַכְתְּ, תְּבָרֵךְ, מְבָרֵךְ   5. וַיְהִי, וְהָיָה – הָלְכוּ, יֵלְכוּ, הוֹלְכִים – לְבַקֵּשׁ   6. וַיְדַבֵּר, וְדִבֶּר, וּמְדַבֵּר – קוּמוּ – וְשׁוּבוּ   7. תְּשַׁלַּח, תְּשַׁלְּחִי, תְּשַׁלְּחוּ, תְּשַׁלַּחְנָה – יָמוּתוּ   8. בָּא, יָבוֹא – צִוָּה, יְצַוֶּה, מְצַוֶּה – לְשַׁלֵּחַ   9. צַו, יְצַו, מְצַוִּים – לִשְׁמֹר   10. בַּקֵּשׁ, יְבַקֵּשׁ, מְבַקֵּשׁ – שָׁבַר, יִשְׁבֹּר, שׁוֹבְרִים, שָׁבְרוּ, יִשְׁבְּרוּ, מְשַׁבְּרִים

1. The father blessed/will bless/is blessing his sons with money, and he will free/and he has freed/and he is freeing them to find their place in the world.   2. Every morning my father commanded/will command/is commanding his sons to return toward the house before evening.   3. The prophets spoke/will speak/are speaking the truth, did/will do/are doing justice, and continually have sought/will seek/are seeking peace.   4. I put/will put/am putting bread and wine in the entrance of your tent, and you blessed/will bless/are blessing me.   5. And there was/and there will be a famine in the land of Moab, and my sons went/will

go/are going to Egypt to seek bread and fruit.   6. And Moses spoke/will speak/is speaking to his brothers, saying: "Arise in the morning and return to the tent of meeting with me."   7. Do not send (with 4 possible speakers: *ms, fs, m pl, f pl*) the rams of the mountain to the desert because they will die there from famine.   8. The army came/is coming/will come to our land, and also it commanded/it will command/it is commanding us to free the slaves.   9. The priests commanded/will command/are commanding our children, all of them, to guard the commandments of the Torah for the sake of our fathers.   10. The king sought/will seek/is seeking peace in his land, and the chiefs of his army broke/will break/are breaking their swords for the sake of his word.

Exercise 5

1. מְשַׁלֵּחַ, יוֹדְעִים, My slaves know that I am setting them free now.   2. הַשּׁוֹלֵחַ, Moses, the one who is sending you to Israel, he also will set you free.

3. מְבַקֵּשׁ, יוֹשֵׁב, שׁוֹפֵט, The judge of the evil camp is sitting in his throne and he is seeking an offering from every family around.   4. וּמְסַפֵּר, יוֹשֵׁב, Abraham is always sitting in the opening of his tent and he is telling about his deeds to his sons.   5. שֹׁמְרֵי, מְבַקְּשֵׁי, In time of famine my brothers are seekers of bread and also guarders of water.   6. מְבַקֵּשׁ, The army of Moab is seeking war for the sake of its land.   7. וּמְצַוֶּה, מְדַבֵּר, עוֹנֶה, Here I am speaking to you and commanding you but you are not answering me and this is a great sin.   8. הַבָּאָה, הַמְדַבְּרִים, The speakers stood and they told us about the clothes of Jerusalem that will be in our midst in the coming year.   9. וּמְבַקֵּשׁ, וְהוֹלֵךְ, שָׂם, I am putting on me (putting on) my good clothes and going to your house and seeking your hand and your heart.

Exercise 6

1. אָבִינוּ יְבָרֵךְ אוֹתָנוּ לְמַעַן בָּנֵינוּ.   2. וַיְדַבֵּר מֹשֶׁה לִבְנֵי יִשְׂרָאֵל לֵאמֹר:"בַּקְּשׁוּ מִשְׁפָּט וְשִׁמְרוּ אֶת הַתּוֹרָה!"   3. וַיְצַו פַּרְעֹה אֶת עֲבָדָיו לִבְנוֹת לוֹ עָרִים גְּדוֹלוֹת.   4. הַמֶּלֶךְ סָפַר כָּל הַזָּהָב, אָז הוּא סִפֵּר לְבָנָיו עָלָיו.   5. דָּוִד תָּמִיד יְבַקֵּשׁ לַעֲשׂוֹת מִלְחָמוֹת, לָקַחַת נָשִׁים, וְלָרֶשֶׁת נַחֲלָה.   6. יוֹסֵף שָׁלַח מַלְאָכִים לְסַפֵּר אֶת כָּל הָאָרֶץ אֲשֶׁר שָׁלַח אֶת הָעֲבָדִים.   7. בִּימֵי הָרָעָב אַנְשֵׁי הַחַיִל שָׁבְרוּ אֶת הַשְּׁעָרִים לִמְצֹא לֶחֶם לֶאֱכֹל וּמַיִם לִשְׁתּוֹת.

Exercise 7

1. I got up in the morning, I put my clothes on (me),
I went out from the opening of the tent and then I
commanded the slaves to give (to) me bread.

א. הֵם קָמוּ בַּבֹּקֶר, שָׂמוּ אֶת בִּגְדֵיהֶם עֲלֵיהֶם, יָצְאוּ
מִפֶּתַח הָאֹהֶל וְאָז צִוּוּ אֶת הָעֲבָדִים לָתֵת לָהֶם לֶחֶם.
ב. קוּם בַּבֹּקֶר, שִׂים אֶת בְּגָדֶיךָ עָלֶיךָ, צֵא מִפֶּתַח
הָאֹהֶל וְאָז צַו אֶת הָעֲבָדִים לָתֵת לְךָ לֶחֶם! ג. הוּא
יָקוּם בַּבֹּקֶר, יָשִׂים אֶת בְּגָדָיו עָלָיו, יֵצֵא מִפֶּתַח הָאֹהֶל
וְאָז יְצַוֶּה אֶת הָעֲבָדִים לָתֵת לוֹ לֶחֶם. ד. תָּקוּמוּ
בַּבֹּקֶר, תָּשִׂימוּ אֶת בִּגְדֵיכֶם עֲלֵיכֶם, תֵּצְאוּ מִפֶּתַח
הָאֹהֶל וְאָז תְּצַוּוּ אֶת הָעֲבָדִים לָתֵת לָכֶם לֶחֶם.

2. When you go out to this war, you will break the
heads of the nations, you will smash their altars, you
will seek their souls and you will free their slaves
continually.

א. כַּאֲשֶׁר הַשָּׂרִים יֵצְאוּ לַמִּלְחָמָה הַזֹּאת, יִשְׁבְּרוּ אֶת
רָאשֵׁי הַגּוֹיִם, יְשַׁבְּרוּ אֶת מִזְבְּחוֹתָם, יְבַקְּשׁוּ אֶת נַפְשָׁם
וְאֶת כָּל עַבְדֵיהֶם יְשַׁלְּחוּ תָּמִיד. ב. כַּאֲשֶׁר דָּוִד יֵצֵא
לַמִּלְחָמָה הַזֹּאת, יִשְׁבֹּר אֶת רָאשֵׁי הַגּוֹיִם, יְשַׁבֵּר אֶת
מִזְבְּחוֹתָם, יְבַקֵּשׁ אֶת נַפְשָׁם וְאֶת כָּל עַבְדֵיהֶם יְשַׁלַּח
תָּמִיד. ג. כַּאֲשֶׁר אַתֶּם תֵּצְאוּ לַמִּלְחָמָה הַזֹּאת, תִּשְׁבְּרוּ
אֶת רָאשֵׁי הַגּוֹיִם, תְּשַׁבְּרוּ אֶת מִזְבְּחוֹתָם, תְּבַקְּשׁוּ אֶת
נַפְשָׁם וְאֶת כָּל עַבְדֵיהֶם תְּשַׁלְּחוּ תָּמִיד. ד. כַּאֲשֶׁר
אֲנַחְנוּ נֵצֵא לַמִּלְחָמָה הַזֹּאת, נִשְׁבֹּר אֶת רָאשֵׁי הַגּוֹיִם,
נְשַׁבֵּר אֶת מִזְבְּחוֹתָם, נְבַקֵּשׁ אֶת נַפְשָׁם וְאֶת כָּל
עַבְדֵיהֶם נְשַׁלַּח תָּמִיד. ה. כַּאֲשֶׁר אֲנִי אֵצֵא לַמִּלְחָמָה
הַזֹּאת, אֶשְׁבֹּר אֶת רָאשֵׁי הַגּוֹיִם, אֲשַׁבֵּר אֶת מִזְבְּחוֹתָם,
אֲבַקֵּשׁ אֶת נַפְשָׁם וְאֶת כָּל עַבְדֵיהֶם אֲשַׁלַּח תָּמִיד.

3. In the month of the famine we did not eat fruit and
we did not drink wine, we only sat in our houses, and
also spoke words of truth.

א. בְּחֹדֶשׁ הָרָעָב לֹא תֹאכְלוּ פְּרִי וְלֹא תִשְׁתּוּ יַיִן, רַק
תֵּשְׁבוּ בְּבָתֵּיכֶם, וְגַם תְּדַבְּרוּ דִּבְרֵי אֱמֶת. ב. בְּחֹדֶשׁ
הָרָעָב הֵם לֹא אוֹכְלִים פְּרִי וְלֹא שׁוֹתִים יַיִן, רַק
יוֹשְׁבִים בְּבָתֵּיהֶם, וְגַם מְדַבְּרִים דִּבְרֵי אֱמֶת.
ג. בְּחֹדֶשׁ הָרָעָב לֹא אָכַלְתִּי פְּרִי וְלֹא שָׁתִיתִי יַיִן, רַק
יָשַׁבְתִּי בְּבֵיתִי, וְגַם דִּבַּרְתִּי דִּבְרֵי אֱמֶת. ד. בְּחֹדֶשׁ
הָרָעָב לֹא אָכַלְתָּ פְּרִי וְלֹא שָׁתִיתָ יַיִן, רַק יָשַׁבְתָּ
בְּבֵיתְךָ, וְגַם דִּבַּרְתָּ דִּבְרֵי אֱמֶת. ה. בְּחֹדֶשׁ הָרָעָב

הוּא לֹא יֹאכַל פְּרִי וְלֹא יִשְׁתֶּה יַיִן, רַק יֵשֵׁב בְּבֵיתוֹ,
וְגַם יְדַבֵּר דִּבְרֵי אֱמֶת.

4. The old man will smash many rocks in order that he
will find the gold which he is seeking.

א. אֲנִי אֲשַׁבֵּר אֲבָנִים רַבּוֹת לְמַעַן אֶמְצָא אֶת הַזָּהָב
אֲשֶׁר אֲנִי מְבַקֵּשׁ. ב. אַתָּה תְּשַׁבֵּר אֲבָנִים רַבּוֹת לְמַעַן
תִּמְצָא אֶת הַזָּהָב אֲשֶׁר אַתָּה מְבַקֵּשׁ. ג. אַתֶּם תְּשַׁבְּרוּ
אֲבָנִים רַבּוֹת לְמַעַן תִּמְצְאוּ אֶת הַזָּהָב אֲשֶׁר אַתֶּם
מְבַקְּשִׁים. ד. אֲנַחְנוּ נְשַׁבֵּר אֲבָנִים רַבּוֹת לְמַעַן נִמְצָא
אֶת הַזָּהָב אֲשֶׁר אֲנַחְנוּ מְבַקְּשִׁים. ה. אַנְשֵׁי בֵּית לֶחֶם
יְשַׁבְּרוּ אֲבָנִים רַבּוֹת לְמַעַן יִמְצְאוּ אֶת הַזָּהָב אֲשֶׁר הֵם
מְבַקְּשִׁים. ו. שָׂרָה תְּשַׁבֵּר אֲבָנִים רַבּוֹת לְמַעַן תִּמְצָא
אֶת הַזָּהָב אֲשֶׁר הִיא מְבַקֶּשֶׁת.

5. My father told me that he will bless me and after
that he will die.

א. אִמִּי סִפְּרָה לִי כִּי תְּבָרֵךְ אוֹתִי וְאַחֲרֵי כֵן תָּמוּת.
ב. הַנְּבִיאִים סִפְּרוּ לִי כִּי יְבָרְכוּ אוֹתִי וְאַחֲרֵי כֵן יָמוּתוּ.
ג. אַתָּה סִפַּרְתָּ לִי כִּי תְּבָרֵךְ אוֹתִי וְאַחֲרֵי כֵן תָּמוּת.
ד. אַתֶּם סִפַּרְתֶּם לִי כִּי תְּבָרְכוּ אוֹתִי וְאַחֲרֵי כֵן תָּמוּתוּ.

6. In the evening we lay down near the water, and the
light in the heavens found favor in our eyes, we heard
the voice of the wind among the trees and thus we knew
that (the) life is good.

א. בָּעֶרֶב אֲנִי שָׁכַבְתִּי עַל יַד הַמַּיִם, וְהָאוֹר בַּשָּׁמַיִם
מָצָא חֵן בְּעֵינַי, שָׁמַעְתִּי אֶת קוֹל הָרוּחַ בֵּין הָעֵצִים וְכֵן
יָדַעְתִּי כִּי הַחַיִּים טוֹבִים. ב. בָּעֶרֶב אַתָּה שָׁכַבְתָּ עַל
יַד הַמַּיִם, וְהָאוֹר בַּשָּׁמַיִם מָצָא חֵן בְּעֵינֶיךָ, שָׁמַעְתָּ אֶת
קוֹל הָרוּחַ בֵּין הָעֵצִים וְכֵן יָדַעְתָּ כִּי הַחַיִּים טוֹבִים.
ג. בָּעֶרֶב לֵאָה שָׁכְבָה עַל יַד הַמַּיִם, וְהָאוֹר בַּשָּׁמַיִם
מָצָא חֵן בְּעֵינֶיהָ, שָׁמְעָה אֶת קוֹל הָרוּחַ בֵּין הָעֵצִים
וְכֵן יָדְעָה כִּי הַחַיִּים טוֹבִים. ד. בָּעֶרֶב אַתֶּם שְׁכַבְתֶּם
עַל יַד הַמַּיִם, וְהָאוֹר בַּשָּׁמַיִם מָצָא חֵן בְּעֵינֵיכֶם,
שְׁמַעְתֶּם אֶת קוֹל הָרוּחַ בֵּין הָעֵצִים וְכֵן יְדַעְתֶּם כִּי
הַחַיִּים טוֹבִים. ה. בָּעֶרֶב דָּוִד שָׁכַב עַל יַד הַמַּיִם,
וְהָאוֹר בַּשָּׁמַיִם מָצָא חֵן בְּעֵינָיו, שָׁמַע אֶת קוֹל הָרוּחַ
בֵּין הָעֵצִים וְכֵן יָדַע כִּי הַחַיִּים טוֹבִים. ו. בָּעֶרֶב
הַמַּלְאָכִים שָׁכְבוּ עַל יַד הַמַּיִם, וְהָאוֹר בַּשָּׁמַיִם מָצָא חֵן
בְּעֵינֵיהֶם, שָׁמְעוּ אֶת קוֹל הָרוּחַ בֵּין הָעֵצִים וְכֵן יָדְעוּ
כִּי הַחַיִּים טוֹבִים.

(Exercise 7 continued)

7. Who will continually take his clothes and then will sit in the opening of the tent of meeting in order that he may speak to the tribe standing around?

א. הַכֹּהֲנִים תָּמִיד יִקְחוּ אֶת בִּגְדֵיהֶם וְאָז יֵשְׁבוּ בְּפֶתַח אֹהֶל מוֹעֵד לְמַעַן יְדַבְּרוּ אֶל הַמַּטֶּה הָעוֹמֵד סָבִיב.

ב. אָנֹכִי תָּמִיד אֶקַּח אֶת בִּגְדִי וְאָז אֵשֵׁב בְּפֶתַח אֹהֶל מוֹעֵד לְמַעַן אֲדַבֵּר אֶל הַמַּטֶּה הָעוֹמֵד סָבִיב.

ג. אַתָּה תָּמִיד תִּקַּח אֶת בְּגָדֶיךָ וְאָז תֵּשֵׁב בְּפֶתַח אֹהֶל מוֹעֵד לְמַעַן תְּדַבֵּר אֶל הַמַּטֶּה הָעוֹמֵד סָבִיב. ד. אַתֶּם תָּמִיד תִּקְחוּ אֶת בִּגְדֵיכֶם וְאָז תֵּשְׁבוּ בְּפֶתַח אֹהֶל מוֹעֵד לְמַעַן תְּדַבְּרוּ אֶל הַמַּטֶּה הָעוֹמֵד סָבִיב.

A TALL TALE: The Fisherman and His Wife

An old fisherman lived with his wife in a small house near the sea and he did not have money. Every morning the man went down to the sea to fish (for) fish and every evening the man returned to his house with fish to eat. And it was (the) day, and the fisherman went down to the sea in the morning and he fished there all day. And it was evening, and the fisherman fished (caught) a fish of gold.

The fish of gold spoke to the fisherman, saying: "Please set me free in order that I will return to the water and I will give you everything that you seek (request) from me." The fisherman answered, saying: "I regularly give food to my wife in the evening. If you will only give me food instead of you, I will set you free to return to the water."

The fish of gold gave meat and bread and fruit and wine to the fisherman. The fish of gold returned to the water and the fisherman returned to his house with the food in his hands. When the fisherman was coming to his house, his wife saw all the food in his hands. She said: "What is all of this food?" The man told his wife everything that was (had happened). His wife commanded him, saying: "Return to the sea! Command the fish of gold to build us a big house and to give us a lot of money!"

The fisherman went down and he came to the sea, and he called in a big voice: "Fish of gold, come up to me!" The fish of gold answered and said: "What do you request from me?" He told to the fish of gold everything that his wife said. The fish of gold spoke, saying: "Please return to your house and I will do that which you request." The fisherman returned to his house and behold everything was as he requested. And his wife was standing in an opening of a very big house with money in her hands.

Three months passed. And it came to pass one morning, the wife of the fisherman arose and she said to herself: "It is not enough for me! We are able (can) to request more from that fish of gold." She called to her husband, saying: "My husband, return to the sea! Speak to the fish of gold and command him to make us kings. And then we will rule over all the land." The fisherman went down and came to the sea, and thus he said: "Fish of gold come up to me!" The fish of gold came up and said: "What are you requesting from me now?" He told the fish of gold everything that his wife said. The fish of gold said, saying: "Please return to your house and everything will be as you requested." The fisherman returned to his house and, behold, everything was as he requested. And his wife was standing in the opening of the house and the clothes of the wife of the king was on her. The fisherman and his wife ruled over all of the land.

And it was after these things, his wife opened her mouth, saying: "Now we are kings. Why will we not be gods? Return to the sea! Command the fish of gold to make us gods and thus we will rule also over the heavens and also over the land!" The fisherman answered and said to his wife: "We are kings. It is enough for us! We have good food, a very big house, and a lot of money. I will not go to request this thing from the fish of gold!" But the wife did not hear his words. She opened her mouth and said to him: "Return to the sea! Do what I commanded you!" The fisherman went down and he came to the sea and he said: "Fish of gold come up to me!" The fish of gold came up and said: "What else are you requesting from me?" The fisherman told the fish of gold everything that his wife requested. The fish of gold said: "The thing that your wife is requesting is not good. Now I will turn away (aside) from you. You will not be gods and also you will not be kings! I will take from you also the big house and also the money! Return to your evil wife! You requested everything and now you will not have a thing."

The fisherman returned to his house and behold every thing was as the fish of gold said. And his wife was standing in the opening of their little house and they did not still have a thing from everything that the fish of gold had given them. Everyday the fisherman returned to go down on his way to the sea to fish (for) fish. But the fish of gold did not again come up to him from the sea.

Chapter 24

Oral Review

1. What shall I send to Abraham in order that he will free the slaves? You may send (to) him gold and cattle in order that he will free the slaves. 2. Will you seek (look for) your wife in your house? I will seek her in the field because she went out to guard the flock. 3. What is Joseph telling his messengers about the holy city? He will tell that there is a big famine and there is no bread in the place. 4. Who will bless the children of Rachel in the coming days (in the days to come)? The prophet will bless them and also judge them concerning their sins. 5. Who smashed the gates in (at) the entrance of the city? The army of David broke its covenant with the king and then smashed his gates. 6. Did you put your

(Oral Review continued)

sword in the tent of meeting? The priest ordered me to put it there and thus I did. 7. Did your father tell about his fathers and his generations? My father counted the good years and continually tells me about them. 8. Who spoke to Pharaoh for the sake of his brothers? Moses spoke to Pharaoh and commanded him to free his people. 9. What did the chief command you in order that you would go to war? He commanded me to take a sword in my hand and to go forth. 10. Did you not see good and great things in your going (when you went) on the road? I saw only famine and evil ones in my going forth (when I went out) and then I returned toward the house (home).

Exercise 1

1. I caused to wear, I threw, I caused to hear, I will cause to wear, I will throw, I will cause to hear   2. you caused to rule (*m sg*), you caused to cross over, you grasped, you caused to hear, you will cause to rule, you will cause to cross over, you will grasp   3. you grasped (*f sg*), you caused to wear, you caused to rule, you caused to stand, you will grasp, you will cause to wear, you will cause to rule   4. he threw, he caused to wear, he caused to rule, he caused to hear, he caused to stand, he caused to cross over, he grasped   5. he will throw, he will cause to wear, he will cause to rule, he will cause to hear, he will cause to stand, he will cause to cross over, he will grasp   6. she threw, she caused to stand, she caused to rule, she grasped, she will throw, she will cause to stand, she will cause to rule   7. we threw, we caused to rule, we caused to cross over, we caused to stand, we will throw, we will cause to rule, we will cause to cross over   8. you caused to hear (*m pl*), you grasped, you caused to wear, you will cause to hear, you will grasp, you will cause to wear   9. they caused to rule, they caused to stand, they caused to hear, they caused to cross over, they grasped, they caused to wear, they threw   10. they will cause to rule, they will cause to stand, they will cause to hear, they will cause to cross over, they will grasp, they will cause to wear, they will throw   11. to cause to hear, to throw, to cause to stand, to grasp, to cause to cross over, to cause to rule

Exercise 2

הִלְבַּשְׁתִּי, הִלְבַּשְׁתָּ, הִלְבַּשְׁתְּ, הִלְבִּישׁ, – perfect
הִלְבִּישָׁה, הִלְבַּשְׁנוּ, הִלְבַּשְׁתֶּם, הִלְבַּשְׁתֶּן, הִלְבִּישׁוּ,
הִלְבִּישׁוּ; אַלְבִּישׁ, תַּלְבִּישׁ, תַּלְבִּישִׁי, – imperfect
יַלְבִּישׁ, תַּלְבִּישׁ, נַלְבִּישׁ, תַּלְבִּישׁוּ, תַּלְבֵּשְׁנָה, יַלְבִּישׁוּ,
תַּלְבֵּשְׁנָה; מַלְבִּישׁ, מַלְבֶּשֶׁת, מַלְבִּישִׁים, – participle
מַלְבִּישׁוֹת; (לְ)הַלְבִּישׁ – infinitive

Exercise 3

1. B   2. F   3. A   4. L   5. C   6. E   7. K   8. H   9. I
10. G   11. J   12. D

Exercise 4

1. Why did his brother throw stones on (at) him? Why did his brother throw stones at him and also command him to sit? Why did his brother throw stones at him, command him to sit, and not cause him to stand? 2. The father transferred his flock to another field. He transferred his flock and also counted them and the number of (the) flock was three hundred. He transferred his flock, counted them and then he announced to the people that the number of the flock was many. 3. Why will the commanders strengthen the army? They will strengthen the army because they will cause it (them) to stand on their border. They will strengthen the army and also cause them to stand on their border and then they will go forth to war. 4. The number of years that David ruled were twenty two. David was able to rule and they did not seek to crown another king. David was able to rule and they did not crown another king until he died. 5. The man is grasping his little son. He is grasping his son and is telling him that there is no good meat or bread in the house. He is grasping him and he is telling him that there is no bread and then they are going out to eat.

Exercise 5

1. הִלְבִּישׁ, יַלְבִּישׁ, מַלְבִּישׁ, הִלְבִּישָׁה, תַּלְבִּישׁ, מַלְבֶּשֶׁת
2. שָׁמְעוּ, יִשְׁמָעוּ, שׁוֹמְעִים – יַשְׁמִיעוּ   3. עָבַר, יַעֲבֹר,
עוֹבֵר – הֶעֱבִיר, יַעֲבִיר, מַעֲבִיר   4. יָשַׁב, יֵשֵׁב, יוֹשֵׁב –
הִשְׁמִיעַ, יַשְׁמִיעַ, מַשְׁמִיעַ   5. הִמְלִיכוּ, יַמְלִיכוּ,
מַמְלִיכִים – הֶעֱמִידוּ יַעֲמִידוּ, מַעֲמִידִים   6. הֶחֱזִיק,
יַחֲזִיק, מַחֲזִיק – הִשְׁלִיךְ, יַשְׁלִיךְ, מַשְׁלִיךְ – יָצָא, יֵצֵא,
יוֹצֵא – מֵתָה, תָּמוּת, מֵתָה

Exercise 6

1. Did you count all of the rams of the field for the sake of the offering? פָּעַל – סָפַרְתָּ, We counted all of them and their number was one hundred and twenty and then we told our brothers about them. פָּעַל – סָפַרְנוּ, פָּעַל – סָפַרְנוּ   2. The chiefs of the tribe transferred the army from the camp to Egypt. הִפְעִיל – הֶעֱבִירוּ, Did the army still cross over the mountains round about? פָּעַל – עָבַר   3. Pharaoh set free the slaves from his land and they will go down toward the sea. פָּעַל – וַיֵּרְדוּ, פָּעַל – שָׁלַח, The slaves did not throw their sins on the water. הִפְעִיל – הִשְׁלִיכוּ   4. Count six days and afterward the Sabbath will come. פָּעַל – תָּבוֹא, פָּעַל – סְפֹר, On the day of the Sabbath turn aside from evil and do good! פָּעַל – סוּר, פָּעַל – וַעֲשֵׂה   5. The judge will announce: "Do not sit

(Exercise 6 continued)

on the throne of honor and do not put your foot
in your mouth!" פָּעַל – תֵּשֵׁב, הִפְעִיל – יַשְׁמִיעַ,
פָּעַל – תָּשִׂים, Only the king will be able to sit on the
throne of honor and to put his foot in his mouth.
פָּעַל – לָשׂוּם, פָּעַל – לָשֶׁבֶת, פָּעַל – יוּכַל

Exercise 7

1. In the evening Joseph grasped the clothes of his son
in his hands, dressed him and then sat with him to eat
and to drink.

א. בָּעֶרֶב הֶחֱזִיקָה שָׂרָה בְּבִגְדֵי בְּנָהּ בְּיָדֶיהָ, הִלְבִּישָׁה
אוֹתוֹ וְאָז יָשְׁבָה עִמּוֹ לֶאֱכֹל וְלִשְׁתּוֹת.   ב. בָּעֶרֶב
הֶחֱזַקְתָּ בְּבִגְדֵי בִּנְךָ בְּיָדֶיךָ, הִלְבַּשְׁתָּ אוֹתוֹ וְאָז יָשַׁבְתָּ
עִמּוֹ לֶאֱכֹל וְלִשְׁתּוֹת.   ג. בָּעֶרֶב הֶחֱזַקְתִּי בְּבִגְדֵי בְּנִי
בְּיָדִי, הִלְבַּשְׁתִּי אוֹתוֹ וְאָז יָשַׁבְתִּי עִמּוֹ לֶאֱכֹל וְלִשְׁתּוֹת.
ד. בָּעֶרֶב הֶחֱזַקְנוּ בְּבִגְדֵי בְּנֵנוּ בְּיָדֵינוּ, הִלְבַּשְׁנוּ אוֹתוֹ
וְאָז יָשַׁבְנוּ עִמּוֹ לֶאֱכֹל וְלִשְׁתּוֹת.   ה. בָּעֶרֶב הֶחֱזַקְתֶּם
בְּבִגְדֵי בִּנְכֶם בְּיָדֵיכֶם, הִלְבַּשְׁתֶּם אוֹתוֹ וְאָז יְשַׁבְתֶּם עִמּוֹ
לֶאֱכֹל וְלִשְׁתּוֹת.   ו. בָּעֶרֶב הֶחֱזִיקוּ הָאָבוֹת בְּבִגְדֵי בְּנָם
בְּיָדֵיהֶם, הִלְבִּישׁוּ אוֹתוֹ וְאָז יָשְׁבוּ עִמּוֹ לֶאֱכֹל וְלִשְׁתּוֹת.

2. The messengers will erect the tents in the midst of
the desert and afterward they will go out under the
heavens to seek the truth.

א. הַכֹּהֵן יַעֲמִיד אֶת הָאֹהָלִים בְּקֶרֶב הַמִּדְבָּר וְאַחֲרֵי כֵן
יֵצֵא תַּחַת הַשָּׁמַיִם לְבַקֵּשׁ אֶת הָאֱמֶת.   ב. אַתֶּם
תַּעֲמִידוּ אֶת הָאֹהָלִים בְּקֶרֶב הַמִּדְבָּר וְאַחֲרֵי כֵן תֵּצְאוּ
תַּחַת הַשָּׁמַיִם לְבַקֵּשׁ אֶת הָאֱמֶת.   ג. אַתָּה תַּעֲמִיד אֶת
הָאֹהָלִים בְּקֶרֶב הַמִּדְבָּר וְאַחֲרֵי כֵן תֵּצֵא תַּחַת הַשָּׁמַיִם
לְבַקֵּשׁ אֶת הָאֱמֶת.   ד. אָנֹכִי אַעֲמִיד אֶת הָאֹהָלִים
בְּקֶרֶב הַמִּדְבָּר וְאַחֲרֵי כֵן אֵצֵא תַּחַת הַשָּׁמַיִם לְבַקֵּשׁ
אֶת הָאֱמֶת.   ה. אֲנַחְנוּ נַעֲמִיד אֶת הָאֹהָלִים בְּקֶרֶב
הַמִּדְבָּר וְאַחֲרֵי כֵן נֵצֵא תַּחַת הַשָּׁמַיִם לְבַקֵּשׁ אֶת
הָאֱמֶת.

3. In the time of the war the men of the army will crown
another chief and they will tell him what to do, and in
the coming year they will say to him to go.

א. בְּעֵת הַמִּלְחָמָה אַתָּה תַּמְלִיךְ שַׂר אַחֵר וְאַתָּה תְּסַפֵּר
לוֹ מַה לַעֲשׂוֹת, וּבַשָּׁנָה הַבָּאָה תֹּאמַר לוֹ לָלֶכֶת.
ב. בְּעֵת הַמִּלְחָמָה אֲנַחְנוּ נַמְלִיךְ שַׂר אַחֵר וַאֲנַחְנוּ נְסַפֵּר

לוֹ מַה לַעֲשׂוֹת, וּבַשָּׁנָה הַבָּאָה נֹאמַר לוֹ לָלֶכֶת.
ג. בְּעֵת הַמִּלְחָמָה אָנֹכִי אַמְלִיךְ שַׂר אַחֵר וְאָנֹכִי אֲסַפֵּר
לוֹ מַה לַעֲשׂוֹת, וּבַשָּׁנָה הַבָּאָה אֹמַר לוֹ לָלֶכֶת.
ד. בְּעֵת הַמִּלְחָמָה אַבְרָהָם יַמְלִיךְ שַׂר אַחֵר וְהוּא יְסַפֵּר
לוֹ מַה לַעֲשׂוֹת, וּבַשָּׁנָה הַבָּאָה יֹאמַר לוֹ לָלֶכֶת.
ה. בְּעֵת הַמִּלְחָמָה אַתֶּם תַּמְלִיכוּ שַׂר אַחֵר וְאַתֶּם תְּסַפְּרוּ
לוֹ מַה לַעֲשׂוֹת, וּבַשָּׁנָה הַבָּאָה תֹּאמְרוּ לוֹ לָלֶכֶת.

4. The prophet announced the words of the
commandments and also wrote them, but he did not
remember to speak about them to his sons or his
daughters.

א. אֲנִי הִשְׁמַעְתִּי אֶת דִּבְרֵי הַמִּצְוֹת וְגַם כָּתַבְתִּי אוֹתָם,
אַךְ לֹא זָכַרְתִּי לְדַבֵּר עֲלֵיהֶם אֶל בָּנַי אוֹ בְּנוֹתַי.
ב. אַתָּה הִשְׁמַעְתָּ אֶת דִּבְרֵי הַמִּצְוֹת וְגַם כָּתַבְתָּ אוֹתָם,
אַךְ לֹא זָכַרְתָּ לְדַבֵּר עֲלֵיהֶם אֶל בָּנֶיךָ אוֹ בְּנוֹתֶיךָ.
ג. רִבְקָה הִשְׁמִיעָה אֶת דִּבְרֵי הַמִּצְוֹת וְגַם כָּתְבָה אוֹתָם,
אַךְ לֹא זָכְרָה לְדַבֵּר עֲלֵיהֶם אֶל בָּנֶיהָ אוֹ בְּנוֹתֶיהָ.
ד. אֲנַחְנוּ הִשְׁמַעְנוּ אֶת דִּבְרֵי הַמִּצְוֹת וְגַם כָּתַבְנוּ אוֹתָם,
אַךְ לֹא זָכַרְנוּ לְדַבֵּר עֲלֵיהֶם אֶל בָּנֵינוּ אוֹ בְּנוֹתֵינוּ.
ה. הַצַּדִּיקִים הִשְׁמִיעוּ אֶת דִּבְרֵי הַמִּצְוֹת וְגַם כָּתְבוּ
אוֹתָם, אַךְ לֹא זָכְרוּ לְדַבֵּר עֲלֵיהֶם אֶל בְּנֵיהֶם אוֹ
בְּנוֹתֵיהֶם.

5. The slaves of Jacob will take the fruit from the tree
and then they will throw it on the ground and thus they
will make wine from it.

א. אֶקַּח אֶת הַפְּרִי מֵהָעֵץ וְאָז אַשְׁלִיךְ אוֹתוֹ עַל הָאֲדָמָה
וְכֵן אֶעֱשֶׂה מִמֶּנּוּ יַיִן.   ב. רוּת תִּקַּח אֶת הַפְּרִי מֵהָעֵץ
וְאָז תַּשְׁלִיךְ אוֹתוֹ עַל הָאֲדָמָה וְכֵן תַּעֲשֶׂה מִמֶּנּוּ יַיִן.
ג. תִּקְחוּ אֶת הַפְּרִי מֵהָעֵץ וְאָז תַּשְׁלִיכוּ אוֹתוֹ עַל
הָאֲדָמָה וְכֵן תַּעֲשׂוּ מִמֶּנּוּ יַיִן.   ד. יִצְחָק יִקַּח אֶת הַפְּרִי
מֵהָעֵץ וְאָז יַשְׁלִיךְ אוֹתוֹ עַל הָאֲדָמָה וְכֵן יַעֲשֶׂה מִמֶּנּוּ
יַיִן.   ה. תִּקַּח אֶת הַפְּרִי מֵהָעֵץ וְאָז תַּשְׁלִיךְ אוֹתוֹ עַל
הָאֲדָמָה וְכֵן תַּעֲשֶׂה מִמֶּנּוּ יַיִן.

A TALL TALE: The Emperor's New Clothes

It came to pass after the death of the old king, the
people of the land crowned a new king. The new king
loved clothes very much and he gave all his money
for the sake of his clothes. Every morning his slaves
dressed him in new clothes. And every day he went
out in front of his people in his new clothes.

In this land there lived two evil ones who sought money
with no work. The two evil ones announced in all of the

(A TALL TALE continued)

land that they know (how) to make clothes better than all others. Only the wise will be able to see these clothes. A man who is not wise will not be able to see them.

The king heard about these clothes and he said to himself: "With clothes like these I will be able to know who is wise and who is not wise in my land. Then I will be a great king." The king sent his slaves to find the makers of those clothes. They found them in another city and they sent them to the house of the king.

The two evil ones came to the house of the king. And they said to the king, saying: "We are makers of clothes. We are able to make clothes for you that there none like them (that are like no others) in all of your land. Only wise people will be able to see these clothes. Give us a lot of money and we will make them for you."

Thus the king said to himself: "With these clothes I will be a greater king than all others. I will be able to know who is wise and who is not wise." The king answered and said to the evil ones: "Here is the money, now make (for) me these clothes!" The two evil ones grasped the money in their hands and they said to the king: "We will return to our house and then we will make the clothes for you."

And it came to pass after many days the king sent his young man to see the work of the makers of the clothes. In his coming to the house the young man saw that there were no clothes there. The young man said to himself: "Only wise ones are able to see the clothes. Am I not wise? Why am I not seeing the clothes? I will not tell to a man (anyone)." And he said to the makers of the clothes: "How beautiful are these clothes. There are none like them in all the land. Now I will return to the king and I will tell him about the new clothes." And thus he did.

And it came to pass after a month the evil ones returned to the house of the king. They grasped a big vessel (container) in their hands and they spoke to all of the household of the king, saying: "Here are the new clothes of the king in the midst of this container."

The king came and he did not open the container and he announced to his people, saying: "In the morning on the day of the Sabbath I will dress in my new clothes and I will go out in front of you. I command you to be near the road in front of the gates at the entrance of the city to see me and my new clothes."

And it came to pass in the light of the morning on the day of the Sabbath the king called to his slave who loved to dress him in his new clothes. The slave opened the container and saw that there was not a thing inside it. The slave said to himself: "Only wise ones will be able to see these clothes. Am I not wise? Why am I not seeing the clothes? I will not tell anyone." And the slave said to the king: "How beautiful are these clothes.

There are none like them in all of your land. Now I will dress you in them."

The king saw in (at) that time that there were no clothes in the container and he said to himself: "Only wise ones are able to see these clothes. A man who is not wise will not be able to see them. Am I not wise? Why am I not seeing the clothes? Am I not able to rule? I will not tell anyone."

The king spoke to the slave, saying: "The clothes are in truth beautiful. There are none like them in all of my land. Now you will dress me in my new clothes."

The slave took the night clothes from the king and put them on the ground. He took the clothes that were not clothes from the container, and he dressed the king in them. But in truth there were no clothes on the king.

The king said to himself: "I do not see one clothes (piece of clothing) on me but my slave sees them. Now I know how wise my slave is." The king spoke to his slave, saying: "I am dressed in beautiful clothes. We will get up and go out before the people of my land because I commanded them to be near the road to see me."

The king went out and came before the people. All the people of the land knew that only wise people would be able to see the clothes of the king. All the people saw and behold there was not a thing on the king. Every man said to himself: "I am not wise because I do not see the clothes of the king."

A small son stood in the middle of all the people. He came with his father to see the clothes of the king. And he saw the king and he announced in a big voice: "See! There are no clothes on the king. The king is naked! The king is naked!"

The people of the land saw the king with opened eyes and they knew that the son spoke (the) truth and the king was naked.

And the king knew that there were no clothes on him and he was standing there naked. The king was very ashamed that he was naked in front of all of the people of his land.

Then the king really knew that he was not wise and that he was not a good king. He would not be able to rule anymore because he loved clothes more than anything. The king announced to his people that on the coming Sabbath the people would be able to crown another king. And thus they did.

Chapter 25

Oral Review

1. My children will wear bad clothes (for) six days. On the day of the Sabbath I will dress them in good clothes. 2. Seven kings ruled in seven countries (for) twenty years. Only the prophet will be able to crown

(Oral Review continued)

another man.   3. The father heard that his wife gave birth to two sons. The father announced in all of his city that he has two sons.   4. The man loved to count the animals roundabout. He recounted to his father about the money which he will have from all of these animals.   5. Why did you throw a bad seed in the midst of the field? I threw the seed on the ground in order that we may eat bread.   6. Do not cause me to stand in front of these four righteous ones. If I will stand in front of them they will see all of my sins. 7. Joseph crossed over the border of his property with three rams and three flocks of sheep. Then he transfered them to my master as a gift.   8. Ten brothers will strengthen the wood of their house from the waters of the heavens. One brother will put the wood near the house and nine brothers will put the wood on the top of the house.   9. David the king announced the death of his son to the chiefs of the tribe. The chiefs of the tribe erected gates to honor the son of David. The number of chiefs of the tribe were twenty-six and all of them guarded the Sabbath.

Exercise 1

1. I threw, I told, I knocked down, I saved, I will throw, I will tell, I will knock down, I will save 2. you announced (*m sg*), you begot, you brought out, you lowered, you will announce, you will beget, you will bring out, you will lower   3. you saved (*f sg*), you knocked down, you told, you threw, you will save, you will knock down, you will tell, you will throw 4. he lowered, he brought out, he begot, he announced, he saved, he told, he knocked down, he threw   5. he will lower, he will bring out, he will beget, he will announce, he will save, he will tell, he will knock down, he will throw   6. she lowered, she told, she announced, she saved, she will lower, she will tell, she will announce, she will save 7. we threw, we knocked down, we told, we saved, we will throw, we will knock down, we will tell, we will save 8. you begot (*m pl*), you announced, you lowered, you will beget, you will announce, you will lower   9. they knocked down, they told, they threw, they saved, they lowered, they brought out, they begot 10. they will knock down, they will tell, they will throw, they will save, they will lower, they will bring out, they will beget, they will announce   11. to tell, to save, to knock down, to throw, to announce, to bring out, to lower

Exercise 2

הוֹדַעְתִּי, הוֹדַעְתָּ, הוֹדַעְתְּ, הוֹדִיעַ, הוֹדִיעָה, – perfect
הוֹדַעְנוּ, הוֹדַעְתֶּם, הוֹדַעְתֶּן, הוֹדִיעוּ, הוֹדִיעוּ;
אוֹדִיעַ, תּוֹדִיעַ, תּוֹדִיעִי, יוֹדִיעַ, תּוֹדִיעַ, – imperfect
נוֹדִיעַ, תּוֹדִיעוּ, תּוֹדַעְנָה, יוֹדִיעוּ, תּוֹדַעְנָה;
מוֹדִיעַ, מוֹדַעַת, מוֹדִיעִים, מוֹדִיעוֹת; – participle
הוֹדֵעַ, הוֹדִיעוּ; – command   (לְ)הוֹדִיעַ – infinitive

Exercise 3

נָפַל, נָפַלְתִּי, נָפַלְתָּ, נָפַלְתְּ, נָפְלָה, – perfect פָּעַל
אֶפֹּל, – imperfect נָפַלְנוּ, נְפַלְתֶּם, נְפַלְתֶּן, נָפְלוּ;
תִּפֹּל, תִּפְּלִי, יִפֹּל, תִּפֹּל, נִפֹּל, תִּפְּלוּ, תִּפֹּלְנָה, יִפְּלוּ;
נוֹפֵל, נוֹפֶלֶת, נוֹפְלִים, נוֹפְלוֹת – participle
(לְ)נְפֹּל, נָפוֹל – infinitives
הִפַּלְתִּי, הִפַּלְתָּ, הִפַּלְתְּ, – perfect הִפְעִיל
הִפַּלְנוּ, הִפַּלְתֶּם, הִפַּלְתֶּן, הִפִּילוּ, הִפִּילוּ;
אַפִּיל, תַּפִּיל, תַּפִּילִי, יַפִּיל, תַּפִּיל, נַפִּיל, – imperfect
תַּפִּילוּ, תַּפֵּלְנָה, יַפִּילוּ, תַּפֵּלְנָה; מַפִּיל – participle
מַפִּילָה, מַפִּילִים, מַפִּילוֹת; (לְ)הַפִּיל – infinitive

Exercise 4

1. Your friend will tell the truth. If your friend will tell the truth he will save his soul. If your friend will tell the truth and also save his soul he will be righteous. 2. Abraham begot Isaac. Abraham begot Isaac and Isaac begot Jacob. Jacob begot Joseph, and then his brothers caused him to go down to Egypt.   3. You will announce the famine in Moab. You will announce the famine and you will bring the tribe out from Moab. You will announce the famine and then you will bring the tribe out in order that you will rescue it (the tribe). 4. The teller (the one who tells) is announcing his name to the people. The teller is announcing to the people and is announcing peace in the tent of meeting. He is announcing to the people and he is announcing in the tent of meeting that bad ones caused the king to fall. 5. The old one did not see the road. He did not see the road and he fell on his face. He did not see the road and he fell on his face and his friend saved him. 6. The commanders strengthened their army for the sake of the war. They strengthened their army and they announced that there will be war. They strengthened their army and they announced the war and they wrote about it in the scroll.

Exercise 5

1. פָּעַל, א.ב.ו.ב, in your coming   2. הִפְעִיל, נ.ג.ד, I told   3. פָּעַל, ש.ל.ח, and to send   4. הִפְעִיל, ק.ז.ח, and the ones (who are) grasping, strengthening 5. פָּעַל, י.ש.ב, in your sitting   6. פָּעַל, נ.ת.ן, to give   7. פָּעַל, ש.י.ם, and we will put   8. פ.ת.ח, the opened ones   9. הִפְעִיל, ע.מ.ד, we erected 10. פָּעַל, צ.ו.ה, and they commanded   11. פָּעַל, מ.ו.ת, and he died   12. הִפְעִיל, י.ר.ד, they will lower   13. פָּעַל, ש.ת.ה, and he drank   14. פָּעַל, י.כ.ל, and I was able   15. פָּעַל, י.ל.ד, to give birth to   16. פָּעַל, ק.ו.ם, you arose   17. פָּעַל, ה.ל.ך,

(Exercise 5 continued)

and in your going   18. שׁ.ל.ח, פָּעַל, to set free   19.
הַפְעִיל, י.צ.א, the one bringing out, the bringing out
20. נ.ג.ד, הִפְעִיל, the   21. ה.י.ה, פָּעַל, he will be
one telling, the teller   22. הִפְעִיל, שׁ.ל.ך, to throw
23. שׁ.כ.ב, פָּעַל, you will lie down   24. שׁ.ב.ר, פָּעַל,
we will break

Exercise 6

1. The messengers returned to Bethlehem and they
sat there.   2. I will not be able to eat fruit or meat and
instead of them I will eat bread.   3. The judge loved to
count all of his judgements but he did not love to tell
about them to his friend.   4. You will come to
Jerusalem and you will also build houses there but do
not erect an altar within the city.   5. The ones bringing
out gold in the mountains are bringing it out from there
and they are not making (it) known to the king.   6. I
will inherit all of the clothes of my mother and I will
wear them but I will not dress my friend in them.
7. Aaron will knock down a man bigger than him when
he will fall.   8. Jacob begot many sons but he was not
able to save the one who he loved.

Exercise 7

1. יָלַד, יֵלֵד, יוֹלֵד, הוֹלִיד, יוֹלִיד, מוֹלִיד – הִמְלִיךְ,
יַמְלִיךְ, מַמְלִיךְ   2. בִּקְשׁוּ, יְבַקְשׁוּ, מְבַקְשִׁים – הוֹצִיאוּ,
יוֹצִיאוּ, מוֹצִיאִים – הוֹדִיעוּ, יוֹדִיעוּ, מוֹדִיעִים   3. נָפְלָה,
תִּפֹּל, נוֹפֶלֶת – הֶעֱמִיד, יַעֲמִיד, מַעֲמִיד   4. יָלְדָה –
יָלַד, הוֹלִיד   5. הִפִּיל, יַפִּיל, מַפִּיל – נָפַל, יִפֹּל, נוֹפֵל
6. הוֹדִיעַ, יוֹדִיעַ, מוֹדִיעַ – יָדַע, יוֹדֵעַ   7. הִצַּלְתִּי,
אַצִּיל, מַצִּיל, מַצִּילָה – הִגַּדְתִּי, אַגִּיד, מַגִּיד, מַגֶּדֶת –
לִשְׁתּוֹת   8. הֶעֱבִירוּ, יַעֲבִירוּ, מַעֲבִירִים   9. שָׁלַח,
יִשְׁלַח, מְשַׁלֵּחַ – לַחֲזֹק, לְהַחֲזִיק

Exercise 8

1. Isaac took a book and he walked on the road and he
went down to the sea and he sat there with friends.

א.וַיִּקַּח סֵפֶר וַיֵּלְכוּ בַּדֶּרֶךְ וַיֵּרְדוּ אֶל הַיָּם וַיֵּשְׁבוּ שָׁם
עִם רֵעִים.   ב.וָאֶקַּח סֵפֶר וָאֵלֵךְ בַּדֶּרֶךְ וָאֵרֵד אֶל
הַיָּם וָאֵשֵׁב שָׁם עִם רֵעִים.   ג.וַנִּקַּח סֵפֶר וַנֵּלֶךְ בַּדֶּרֶךְ
וַנֵּרֶד אֶל הַיָּם וַנֵּשֶׁב שָׁם עִם רֵעִים.   ד.וַתִּקַּח סֵפֶר
וַתֵּלֶךְ בַּדֶּרֶךְ וַתֵּרֶד אֶל הַיָּם וַתֵּשֶׁב שָׁם עִם רֵעִים.
ה.וַתִּקְחוּ סֵפֶר וַתֵּלְכוּ בַּדֶּרֶךְ וַתֵּרְדוּ אֶל הַיָּם וַתֵּשְׁבוּ
שָׁם עִם רֵעִים.

2. You will go out from Egypt and you will bring out all
your slaves and you will bring them down with you
when you go down toward the desert.

א.אֵצֵא מִמִּצְרַיִם וְהוֹצֵאתִי אֶת כָּל עֲבָדַי וְהוֹרַדְתִּי
אוֹתָם עִמִּי כַּאֲשֶׁר אֵרֵד מִדְבָּרָה.   ב.תֵּצֵא מִמִּצְרַיִם
וְהוֹצֵאתָ אֶת כָּל עֲבָדֶיךָ וְהוֹרַדְתָּ אוֹתָם עִמְּךָ כַּאֲשֶׁר
תֵּרֵד מִדְבָּרָה.   ג.הוּא יֵצֵא מִמִּצְרַיִם וְהוֹצִיא אֶת כָּל
עֲבָדָיו וְהוֹרִיד אוֹתָם עִמּוֹ כַּאֲשֶׁר יֵרֵד מִדְבָּרָה.
ד.הֵם יֵצְאוּ מִמִּצְרַיִם וְהוֹצִיאוּ אֶת כָּל עַבְדֵיהֶם וְהוֹרִידוּ
אוֹתָם עִמָּם כַּאֲשֶׁר יֵרְדוּ מִדְבָּרָה.

3. If you know all the commandments of the scroll
(book) of the law and you announce these words then
you will be a prophet.

א.אִם צַדִּיק יוֹדֵעַ אֶת כָּל מִצְוֹת סֵפֶר הַתּוֹרָה וּמַשְׁמִיעַ
אֶת הַדְּבָרִים הָאֵלֶּה אָז יִהְיֶה נָבִיא.   ב.אִם אֲנִי יוֹדֵעַ
אֶת כָּל מִצְוֹת סֵפֶר הַתּוֹרָה וּמַשְׁמִיעַ אֶת הַדְּבָרִים
הָאֵלֶּה אָז אֶהְיֶה נָבִיא.   ג.אִם אַתֶּם יוֹדְעִים אֶת כָּל
מִצְוֹת סֵפֶר הַתּוֹרָה וּמַשְׁמִיעִים אֶת הַדְּבָרִים הָאֵלֶּה אָז
תִּהְיוּ נְבִיאִים.   ד.אִם הָרְשָׁעִים יוֹדְעִים אֶת כָּל מִצְוֹת
סֵפֶר הַתּוֹרָה וּמַשְׁמִיעִים אֶת הַדְּבָרִים הָאֵלֶּה אָז יִהְיוּ
נְבִיאִים.   ה.אִם לֵאָה יוֹדַעַת אֶת כָּל מִצְוֹת סֵפֶר
הַתּוֹרָה וּמַשְׁמַעַת אֶת הַדְּבָרִים הָאֵלֶּה אָז תִּהְיֶה נָבִיא.

4. Abraham rescued Sarah from an evil place and from
death and then he fell on his face before her because
she found favor in his eyes.

א.הִצַּלְתִּי אֶת שָׂרָה מִמָּקוֹם רַע וּמִמָּוֶת וְאָז נָפַלְתִּי עַל
פָּנַי לְפָנֶיהָ כִּי מָצְאָה חֵן בְּעֵינַי.   ב.הִצִּילוּ עֲשָׂרָה
רֵעִים אֶת שָׂרָה מִמָּקוֹם רַע וּמִמָּוֶת וְאָז נָפְלוּ עַל פְּנֵיהֶם
לְפָנֶיהָ כִּי מָצְאָה חֵן בְּעֵינֵיהֶם.   ג.הִצַּלְתָּ אֶת שָׂרָה
מִמָּקוֹם רַע וּמִמָּוֶת וְאָז נָפַלְתָּ עַל פָּנֶיךָ לְפָנֶיהָ כִּי
מָצְאָה חֵן בְּעֵינֶיךָ.   ד.הִצַּלְתֶּם אֶת שָׂרָה מִמָּקוֹם רַע
וּמִמָּוֶת וְאָז נְפַלְתֶּם עַל פְּנֵיכֶם לְפָנֶיהָ כִּי מָצְאָה חֵן
בְּעֵינֵיכֶם.

5. Aaron spoke to all of the people in his city and he
told them that he was seeking a place to live and work
to do.

א.הַשָּׂרִים דִּבְּרוּ לְכָל אַנְשֵׁי עִירָם וַיְסַפְּרוּ לָהֶם כִּי
מְבַקְשִׁים מָקוֹם לָשֶׁבֶת וַעֲבוֹדָה לַעֲשׂוֹת.   ב.רָחֵל
דִּבְּרָה לְכָל אַנְשֵׁי עִירָהּ וַתְּסַפֵּר לָהֶם כִּי מְבַקֶּשֶׁת
מָקוֹם לָשֶׁבֶת וַעֲבוֹדָה לַעֲשׂוֹת.   ג.דִּבַּרְתִּי לְכָל אַנְשֵׁי

(Exercise 8 continued)

עִירִי וַאֲסַפֵּר לָהֶם כִּי מְבַקֵּשׁ מָקוֹם לָשֶׁבֶת וַעֲבוֹדָה
לַעֲשׂוֹת. ד.דִּבַּרְתָּ לְכָל אַנְשֵׁי עִירְךָ וַתְּסַפֵּר לָהֶם כִּי
מְבַקֵּשׁ מָקוֹם לָשֶׁבֶת וַעֲבוֹדָה לַעֲשׂוֹת.

A TALL TALE: Rumpelstiltskin

Once upon a time in those days there lived in the land a poor man and he had only one daughter. It came to pass in his going to the field the man saw the king of his land.

He came before the king and he spoke to him, saying: "Good morning my lord the king. Did you hear about my daughter? She will be able to make gold from the grass of the field." The king answered: "What?! Your daughter will be able to make gold from grass? In truth? If thus (if this is so), may you cause her to stand before the throne of my honor in the evening. And do not make (this) known to a man (anyone)!"

And his daughter stood in front of the throne of the king and she did not know why. The king took her to a small room and there was much grass in it. The king said to her, saying: "Your father told me that you will be able to make gold (from) the grass. Make me gold from all the grass in this room! I will return in the morning and if I will not see gold instead of grass, you will surely die." And the king went out of the room.

The young woman fell on her face and cried. She called (out): "I do not know (how) to make gold from grass and in the morning I will die. What shall I do? Who will rescue me?" And behold at that time a little man arose from under the grass and said to her: "Why are you sitting in the midst of the grass and why are you crying?"

The young woman answered: "The king told me to make gold from this grass and if not, I will die in the morning. And I do not know how to make gold. Will you please be able to rescue me?"

Thus said the little man: "What will you give me in order that I will rescue you?" The young woman answered and she said: "I will give you this cloak that I am wearing." The little man put his hand on the cloak and said: "Now I will rescue you. I will make gold from all this grass." And thus he did.

In the morning the king returned to the entrance of the room and he saw the young woman sitting among all of the gold and he said: "I commanded you to make gold from grass and thus you did. This finds favor in my eyes (I like this). How good you are." The king said to himself: "Will she be able to make it again?" The king took out all the gold from the room. And he took the young woman to another room, a room bigger than the first room. And in it there was more grass than the grass in the first room. The king commanded the young woman, saying: "I will return in the morning and

if I will not see gold in place of grass, you will surely die."

The young woman fell on her face and cried again. And she called out: "I do not know how to make gold from grass and in the morning I will die. Who will rescue me today?" And behold in (at) that time the little man arose from under the grass and said to her: "What can you give me today in order that I will make you gold from all this grass?" And the young woman answered and she said: "I will give you this jewel." And the little man put his hand on the jewel and he said: "Today I will rescue you again. I will make gold from all this grass." And thus he did.

In the morning the king returned to the entrance of the other room and saw the young woman sitting among all the gold and said: "I commanded you to make gold from the grass and thus you did. It finds much favor in my eyes (I like it a lot). If you will be able to make gold from grass also tonight I will bless you and also I will take you for my wife. But if not, you will surely die." The king took all the gold from the room. And he took the young woman to another room, very large and inside of it there was very much grass.

The young woman opened her mouth and cried in a big (loud) voice because she knew that she did not have a thing to give the little man tonight. And behold at that time the little man arose from under the grass and said to her: "Why are you crying tonight? Do you not know that I will come to rescue you? What will you give me now?" And the young woman answered him: "I do not have a thing anymore. You took everything I had!" The little man told the young woman: "If I will make gold for you from all this grass the king will take you for his wife. Then you will give me your first son." And she said to herself: "Who knows what will be (happen)?" And she answered the little man: "I will give you whatever you seek. Only make gold for me tonight." And thus he did.

The king returned with the light of the morning and he saw the gold. He blessed the young woman and took her for his wife.

It came to pass after one year the wife of the king gave birth to a son. She did not remember what she told the little man. And was one day and the little man arose before her and requested her son. The wife of the king remembered all that was (everything that had happened) and she cried much and she said to the little man: "Do not take my son from me!" The little man said: "Do not cry! I will return to you after three days. If you will know my name I will not take your son from you."

In the coming of the little man (when the little man came) on the first day, the wife of the king said to him: "Is your name Pharaoh?" And he answered: "No!" And she said: "Is your name Moses?" And he answered: "No!" And she said: "Is your name David?" And also this was not his name. And she said many more names to him and his name was not among them.

(A TALL TALE continued)

The wife of the king sent messengers to all the land and to all the lands around in order that she will know (find out) the name of the man.

And it came to pass on the second day when the little man came she said to him: "Is your name Ali-Baba?" "Is your name Goldilocks?" "Is your name Nebuchadnezzar?" And she said many more names. And his name was not among these names.

And it came to pass on the third day in the light of the morning, the wife of the king arose with her son and she cried in a loud voice. She said to herself: "Today the little man will take my son from me because I do not know his name. The messengers also did not know his name. Who will rescue me and my son now?" And there came one from (of) the messengers and he told her: "I went in all the land from place to place and I did not find a man who knows the name of the little man. But in my returning (when I returned) to you, I saw in the midst of the field a little man standing on his little feet and calling in a loud voice: 'Today I will take her son from the wife of the king. She does not know that my name is Rumpelstiltskin. My name is Rumplestiltskin!' Thus I heard."

These words found favor in the eyes of the wife of the king. When the little man came she said to him: "Is your name Abraham?" And he answered: "No! My name is not Abraham!" And she said: "Is your name Isaac?" And he answered: "No! My name is not Isaac!" And she said: "Is your name Jacob?" And he answered: "No! My name is not Jacob! Now give me your son!" And the wife of the king said: "Is your name ...Rumpelstiltskin?" And Rumpelstiltskin called out: "Augggg! That is in truth (truly) my name. Who told you?"

And Rumpelstiltskin went out from the house of the king and no man has seen him up to this (very) day.

CHAPTER 26

Oral Review

1. Two wicked ones threw stones in the ark of holiness and we sent them away from our land.   2. Why did Moses cause his army to stand outside of the camp and he stood in front of it?   3. The rams will knock down the old one and they will break his legs if he will not grasp my hand.   4. Do not tell me what to wear when I go outside.   5. Aaron crossed over to the border of Moab and he transferred his flock of sheep with him. 6. The chief of the army commanded his men to strengthen the gates of the city.   7. The woman announced to her husband that she knew his deeds and his sins.   8. We will go outside and also we will bring out the slave in order that he will bring down the fruit from the tree for us.   9. It is written in the scroll of the law that the prophet will crown David instead of the other king.   10. The priests will dress Pharoh in garments of a king and they will dress in clothing of honor.   11. Jacob announced to his friend that he will not be obeying (listening to the voice of) his mother. 12. I fell to (in) the midst of the sea and my friend saved me from death.

Exercise 1

1. I brought, I hit, I established, I prepared, I will bring, I will hit, I will establish, I will prepare   2. you killed (*m sg*), you brought, you prepared, you hit, you will kill, you will bring, you will prepare, you will hit 3. you hit (*f sg*), you killed, you established, you brought, you will hit, you will kill, you will establish, you will bring   4. he brought, he prepared, he killed, he brought back, he established, he hit, he begot, he saved 5. he will bring, he will prepare, he will kill, he will bring back, he will establish, he will hit, he will lower, he will save   6. she brought back, she established, she killed, she hit, she will bring back, she will establish, she will kill, she will hit   7. we brought, we hit, we killed, we brought back, we will bring, we will hit, we will kill, we will bring back   8. you hit (*m pl*), you established, you brought back, you prepared, you hit, you will establish, you will bring back   9. they hit, they prepared, they killed, they brought back, they brought, they established, they begot, they saved 10 they will hit, they will prepare, they will kill, they will bring back, they will bring, they will establish, they will beget, they will save   11. to bring, to prepare, to kill, to bring back, to establish, to hit, to knock down

Exercise 2

1. B   2. G   3. E   4. K   5. N   6. T   7. X   8. V   9. A 10. H   11. O   12. W   13. Q   14. U   15. R   16. C 17. L   18. S   19. I   20. P   21. D   22. M   23. J   24. F

Exercise 3

פָּעַל – perfect, שַׁבְתִּי, שַׁבְתָּ, שַׁבְתְּ, שָׁב, שָׁבָה, שַׁבְנוּ, שַׁבְתֶּם, שַׁבְתֶּן, שָׁבוּ, שָׁבוּ; imperfect – אָשׁוּב, תָּשׁוּב, תָּשׁוּבִי, יָשׁוּב, תָּשׁוּב, נָשׁוּב, תָּשׁוּבוּ, תָּשֹׁבְנָה, יָשׁוּבוּ, תָּשֹׁבְנָה; participle – שָׁב, שָׁבָה, שָׁבִים, שָׁבוֹת; command – שׁוּב, שׁוּבִי, שׁוּבוּ; infinitives: regular – (לְ)שׁוּב, emphasis – שׁוֹב

הִפְעִיל – perfect, הֲשִׁיבוֹתִי, הֲשִׁיבוֹתָ, הֲשִׁיבוֹת, הֵשִׁיב, הֵשִׁיבָה, הֲשִׁיבוֹנוּ, הֲשִׁיבוֹתֶם, הֲשִׁיבוֹתֶן, הֵשִׁיבוּ, הֵשִׁיבוּ; imperfect – אָשִׁיב, תָּשִׁיב, תָּשִׁיבִי, יָשִׁיב, תָּשִׁיב, נָשִׁיב, תָּשִׁיבוּ, תָּשֵׁבְנָה, יָשִׁיבוּ, תָּשֵׁבְנָה; participle – מֵשִׁיב, מְשִׁיבָה, מְשִׁיבִים, מְשִׁיבוֹת; command – הָשֵׁב, הָשִׁיבִי, הָשִׁיבוּ; infinitives: regular – (לְ)הָשִׁיב, emphasis – הָשֵׁב

Exercise 4

1. Joseph brought the bones of Jacob to his land.
2. The righteous one will establish his covenant with the tribes of the nations.   3. An animal will be able to kill a person with the sole of her foot.   4. I brought the book back to its place lest it will fall in the dust roundabout.   5. The brothers hit Joseph on the head three times.   6. Pharaoh hit his daughter and she fell in the dust and she died.   7. I prepared fruit and meat for them and they sat and they ate in front of the entrance.   8. The young men will hit the ram many times lest he will kill them.   9. My sons brought dust to the house on the soles of their feet.   10 The prophets established a holy scroll and commanded the people to know it.

Exercise 5

1.דָּוִד בָּא לְבֵיתִי, וַיָּבֵא אִישׁ קָדוֹשׁ. 2.פַּעַם קָם אַבְרָהָם וַיָּקֶם בְּרִית.   3.הַשַּׂר לָקַח אֶת הַכֶּסֶף מִן הָעֶבֶד וְלֹא הֵשִׁיב אֹתוֹ.   4.מֹשֶׁה הֵמִית אֶת רֵעֵהוּ, וְאָז שָׂם אֶת עַצְמוֹתָיו בֶּעָפָר.   5.הַנָּבִיא יָכִין אֶת הַיַּיִן הַקָּדוֹשׁ לַכֹּהֵן.   6.הִשְׁלַכְתִּי אֶת הַכֵּלִים, וְאַכֶּה אֶת אִישִׁי.   7.שָׁמַעְתִּי עַל הַמִּלְחָמָה, וַאַשְׁמִיעַ אוֹתוֹ שֶׁבַע פְּעָמִים.   8.תַּעֲמֹד נֶגֶד הַמִּזְבֵּחַ, וְהֶעֱמַדְתָּ אֶת רֵעֲךָ לְפָנֶיךָ.

Exercise 6

1. My brother arose in the morning and he established a camp opposite the sea.   2. Pharaoh hit his slave with the palm of his hand and the slave died.   3. The prophet brought sanctified wine and he drank it.
4. The chief built an altar from dust and stones and he put an offering on it.   5. David brought back the dish to the priest and he returned to his tent.

Exercise 7

1.וְשׁוֹפֵט ,וְשָׁפַט ,וַיִּשְׁפֹּט – מֵקִים ,יָקִים ,הֵקִים. The seed of Abraham established/will establish/is establishing a house of justice opposite the mountain and he judged /will judge/is judging from there.
2.וּמֵשִׁיב ,וְהֵשִׁיב ,וַיָּשֶׁב ,וְלוֹקֵחַ ,וְלָקַח ,וַיִּקַּח – Abraham took/will take /is taking the holy book and he returned/will return/is returning it to the tent of meeting.   3.יַעֲמִיד ,הֶעֱמִיד – מֵכִין ,יָכִין ,הֵכִין ,מַעֲמִיד, The army of Egypt prepared/ will prepare/is preparing sword(s) lest it was caused to stand/will be caused to stand/is caused to stand opposite a force bigger than it.   4.וְהֵמִית ,וַיָּמֶת – וְקָם ,וְקָם ,וַיָּקָם,

יְהִי ,הָיוּ ,הָיוּ – וָמֵמִית, The great ram arose/will arise/is arising and he killed/will kill/is killing the little animal and blood and bones (guts) were/will be/(are) in the dust of the field.   5.הֵכָה, וְהִפִּיל ,וַיַּפֵּל – מַכֶּה ,יַכֶּה ,הִכָּה, וּמַפִּיל, The evil one hit/will hit/is hitting the elder (with) a big blow and knocked/will knock/is knocking him in the dust.   6.וַיָּרֶד ,וַיֵּרֶד – סוֹפֵר ,יִסְפֹּר ,סָפַר, וְיוֹרֵד, The righteous one counted/will count/is counting the commandments in the law and went down/will go down/is going down to rule over the nation.   7.יָלַד, וְיִירְשׁוּ ,יָרְשׁוּ – הוֹלִיד ,יָלַד – הוֹלִיד, Abraham begot/will beget Isaac and Isaac begot/will beget Jacob and their generations inherited/will inherit the land.
8.וַיַּעֲמִידוּ – וַיַּעֲבִירוּ – הוֹצִיאוּ, Moses and Aaron brought the children of Israel out from the land of Egypt and transferred them to the desert and caused them to stand across from the mountain.

Exercise 8

1. The head of the army of Moab arose and attacked the army of Egypt and knocked it into the dust and established a holy altar.

א.וַיָּקוּמוּ אֲדוֹנֵי הַמִּדְבָּר וַיַּכּוּ אֶת חֵיל מִצְרַיִם וַיַּפִּילוּ אוֹתוֹ אֶל הֶעָפָר וַיָּקִימוּ מִזְבֵּחַ קָדוֹשׁ.   ב.וַתָּקָם וַתַּכֶּה אֶת חֵיל מִצְרַיִם וַתַּפֵּיל אוֹתוֹ אֶל הֶעָפָר וַתָּקֵם מִזְבֵּחַ קָדוֹשׁ.   ג.וַנָּקָם וַנַּכֶּה אֶת חֵיל מִצְרַיִם וַנַּפִּיל אוֹתוֹ אֶל הֶעָפָר וַנָּקִים מִזְבֵּחַ קָדוֹשׁ.   ד.וַתָּקוּמוּ וַתַּכּוּ אֶת חֵיל מִצְרַיִם וַתַּפִּילוּ אוֹתוֹ אֶל הֶעָפָר וַתָּקִימוּ מִזְבֵּחַ קָדוֹשׁ.   ה.וָאָקוּם וָאַכֶּה אֶת חֵיל מִצְרַיִם וָאַפִּיל אוֹתוֹ אֶל הֶעָפָר וָאָקִים מִזְבֵּחַ קָדוֹשׁ.

2. I prepared for me (myself) bread and fruit to eat lest I would die from hunger.

א.אַתָּה הֲכִינוֹתָ לְךָ לֶחֶם וּפְרִי לֶאֱכֹל פֶּן תָּמוּת מֵרָעָב.   ב.הוּא הֵכִין לוֹ לֶחֶם וּפְרִי לֶאֱכֹל פֶּן יָמוּת מֵרָעָב.   ג.הִיא הֵכִינָה לָהּ לֶחֶם וּפְרִי לֶאֱכֹל פֶּן תָּמוּת מֵרָעָב.   ד.אֲנַחְנוּ הֲכִינוֹנוּ לָנוּ לֶחֶם וּפְרִי לֶאֱכֹל פֶּן נָמוּת מֵרָעָב.   ה.אַתֶּם הֲכִינוֹתֶם לָכֶם לֶחֶם וּפְרִי לֶאֱכֹל פֶּן תָּמוּתוּ מֵרָעָב.   ו.הֵמָּה הֵכִינוּ לָהֶם לֶחֶם וּפְרִי לֶאֱכֹל פֶּן יָמוּתוּ מֵרָעָב.

3. After the death of Pharaoh his slaves brought him outside and they brought back his bones to the dust and then they returned to their home.

(Exercise 8 continued)

א.אַחֲרֵי מוֹת פַּרְעֹה הוֹצִיא בְּנוֹ אוֹתוֹ הַחוּצָה וְאֶת
עַצְמוֹתָיו הֵשִׁיב אֶל הֶעָפָר וְאָז שָׁב אֶל בֵּיתוֹ.
ב.אַחֲרֵי מוֹת פַּרְעֹה הוֹצִיאָתַם אוֹתוֹ הַחוּצָה וְאֶת
עַצְמוֹתָיו הֵשִׁיבוֹתַם אֶל הֶעָפָר וְאָז שַׁבְתֶּם אֶל בֵּיתְכֶם.
ג.אַחֲרֵי מוֹת פַּרְעֹה הוֹצִיאנוּ אוֹתוֹ הַחוּצָה וְאֶת עַצְמוֹתָיו
הֵשִׁיבוֹנוּ אֶל הֶעָפָר וְאָז שַׁבְנוּ אֶל בֵּיתֵנוּ.   ד.אַחֲרֵי
מוֹת פַּרְעֹה הוֹצֵאתָ אוֹתוֹ הַחוּצָה וְאֶת עַצְמוֹתָיו הֵשִׁיבוֹתָ
אֶל הֶעָפָר וְאָז שַׁבְתָּ אֶל בֵּיתֶךָ.   ה.אַחֲרֵי מוֹת פַּרְעֹה
הוֹצֵאתִי אוֹתוֹ הַחוּצָה וְאֶת עַצְמוֹתָיו הֵשִׁיבוֹתִי אֶל
הֶעָפָר וְאָז שַׁבְתִּי אֶל בֵּיתִי.   ו.אַחֲרֵי מוֹת פַּרְעֹה
הוֹצִיאָה אִשְׁתּוֹ אוֹתוֹ הַחוּצָה וְאֶת עַצְמוֹתָיו הֵשִׁיבָה אֶל
הֶעָפָר וְאָז שָׁבָה אֶל בֵּיתֶךָ.

4. Joseph prepared his sword and he hit the bad one
and he saved the young woman from him.

א.וַתָּכֵן אֶת חַרְבְּךָ וַתַּכֶּה אֶת הָרָשָׁע וַתַּצִּיל אֶת
הַנַּעֲרָה מִמֶּנּוּ.   ב.וַתָּכִינוּ אֶת חַרְבְּכֶם וַתַּכּוּ אֶת הָרָשָׁע
וַתַּצִּילוּ אֶת הַנַּעֲרָה מִמֶּנּוּ.   ג.וַיָּכִינוּ אֶת חַרְבָּם וַיַּכּוּ אֶת
הָרָשָׁע וַיַּצִּילוּ אֶת הַנַּעֲרָה מִמֶּנּוּ.   ד.וָאָכִין אֶת חַרְבִּי
וָאַכֶּה אֶת הָרָשָׁע וָאַצִּיל אֶת הַנַּעֲרָה מִמֶּנּוּ.

5. David found the bones of his ancestors in the desert
and he brought them out and he brought them to
Bethlehem.

א.וַתִּמְצָא אֶת עַצְמוֹת אֲבוֹתֶיךָ בַּמִּדְבָּר וַתּוֹצִיא אוֹתָן
וַתָּבִיא אוֹתָן אֶל בֵּית לֶחֶם.   ב.וַיִּמְצְאוּ הַמַּלְאָכִים אֶת
עַצְמוֹת אֲבוֹתֵיהֶם בַּמִּדְבָּר וַיּוֹצִיאוּ אוֹתָן וַיָּבִיאוּ אוֹתָן
אֶל בֵּית לֶחֶם.   ג.וָאֶמְצָא אֶת עַצְמוֹת אֲבוֹתַי בַּמִּדְבָּר
וָאוֹצִיא אוֹתָן וָאָבִיא אוֹתָן אֶל בֵּית לֶחֶם.   ד.וַנִּמְצָא
אֶת עַצְמוֹת אֲבוֹתֵינוּ בַּמִּדְבָּר וַנּוֹצִיא אוֹתָן וַנָּבִיא אוֹתָן
אֶל בֵּית לֶחֶם.   ה.וַתִּמְצְאוּ אֶת עַצְמוֹת אֲבוֹתֵיכֶם
בַּמִּדְבָּר וַתּוֹצִיאוּ אוֹתָן וַתָּבִיאוּ אוֹתָן אֶל בֵּית לֶחֶם.

A TALL TALE: Hansel and Gretel

And it came to pass in those days, there were young
people living in a little house opposite the trees and
their name(s) were Hansel and Gretel. And it came to
pass after the death of their mother, their father took
another wife. The father had little work and he
brought little money home. They did not have meat or
fruit to eat nor wine to drink. Everyday they ate only
bread and water.

And it came to pass one evening, and there was not
bread in the house, and the wife of the father sent
Hansel and Gretel to lie down (to sleep) with no bread to
eat. She announced to her husband in a big voice: "Our
life is very bad! There is not bread also for us and also
for your children.If we bring your children out from the
house we will have all of the bread. We will bring them
in the morning to a place in the midst of the trees and
they will not be able to remember their way home. And
then the bread will be only for us." The father
answered: "No! This thing does not find favor in my
eyes! I will not be able to cause them to go out from my
house! These are my children!" His wife declared:
"There is no work and there is no money and there is no
bread. If you will not turn aside from your children, I
will abandon you and I will return to my people." The
father answered: "Do not go. I will do what you seek
from me."

Hansel lay down in his place and heard the words of
the wife of his father.He knew what the wife of his
father planned for him and for Gretel. Hansel said to
himself: "I will take a little bread and I will break it
(into) pieces and these I will put in my clothes. And in
the dust of the road, I will throw them in order that we
will find the way to return home."

The wife arose in the light of the morning and she
prepared bread and water for the road. The father and
his two children arose and all of them walked among
the trees. In their walking on the road, Hansel threw
the bread from his clothes behind him in the dust of the
road.

In their coming to the place (when they came to the
place) in the midst of the trees, the wife of their father
told (to) Hansel and Gretel: "Here is a little bread and
water. Sit under these trees and eat the bread and I
and your father will return tonight to bring you home."

And it was after these things, Hansel said to Gretel,
saying: "They will not return. I listened in the night
and the wife of our father said that there is no bread in
our house. She told our father that they will bring us
out from their house to this place to abandon us. And
thus they did. But I will save you! I took bread and I
broke it into little pieces. On all of the way, I threw
them. In the morning we will see the pieces and we will
find our way home." Gretel said: "My father will not do
a thing like this to me. He will return."

And it was at that time a small bird came and ate all of
the bread that was in the dust of the road.

Hansel and Gretel sat there under the trees all day.
And it was the evening, and Hansel said to Gretel:
"They did not return. We will lie down on the ground
and the spirit of the heavens will guard us, and in the
morning we will find the way home."

Hansel and Gretel arose in the morning and went up to
find their way home. But they did not see the bread
because the bird ate it and they did not know their way
home.

(A TALL TALE continued)

Hansel and Gretel walked all day among the trees and they did not eat a thing. And it was while (as) they were walking among the trees, they saw a little house made from good bread. They came to the house and ate from it. They were really eating from the bread of

the house until they heard a voice of an old one from within the house. "Who is it eating from my house?" Hansel answered: "My name is Hansel and her name is Gretel. We were crossing over among the trees all day and we did not have bread or water. Behold we found this house that is made from bread. We saw that it was good. Therefore we took down pieces and we really ate." The old one said to them: "Come and sit in my house. Now it is evening. In the night you will not be able to find your way. In the light of the morning you will return home."

The old one brought the young people within her house and she took Hansel and bound him to the chair by the palms of his hands and by the soles of his feet.

She told them: "I love to eat young people. But this young man, all of him is bones (he is all bones). I will give him bread and much meat to eat until he will be very big. Then I will put him on the fire and I will eat him." The old one told Gretel: "You will be my slave. All day you will prepare, and also you will bring, and also you will do all that I will command you."

And Gretel was truly a slave to the old one. She prepared bread and meat and brought it to Hansel every day. The eyes of the old one were bad and she did not see well. And it came to pass one time Gretel brought a bone to Hansel when she brought him his food. Every day the old one said to Hansel: "I do not see your face. Give me your hand in order that I will know if you are big (fat) today." And Hansel gave her the bone instead of his hand. And every day the old one said: "The young man is not big. Gretel, give him more bread and more meat in order that he will eat many times every day!"

After a month of days the old one announced to Gretel: "Today you will prepare wood and you will bring it in the middle of the house and then you will make a big fire.

Because today I will eat Hansel!" And Gretel said to herself: "I will save him. I will surely kill the old one."

Gretel prepared wood and brought it in the middle of the house and she made a big fire. And she called the old one saying: "Come to see the fire." And it came to pass when the old one was standing near the fire, Gretel hit her and knocked her (down), and she broke her head and she threw her into the midst of the fire. And she killed the old one.

After these things Gretel freed Hansel from the chair. And they found much silver and gold in the house of the

old one. They took all the silver and gold and they returned home.

When Hansel and Gretel were home their father blessed them and said: "My evil wife died. Return to me my children! Please tell all that you did!"

Hansel and Gretel told (to) their father all the bad and all the good. They gave their father all the silver and the gold. This little family had goodness forever and ever.

Chapter 27

Oral Review: A Word to the Wise....

1. Sticks (wood) and stones will break my bones but names will not (never) hit me.   2. If there is no bread there is no law.   3. Am I my brother's keeper?   4. A woman of valor who can find....   5. Time is money. 6. If I am not for myself, who is for me? If I am only for myself, what am I?   7. Go down Moses to Egypt (land)! Tell the old Pharaoh to let my people go!   8. Lizzie Borden took an ax (sword). She gave her mother forty whacks (hits). When she saw what she had done, she gave her father forty-one.   9. May you proclaim liberty in the land and to all the inhabitants in it.   10. To everything there is a season and a time to every purpose under the heavens.   A time to give birth and a time to die....a time to keep and a time to make discard....a time for war and a time for peace.

Exercise 1

1. I will gather the tribes of Israel and I will send them to destroy the altar of Moab.   2. The nations from the desert will not live again because Pharaoh attacked them and killed them.   3. Do not rule over your sons lest they will fear you.   4. The prophet went up toward the mountain and he caused his flock to go up with him. 5. You did not make a covenant (cut a deal) with me, therefore I will destroy you.   6. May you continue to recount your words and may you write them in the book.   7. Moses struck the stone and he hit it many times.   8. The king lifted his eyes to the captain and commanded him to gather the army.

Exercise 2

1. I gathered, I lived, I continued, I feared, I will gather, I will live, I will continue, I will be in awe of 2. you cut (*m sg*), you destroyed, you lifted, you raised, you will cut, you will destroy, you will lift, you will raise 3. you feared (*f sg*), you continued, you lived, you gathered, you will fear, you will continue, you will live, you will gather   4. he cut, he destroyed, he lifted, he raised, he gathered, he lived, he continued, he feared 5. he will cut, he will destroy, he will lift, he will go up/he will raise, he will gather, he will live, he will continue, he will fear   6. she gathered, she lived, she feared, she lifted, she will gather, she will live, she will fear, she will lift   7. we gathered, we lived, we feared, we cut, we will gather, we will live, we will fear, we will

(Exercise 2 continued)

cut   8. you destroyed (*m pl*), you lifted, you raised, you gathered, you will destroy, you will lift, you will go up/you will raise   9. they lived, they continued, they feared, they cut, they destroyed, they lifted, they raised, they gathered   10. they will live, they will continue, they will fear, they will cut, they will destroy, they will lift up, they will go up/they will raise, they will gather   11. to gather, to raise, to lift, to destroy, to cut, to fear, to continue

Exercise 3

1. he will take me............יִקַּח אוֹתִי
2. they found me............מָצְאוּ אֹתִי
3. they will bring him........יָבִיאוּ אֹתוֹ
4. he commanded us..........צִוָּה אֹתָנוּ
5. he sent me................שָׁלַח אוֹתִי
6. I gave you................נָתַתִּי אוֹתְךָ
7. you (*m sg*) wrote them...כָּתַבְתָּ אוֹתָם
8. may he bless you.........יְבָרֶךְ אוֹתְךָ
9. he hit him................הִכָּה אוֹתוֹ
10. they will kill him........יָמִיתוּ אוֹתוֹ
11. he will eat them........יֹאכַל אוֹתָם
12. he brought me...........הֵבִיא אוֹתִי
13. they knew them.........יָדְעוּ אוֹתָם
14. announce me!..........הוֹדַע אוֹתִי!
15. he will bring me out......יוֹצִיא אֹתִי
16. they will fear you.......יִירְאוּ אוֹתְךָ
17. he will do it.............יַעֲשֶׂה אֹתִי
18. I called you............קָרָאתִי אוֹתְךָ
19. listen (*m pl*) to me!......שִׁמְעוּ אֹתִי!
20. I returned them.......הֲשִׁיבוֹתִי אֹתָם

Exercise 4

1. Once I took a wife. I took a wife and begat children. I took a wife and I begat children and I established a family.   2. I will lift my eyes to the throne of glory. I will lift my eyes to it and I will see a man on it. I will lift my eyes to it and I will see a man on it and I will not fear it. 3. Joseph will continue to put gold in the earth. Joseph will continue to put gold in it and he will not speak about it. Joseph will continue to put gold in it and he will not speak about it lest the king take it from him.   4. In the year of the famine the children of Rachel gathered the seed in their hands. They gathered the seed and they brought it to their family to make bread. They gathered it and they brought it to make bread and they ate on the Sabbath.   5. I will make (cut) a covenant with you. I will make a covenant with you and I will love you forever. I will make a covenant with

you and I will keep you in my heart and I will love you forever.   6. David caused his army to stand across from the sea. He caused his army to stand in order that it will destroy the force of the evil ones. David caused his army to stand and he destroyed evil ones and he lived in peace.   7. They did not find me in my tent. They did not find me in my tent and they did not know me in the city or in the camp. They did not find me and they did not know me because I am the wife of the king.

Exercise 5

1. The men went up towards Jerusalem and caused their sons to go up with them.   2. And it came to pass in those days a man lived a hundred years.   3. I will make bread and in front of my sons I will lift it and then they will eat it. 4. Thus the messenger said to the king: "Throw your sword in the dust and do not send flesh and blood to war."   5. The children of Jacob saw the strength of their brothers but did not fear it.   6. I counted the sins of my brothers but I also told about their good deeds.

Exercise 6

1. נָשְׂאוּ ,יִשְׂאוּ – נוֹשְׂאִים ,וַיַּעֲלוּ ,וְהֶעֱלוּ ,וּמַעֲלִים, Two righteous ones lifted/will lift/are lifting the ark of the law and raised/will raise/are raising it in front of the gates.   2. שׁוֹכֶבֶת ,חָיִיתִי – חָיָה ,אֶחְיֶה ,שָׁכַבְתִּי ,אֶשְׁכַּב, יוֹלֶדֶת ,יָלַדְתִּי ,אֵלֵד, I lived/will live/am living with you many years, I lay/will lie/am lying with you and also I gave birth to/will give birth to/am giving birth to your sons.   3. וְלִחְיוֹת – לָשֶׁבֶת ,כָּרַת ,יִכְרֹת ,כּוֹרֵת, The judge made/will make/is making a covenant with the people of Moab to settle with them near the border and to live in peace.   4. יֵרֵא ,יִירָא, יָרֵא – הָלַךְ ,יֵלֵךְ ,הוֹלֵךְ, The small one feared/will fear/fears the wind in the night, therefore he always walked/will walk/is walking in the light of the day.   5. אָסַף ,יֶאֱסֹף – אוֹסֵף ,וַיְדַבֵּר ,דִּבֵּר ,מְדַבֵּר, Jacob gathered/will gather/is gathering the women with their sons and spoke/will speak/is speaking to them about the words of the law written in this scroll.   6. הוֹסִיף, יוֹסִיף ,מוֹסִיף – לִנְפֹּל ,שָׁתָה ,יִשְׁתֶּה ,שׁוֹתֶה, The young man continued/will continue/is continuing to fall on his face because he drank/will drink/is drinking a lot of wine instead of water.   7. – מֵקִים ,יָקִים ,הֵקִים, סָרוּ ,יָסוּרוּ ,סָרִים, Aaron established/will establish/is establishing a covenant with the children of Israel and they did not turn aside/will not turn aside/are not turning aside from it.

Exercise 7

1. Abraham prepared the palms of his hands in order that he will lift a holy scroll and will put it in the tent of meeting.

א. וָאָכִין אֶת כַּפּוֹת יָדַי לְמַעַן אֶשָּׂא סֵפֶר קָדוֹשׁ וְשַׂמְתִּי אוֹתוֹ בְּאֹהֶל מוֹעֵד. ב. וַתָּכִין אֶת כַּפּוֹת יָדֶיךָ לְמַעַן תִּשָּׂא סֵפֶר קָדוֹשׁ וְשַׂמְתָּ אוֹתוֹ בְּאֹהֶל מוֹעֵד. ג. וַתָּכִינוּ אֶת כַּפּוֹת יְדֵיכֶם לְמַעַן תִּשְׂאוּ סֵפֶר קָדוֹשׁ וְשַׂמְתֶּם אוֹתוֹ בְּאֹהֶל מוֹעֵד. ד. וַיָּכִינוּ הַקְּדוֹשִׁים אֶת כַּפּוֹת יְדֵיהֶם לְמַעַן יִשְׂאוּ סֵפֶר קָדוֹשׁ וְשָׂמוּ אוֹתוֹ בְּאֹהֶל מוֹעֵד. ה. וַנָּכִין אֶת כַּפּוֹת יָדֵינוּ לְמַעַן נִשָּׂא סֵפֶר קָדוֹשׁ וְשַׂמְנוּ אוֹתוֹ בְּאֹהֶל מוֹעֵד.

2. Isaac lived many years and he saw good and evil but he did not fear man or beast.

א. וָאֶחְיֶה שָׁנִים רַבּוֹת וָאֶרְאֶה טוֹב וָרָע אַךְ לֹא יָרֵאתִי אִישׁ אוֹ בְּהֵמָה. ב. וַתִּחְיֶה שָׁנִים רַבּוֹת וַתִּרְאֶה טוֹב וָרָע אַךְ לֹא יָרֵאתָ אִישׁ אוֹ בְּהֵמָה. ג. וַתִּחְיוּ שָׁנִים רַבּוֹת וַתִּרְאוּ טוֹב וָרָע אַךְ לֹא יְרֵאתֶם אִישׁ אוֹ בְּהֵמָה. ד. וַיִּחְיוּ שָׁנִים רַבּוֹת וַיִּרְאוּ טוֹב וָרָע אַךְ לֹא יָרְאוּ אִישׁ אוֹ בְּהֵמָה. ה. וַנִּחְיֶה שָׁנִים רַבּוֹת וַנִּרְאֶה טוֹב וָרָע אַךְ לֹא יָרֵאנוּ אִישׁ אוֹ בְּהֵמָה.

3. The priest brought the vessel with him to his house lest the evil ones would knock it down in the dust and thus will smash it.

א. וַיָּבִיאוּ הַצַּדִּיקִים אֶת הַכְּלִי אִתָּם אֶל בֵּיתָם פֶּן יַפִּילוּהוּ הָרְשָׁעִים בֶּעָפָר וְכֵן יְשַׁבְּרוּהוּ. ב. וַתָּבִיא אֶת הַכְּלִי אִתָּךְ אֶל בֵּיתָךְ פֶּן יַפִּילוּהוּ הָרְשָׁעִים בֶּעָפָר וְכֵן יְשַׁבְּרוּהוּ. ג. וָאָבִיא אֶת הַכְּלִי אִתִּי אֶל בֵּיתִי פֶּן יַפִּילוּהוּ הָרְשָׁעִים בֶּעָפָר וְכֵן יְשַׁבְּרוּהוּ. ד. וַתָּבִיאוּ אֶת הַכְּלִי אִתְּכֶם אֶל בֵּיתְכֶם פֶּן יַפִּילוּהוּ הָרְשָׁעִים בֶּעָפָר וְכֵן יְשַׁבְּרוּהוּ.

4. My father will return to his land but he will not bring his sons with him lest he will not be able to guard them on the road.

א. אָשׁוּב אֶל אַרְצִי אַךְ לֹא אָשִׁיב אֶת בָּנַי אִתִּי פֶּן לֹא אוּכַל לִשְׁמוֹר אוֹתָם בַּדֶּרֶךְ. ב. תָּשׁוּבוּ אֶל אַרְצְכֶם אַךְ לֹא תָּשִׁיבוּ אֶת בְּנֵיכֶם אִתְּכֶם פֶּן לֹא תוּכְלוּ לִשְׁמוֹר אוֹתָם בַּדֶּרֶךְ. ג. תָּשׁוּב אֶל אַרְצְךָ אַךְ לֹא תָּשִׁיב אֶת בָּנֶיךָ אִתְּךָ פֶּן לֹא תוּכַל לִשְׁמוֹר אוֹתָם בַּדֶּרֶךְ.

ד. הָאָבוֹת יָשׁוּבוּ אֶל אַרְצָם אַךְ לֹא יָשִׁיבוּ אֶת בְּנֵיהֶם אִתָּם פֶּן לֹא יוּכְלוּ לִשְׁמוֹר אוֹתָם בַּדֶּרֶךְ. ה. נָשׁוּב אֶל אַרְצֵנוּ אַךְ לֹא נָשִׁיב אֶת בָּנֵינוּ אִתָּנוּ פֶּן לֹא נוּכַל לִשְׁמוֹר אוֹתָם בַּדֶּרֶךְ.

5. The prophet will tell to the people the judgements and the commandments and he will command them to make a covenant with him and afterwards he will bless them.

א. וְסִפַּרְתָּ לָאֲנָשִׁים אֶת הַמִּשְׁפָּטִים וְהַמִּצְוֹת וְצִוִּיתָ אוֹתָם לִכְרֹת אִתָּךְ בְּרִית וְאַחֲרֵי כֵן תְּבָרֵךְ אוֹתָם. ב. וְסִפַּרְתִּי לָאֲנָשִׁים אֶת הַמִּשְׁפָּטִים וְהַמִּצְוֹת וְצִוִּיתִי אוֹתָם לִכְרֹת אִתִּי בְּרִית וְאַחֲרֵי כֵן אֲבָרֵךְ אוֹתָם. ג. וְסִפַּרְתֶּם לָאֲנָשִׁים אֶת הַמִּשְׁפָּטִים וְהַמִּצְוֹת וְצִוִּיתֶם אוֹתָם לִכְרֹת אִתְּכֶם בְּרִית וְאַחֲרֵי כֵן תְּבָרְכוּ אוֹתָם. ד. וְסִפְּרוּ הַכֹּהֲנִים לָאֲנָשִׁים אֶת הַמִּשְׁפָּטִים וְהַמִּצְוֹת וְצִוּוּ אוֹתָם לִכְרֹת אִתָּם בְּרִית וְאַחֲרֵי כֵן יְבָרְכוּ אוֹתָם.

6. The young men gathered the rams from the field of their father and they continued to gather in the fields of the others and they caused them to go up to the top of the mountain.

א. אָסַפְתִּי אֶת הָאֵילִים מִשְּׂדֵה אָבִי וָאוֹסִיף לֶאֱסֹף בִּשְׂדֵי הָאֲחֵרִים וַאַעֲלֶה אוֹתָם לְרֹאשׁ הָהָר. ב. אָסַפְתָּ אֶת הָאֵילִים מִשְּׂדֵה אָבִיךָ וַתּוֹסִיף לֶאֱסֹף בִּשְׂדֵי הָאֲחֵרִים וַתַּעֲלֶה אוֹתָם לְרֹאשׁ הָהָר. ג. אַבְרָהָם אָסַף אֶת הָאֵילִים מִשְּׂדֵה אָבִיו וַיּוֹסִיף לֶאֱסֹף בִּשְׂדֵי הָאֲחֵרִים וַיַּעֲלֶה אוֹתָם לְרֹאשׁ הָהָר. ד. אָסַפְנוּ אֶת הָאֵילִים מִשְּׂדֵה אָבִינוּ וַנּוֹסִיף לֶאֱסֹף בִּשְׂדֵי הָאֲחֵרִים וַנַּעֲלֶה אוֹתָם לְרֹאשׁ הָהָר. ה. אֲסַפְתֶּם אֶת הָאֵילִים מִשְּׂדֵה אֲבִיכֶם וַתּוֹסִיפוּ לֶאֱסֹף בִּשְׂדֵי הָאֲחֵרִים וַתַּעֲלוּ אוֹתָם לְרֹאשׁ הָהָר.

7. The priest opened his mouth and he announced to his people that he transfered his gift to another place.

א. וָאֶפְתַּח אֶת פִּי וָאַשְׁמִיעַ לְעַמִּי כִּי הֶעֱבַרְתִּי אֶת מִנְחָתִי אֶל מָקוֹם אַחֵר. ב. וַיִּפְתְּחוּ אֶת פִּיהֶם וַיַּשְׁמִיעוּ לְעַמָּם כִּי הֶעֱבִירוּ אֶת מִנְחָתָם אֶל מָקוֹם אַחֵר. ג. וַתִּפְתַּח אֶת פִּיהָ וַתַּשְׁמִיעַ לְעַמָּהּ כִּי הֶעֱבִירָה אֶת מִנְחָתָהּ אֶל מָקוֹם אַחֵר. ד. וַתִּפְתַּח אֶת פִּיךָ וַתַּשְׁמִיעַ לְעַמְּךָ כִּי הֶעֱבַרְתָּ אֶת מִנְחָתְךָ אֶל מָקוֹם אַחֵר.

A TALL TALE: Rapunzel

Chapter 1

And it came to pass in those days there lived a man and and his name was Moses and a woman and her name was Sarah. They lived in their house across from a field of an evil woman. In the midst of that field there was a large fruit tree.

One day Sarah saw the fruit that was on the the tree in the field. The fruit found great favor in her eyes. Sarah said to her man (husband): "I saw the most beautiful fruit and it found great favor in my eyes. Go please and bring me this fruit to eat! If you will not bring it to me I will surely die." Moses answered: "Don't die! I will bring you this fruit but remember that that tree is in the field of the evil woman and what will I give her in order that she will give me the fruit?" And Sarah answered: "Give her everything that she will seek (wants)."

Moses crossed over to the field of the evil woman and in his coming (when he was coming) he raised his eyes and he saw and the woman was standing near the tree of fruit. The evil woman spoke to him in a wicked (mean) voice saying: "What are you doing on my land? And what do you want from me?" Moses was afraid and he answered: "I seek fruit for my wife. You have fruit in this field that has found favor in the eyes of my wife. She saw it from the window of our house. If I will not bring her the fruit to eat she will surely die." The evil woman answered: "The fruit is my inheritance. I will give it to you only if you will give me your daughter that your wife will have (give birth to)."

Moses was very afraid and he said to her: "My wife said to me to give (to) you everything that you seek. We will give you our daughter if my wife gives birth." And Moses did not know that his wife would have a daughter. The evil woman answered and she said: "I will give you the fruit for your wife now and afterwards you will bring me your daughter."

Sarah did give birth to a daughter after five months. The evil woman came and took the daughter from them and she brought her to her house. The evil woman called (named) the daughter Rapunzel. And Rapunzel did not see her mother or her father (ever) again.

Chapter 2

And this is the life of Rapunzel. Rapunzel lived with the evil woman and she continued to live with her in her house (for) many years. And it came to pass when Rapunzel was sixteen years old she was very beautiful and she had hair of gold. The evil woman brought out Rapunzel from her house and she put her in a tower in the midst of large trees. Rapunzel was very afraid because in the tower there was no entrance and the window was very high. And there was no ladder to go up or to go down. And it came to pass when the evil woman came to see Rapunzel she stood under the window and she called to her:

"Rapunzel, Rapunzel, let down your hair!
In order that I will go up to see your face."

And it came to pass when Rapunzel heard the voice of the evil woman she let down her hair and the evil woman went (climbed) up on it. Afterwards Rapunzel brought up her hair into the midst of the tower. And Rapunzel continued to let down her hair and bring it up (for) many days.

Chapter 3

And it came to pass after three years a son of a king (a prince) walked among the trees near the tower. The prince heard a voice calling:

"Rapunzel, Rapunzel, let down your hair!
In order that I will go up to see your face."

The prince lifted his eyes and he saw and behold in the window of the tower was a beautiful young woman and she had hair of gold. When he saw the young woman in the window he knew that he loved her.

The prince saw the young woman and behold she was letting down her hair from the window. He saw a woman go up on the hair of gold. And after that the young woman let down her hair and the woman came down on it and then she went on her way. The prince knew when he saw these things that he also would go up to the young woman.

The prince went and he stood under the window of the tower and he called:

"Rapunzel, Rapunzel, let down your hair!
In order that I will go up to see your face"

Rapunzel let down her hair and the prince went up on it and he came within (into) the the tower. And it came to pass when she saw the prince, she was very afraid. Afterwards she raised her eyes and she saw his wise face and she knew that she loved him. And Rapunzel was not afraid again.

Thus the prince said: "Do not be afraid! I heard your voice and I also saw your good face and then I knew that I loved you with all of my heart. Will you be my wife?" Rapunzel answered: "In my seeing (when I saw) your wise face I also knew that I loved you. I would be your wife today but I do not know how to go outside. Will you be able to rescue me?" The prince answered: "I will be able to bring you a piece of a rope every day. Will you be able to prepare a ladder from rope?" Thus Rapunzel said: "If you will bring me rope I will prepare a ladder but remember to come only in the evening because the evil woman comes regularly in the morning!" Rapunzel and the prince made a covenant at that time to go down from the tower and afterwards to be man and wife.

(A TALL TALE continued)

And it came to pass the prince brought a piece of rope every evening. Rapunzel prepared a piece of a ladder with the rope. And every morning, Rapunzel put the ladder under her clothes lest the evil woman would see it. And they continued to prepare the ladder (for) many days.

Chapter 4

And it came to pass when the ladder was large and long, the prince came to let down Rapunzel from the

tower. And behold at that time the evil woman returned to see Rapunzel in the evening. And behold she saw a man letting down Rapunzel on a ladder from the tower. She called in a wicked voice: "Who are you? And why are you bringing out Rapunzel my daughter from the tower? I am commanding you to return Rapunzel!" Rapunzel said: "I will not return to you. I will go with this prince and I will be his wife. We made a covenant." The evil woman called: "No! No! No! He will not rescue you!"

The evil woman grasped Rapunzel with (by) her head and she took a sword in her hand and she cut all of the hair of gold from the head of Rapunzel. The evil woman said to Rapunzel: "Now there is not a man who will take you for his wife and you will continue to live with me forever." The prince called in a big voice saying: "I love her and I will continually love her. I will take her for my wife with no hair on her head." The evil woman said to the prince, saying: "I will grasp my sword and I will hit you and I will knock you down to the dust and I will destroy you and you will surely die." The prince took the sword of the evil woman from her hand and he hit her and he knocked her down to the dust and he destroyed her and he killed her.

And it came to pass after the death of the evil woman the prince took Rapunzel for his wife. They built a house and they established a family. And they recounted to their children (about) these things. Their children recounted to the children of their children, from generation to generation until this (very) day.

CHAPTER 28

Oral Review

1. Abraham did the commandment because his king commanded him to do it. Abraham did it because his king commanded him to do it. 2. I feared that you would throw me from the top of the tree to kill me. I feared that you would throw me from the top of the tree to kill me. 3. In the days of the famine, the righeous ones saw a ram and they killed it and they gave its meat to the people. The righteous ones saw a ram and they killed it and they gave it to the people. 4. The priest brought you in front of the mountain and he blessed you and he guarded you. The priest brought

you in front of the mountain and he blessed you and he guarded you. 5. The prophet sent an angel and he brought us out from Egypt. The prophet sent an angel and he gathered us and he brought us out from Egypt. 6. Joseph announced that he loved me and he sent me to his mother. He announced to me that he loved me and he sent me to his mother. 7. The women went with you in the day but they feared you in the night. The women went with you in the day and they feared you in the night. 8. The king will take his army and he will cause it to stand on the mountain and he will command it to destroy a city. The king took it and he caused it to stand on the mountain and he commanded it to destroy the city opposite it. 9. I called you and I also commanded you to go with me to the entrance of my tent. I called you and I also commanded you to go with me to the entrance of my tent. 10. His father told his son to make the covenant with him and his son made it. His father told him to make the covenant with him and he did it.

Exercise 1

1. I was guarded, I was heard, I was broken, I fought, I will be guarded, I will be heard, I will be broken, I will fight 2. you were seen (*m sg*), you fought, you were found, you were made, you will be seen, you will fight, you will be found, you will be made 3. you fought (*f sg*), you were called, you were seen, you were remembered, you will fight, you will be called, you will be seen, you will be remembered 4. he was guarded, he was heard, it was broken, he was seen, he was called, it was done, he was found, he fought 5. he will be guarded, he will be heard, it will be broken, he will be seen, he will be called, it will be done, he will be found, he will fight 6. it was said, it was gathered, it was built, he was remembered, he was known, he was born, it was given, he was cut off 7. it will be said, it will be gathered, it will be built, he will be remembered, he will be known, he will be born, he will be given, he will be cut off 8. it was built, she was given, it was said, she was born, it will be built, it will be given, it will be said, she will be born 9. we were gathered, we were known, we were found, we were heard, we will be gathered, we will be known, we will be found, we will be heard 10. you were known (*m pl*), you were born, you were seen, you were given, you will be known, you will be born, you will be lifted, you will be given 11. they were guarded, they were heard, they were broken, they were remembered, they were cut off, they fought, they were found, they were called 12. they will be said, they will be gathered, they will be built, they will be born, they will be known, they will be given, they will be done, they will be seen

Exercise 2

פָּעַל – perfect, שָׁבַרְתִּי, שָׁבַרְתָּ, שָׁבַרְתְּ, שָׁבַר, שָׁבְרָה,
שָׁבַרְנוּ, שְׁבַרְתֶּם, שְׁבַרְתֶּן, שָׁבְרוּ, שָׁבְרוּ

אֶשְׁבֹּר – imperfect, תִּשְׁבֹּר, תִּשְׁבְּרִי, יִשְׁבֹּר, תִּשְׁבֹּר,
נִשְׁבֹּר, תִּשְׁבְּרוּ, תִּשְׁבֹּרְנָה, יִשְׁבְּרוּ, תִּשְׁבֹּרְנָה

(Exercise 2 continued)

שׁוֹבֵר, שׁוֹבֶרֶת, שׁוֹבְרִים, שׁוֹבְרוֹת – participle

(לִ)שְׁבֹּר – infinitive

פָּעַל, שָׁבַרְתִּי, שָׁבַרְתָּ, שָׁבַרְתְּ, שָׁבַר, שָׁבְרָה, – perfect
שָׁבַרְנוּ, שְׁבַרְתֶּם, שְׁבַרְתֶּן, שָׁבְרוּ, שָׁבְרוּ

אֶשָּׁבֵר, תִּשָּׁבֵר, תִּשָּׁבְרִי, יִשָּׁבֵר, תִּשָּׁבֵר, – imperfect
נִשָּׁבֵר, תִּשָּׁבְרוּ, תִּשָּׁבַרְנָה, יִשָּׁבְרוּ, תִּשָּׁבַרְנָה

מְשַׁבֵּר, מְשַׁבֶּרֶת, מְשַׁבְּרִים, מְשַׁבְּרוֹת – participle

נִפְעַל, נִשְׁבַּרְתִּי, נִשְׁבַּרְתָּ, נִשְׁבַּרְתְּ, נִשְׁבַּר, – perfect
נִשְׁבְּרָה, נִשְׁבַּרְנוּ, נִשְׁבַּרְתֶּם, נִשְׁבַּרְתֶּן, נִשְׁבְּרוּ, נִשְׁבְּרוּ

אֶשָּׁבֵר, תִּשָּׁבֵר, תִּשָּׁבְרִי, יִשָּׁבֵר, תִּשָּׁבֵר, – imperfect
נִשָּׁבֵר, תִּשָּׁבְרוּ, תִּשָּׁבַרְנָה, יִשָּׁבְרוּ, תִּשָּׁבַרְנָה

נִשְׁבָּר, נִשְׁבֶּרֶת, נִשְׁבָּרִים, נִשְׁבָּרוֹת – participle

Exercise 3

1. J   2. O   3. S   4. E   5. L   6. C   7. N   8. H   9. P
10. A   11. Q   12. G   13. T   14. R   15. B   16. K
17. M   18. D   19. I   20. F

Exercise 4

l. The young man brought bulls down to the river. He brought down bulls in order that they may drink water of (from) a river. He brought them down four times every day, it came to pass twice in the morning and twice in the evening.   2. It came to pass after a year Rachel gave birth to one daughter. It came to pass after two years Rachel gave birth to two daughters. It came to pass after five years Rachel gave birth to a son to inherit the name of the family.   3. Your fathers established a righteous covenant with us. They established a righteous covenant but a sin was done. They established a covenant but a sin was done and the covenant was broken.   4. The chiefs of Moab fought with all their strength. They fought with the army of Pharaoh and they destroyed him. They destroyed him and his sword was broken and his blood was seen in the dust.   5. A son will be born the family of Abraham. A son was born and his name was called Isaac (they named him Isaac). A son was born and was called Isaac and he was known as a prophet. 6. My ears heard that the gold was found in the river. It was found in the river and it was gathered from the river twice. It was found in the river and it was gathered from the river and it was given to the king. 7. The writings will be known in two more years. They will be known in two more years and they will be given to the priests. The writings will be known and they will be given to the priests and they will gather them for a scroll of honor.

Exercise 5

1. נִבְנֶה, יִבָּנֶה, נִבְנָה, The ark of holiness was built/will be built/is being built from wood and from stone.
2. מְדַבֵּר, יְדַבֵּר, דִּבֶּר – נִרְאֶה, יֵרָאֶה, נִרְאָה, The strength of my lord was seen/will be seen/is seen on his face when he spoke/will speak/is speaking with his people.   3. יִזָּכְרוּ, נִזְכְּרוּ, יִדָעִים, יֵדְעוּ, נוֹדְעוּ – נוֹדָעִים, נִזְכָּרִים, Words of righteousness were known/will be known/are known and also were remembered/will be remembered/are being remembered in our generations.
4. נִשְׁמְעוּ – יוֹרֶדֶת, יוֹרֵד, תֵּרֵד, יֵרֵד, יָרְדָה, יָרַד, נִשְׁמָעוֹת, יִשָּׁמְעוּ, In that time the sun descended/will descend/is descending and the wings of the birds were heard/will be heard/are being heard on the shore of the sea.

Exercise 6

1. The bull will be seen in the field and he will see the young man who will fear him.   2. I will make a covenant with my brothers lest I will be cut off from my people and it will destroy me.   3. The prophet will announce a word and his word will be heard and also it will be done.   4. A strength of righteousness will be found in a law of truth and the people will also find it on the lip(s) of the prophet.   5. Do not do a sin twice lest you will do it three times and then it will be done many more times.   6. The priest will go up towards Jerusalem every year, and every two years he will bring up a bull on the altar.

Exercise 7

1. My eyes saw and my ears heard and my mouth told my sin and my transgression which I did.

א. עֵינֶיךָ רָאוּ וְאָזְנֶיךָ שָׁמְעוּ וּפִיךָ הִגִּיד אֶת חַטָּאתְךָ
וַעֲוֹנְךָ אֲשֶׁר עָשִׂיתָ.   ב. עֵינָיו רָאוּ וְאָזְנָיו שָׁמְעוּ וּפִיו
הִגִּיד אֶת חַטָּאתוֹ וַעֲוֹנוֹ אֲשֶׁר עָשָׂה.   ג. עֵינֵיכֶם רָאוּ
וְאָזְנֵיכֶם שָׁמְעוּ וּפִיכֶם הִגִּידוּ אֶת חַטָּאתְכֶם וַעֲוֹנוֹתֵיכֶם
אֲשֶׁר עֲשִׂיתֶם.   ד. עֵינֵיהֶם רָאוּ וְאָזְנֵיהֶם שָׁמְעוּ וּפִיהֶם
הִגִּידוּ אֶת חַטָּאתָם וַעֲוֹנוֹתֵיהֶם אֲשֶׁר עָשׂוּ.

2. David fought with the nations around and he made a covenant with all of them in order that a city would be built and his name would be remembered.

א. נִלְחַמְתִּי בַּגּוֹיִם סָבִיב וָאֶכְרֹת בְּרִית אֶת כֻּלָּם לְמַעַן
תִּבָּנֶה עִיר וּשְׁמִי יִזָּכֵר.   ב. הֵמָּה נִלְחֲמוּ בַּגּוֹיִם סָבִיב
וַיִּכְרְתוּ בְּרִית אֶת כֻּלָּם לְמַעַן תִּבָּנֶה עִיר וּשְׁמָם יִזָּכֵר.

(Exercise 7 continued)

ג. נִלְחַמְתָּ בַּגּוֹיִם סָבִיב וַתִּכְרֹת בְּרִית אֶת כֻּלָּם לְמַעַן תִּבָּנֶה עִיר וְשִׁמְךָ יִזָּכֵר.   ד. נִלְחַמְתֶּם בַּגּוֹיִם סָבִיב וַתִּכְרְתוּ בְּרִית אֶת כֻּלָּם לְמַעַן תִּבָּנֶה עִיר וְשִׁמְכֶם יִזָּכֵר.   ה. נִלְחֲמוּ בַּגּוֹיִם סָבִיב וַנִּכְרֹת בְּרִית אֶת כֻּלָּם לְמַעַן תִּבָּנֶה עִיר וּשְׁמֵנוּ יִזָּכֵר.

3. The young man was seen in the house of the young woman and he was heard within it and he was found there as (with) the coming of the sun.

א. נִרְאֵיתִי בְּבֵית הַנַּעֲרָה וָאֶשָּׁמַע בְּתוֹכוֹ וָאֶמָּצֵא שָׁם כְּבוֹא הַשֶּׁמֶשׁ.   ב. נִרְאֵיתָ בְּבֵית הַנַּעֲרָה וַתִּשָּׁמַע בְּתוֹכוֹ וַתִּמָּצֵא שָׁם כְּבוֹא הַשֶּׁמֶשׁ.   ג. נִרְאֵינוּ בְּבֵית הַנַּעֲרָה וַנִּשָּׁמַע בְּתוֹכוֹ וַנִּמָּצֵא שָׁם כְּבוֹא הַשֶּׁמֶשׁ.   ד. נִרְאֵיתֶם בְּבֵית הַנַּעֲרָה וַתִּשָּׁמְעוּ בְּתוֹכוֹ וַתִּמָּצְאוּ שָׁם כְּבוֹא הַשֶּׁמֶשׁ.   ה. הֵמָּה נִרְאוּ בְּבֵית הַנַּעֲרָה וַיִּשָּׁמְעוּ בְּתוֹכוֹ וַיִּמָּצְאוּ שָׁם כְּבוֹא הַשֶּׁמֶשׁ.

4. The king was known as a man of power and he ruled as a good man until he killed his brother and he was cut off from his people.

א. וָאִוָּדַע כְּאִישׁ חַיִל וָאֶמְלֹךְ כְּאִישׁ טוֹב עַד אֲשֶׁר הֵמַתִּי אֶת אָחִי וָאֶכָּרֵת מֵעַמִּי.   ב. וַתִּוָּדַע כְּאִישׁ חַיִל וַתִּמְלֹךְ כְּאִישׁ טוֹב עַד אֲשֶׁר הֵמַתָּ אֶת אָחִיךָ וַתִּכָּרֵת מֵעַמְּךָ.   ג. וַתִּוָּדַע שָׂרָה כְּאֵשֶׁת חַיִל וַתִּמְלֹךְ כְּאִשָּׁה טוֹבָה עַד אֲשֶׁר הֵמִיתָה אֶת אָחִיהָ וַתִּכָּרֵת מֵעַמָּהּ.   ד. וַנִּוָּדַע כְּאַנְשֵׁי חַיִל וַנִּמְלֹךְ כַּאֲנָשִׁים טוֹבִים עַד אֲשֶׁר הֵמַתְנוּ אֶת אָחִינוּ וַנִּכָּרֵת מֵעַמֵּנוּ.   ה. הֵם וַיִּוָּדְעוּ כְּאַנְשֵׁי חַיִל וַיִּמְלְכוּ כַּאֲנָשִׁים טוֹבִים עַד אֲשֶׁר הֵמִיתוּ אֶת אֲחִיהֶם וַיִּכָּרְתוּ מֵעַמָּם.

5. The chiefs of Pharaoh crossed over the river and they fought there and they were broken and they were carried to another country as slaves.

א. עָבַרְתָּ אֶת הַנָּהָר וַתִּלָּחֶם שָׁם וַתִּשָּׁבֵר וַתִּנָּשֵׂא לְאֶרֶץ אַחֶרֶת כְּעֶבֶד.   ב. עָבַרְנוּ אֶת הַנָּהָר וַנִּלָּחֶם שָׁם וַנִּשָּׁבֵר וַנִּנָּשֵׂא לְאֶרֶץ אַחֶרֶת כַּעֲבָדִים.   ג. עֲבַרְתֶּם אֶת הַנָּהָר וַתִּלָּחֲמוּ שָׁם וַתִּשָּׁבְרוּ וַתִּנָּשְׂאוּ לְאֶרֶץ אַחֶרֶת כַּעֲבָדִים.   ד. עָבַרְתִּי אֶת הַנָּהָר וָאֶלָּחֵם שָׁם וָאֶשָּׁבֵר וָאֶנָּשֵׂא לְאֶרֶץ אַחֶרֶת כְּעֶבֶד.

6. The slave will kill the bird on the shore of the river and he will transfer it from the waters of the river and he will bring it to the tent and he will prepare it and he will give it to his king to eat.

א. וְהֵמַתִּי אֶת הָעוֹף עַל שְׂפַת הַנָּהָר וְהֶעֱבַרְתִּי אֹתוֹ מִמֵּי הַנָּהָר וְהֵבֵאתִי אֹתוֹ אֶל הָאֹהֶל וַהֲכִינוֹתִי אֹתוֹ וְנָתַתִּי אֹתוֹ אֶל מַלְכִּי לֶאֱכֹל.   ב. וְהֵמַתָּ אֶת הָעוֹף עַל שְׂפַת הַנָּהָר וְהֶעֱבַרְתָּ אֹתוֹ מִמֵּי הַנָּהָר וְהֵבֵאתָ אֹתוֹ אֶל הָאֹהֶל וַהֲכִינוֹתָ אֹתוֹ וְנָתַתָּ אֹתוֹ אֶל מַלְכְּךָ לֶאֱכֹל.   ג. וְהֵמַתְנוּ אֶת הָעוֹף עַל שְׂפַת הַנָּהָר וְהֶעֱבַרְנוּ אֹתוֹ מִמֵּי הַנָּהָר וְהֵבֵאנוּ אֹתוֹ אֶל הָאֹהֶל וַהֲכִינוֹנוּ אֹתוֹ וְנָתַנּוּ אֹתוֹ אֶל מַלְכֵּנוּ לֶאֱכֹל.   ד. וְהֵמִיתוּ אֶת הָעוֹף עַל שְׂפַת הַנָּהָר וְהֶעֱבִירוּ אֹתוֹ מִמֵּי הַנָּהָר וְהֵבִיאוּ אֹתוֹ אֶל הָאֹהֶל וְהֵכִינוּ אֹתוֹ וְנָתְנוּ אֹתוֹ אֶל מַלְכָּם לֶאֱכֹל.

7. The prophet crowned a good king over the people. He dressed him in clothing of the Sabbath and he gave him a throne of silver and he only requested from him to turn aside from work of evil and to do deeds of peace.

א. וַיַּמְלִיךְ מֶלֶךְ טוֹב עַל הָעָם. וַיַּלְבֵּשׁ אֹתוֹ בְּבִגְדֵי שַׁבָּת וַיִּתֶּן לוֹ כִּסֵּא כֶסֶף וַיְבַקֵּשׁ מִמֶּנּוּ רַק לָסוּר מֵעֲבוֹדַת רֶשַׁע וְלַעֲשׂוֹת מַעֲשֵׂי שָׁלוֹם.   ב. וַתַּמְלִיךְ מֶלֶךְ טוֹב עַל הָעָם. וַתַּלְבֵּשׁ אֹתוֹ בְּבִגְדֵי שַׁבָּת וַתִּתֶּן לוֹ כִּסֵּא כֶסֶף וַתְּבַקֵּשׁ מִמֶּנּוּ רַק לָסוּר מֵעֲבוֹדַת רֶשַׁע וְלַעֲשׂוֹת מַעֲשֵׂי שָׁלוֹם.   ג. וַתַּמְלִיךְ רָחֵל מֶלֶךְ טוֹב עַל הָעָם. וַתַּלְבֵּשׁ אֹתוֹ בְּבִגְדֵי שַׁבָּת וַתִּתֶּן לוֹ כִּסֵּא כֶסֶף וַתְּבַקֵּשׁ מִמֶּנּוּ רַק לָסוּר מֵעֲבוֹדַת רֶשַׁע וְלַעֲשׂוֹת מַעֲשֵׂי שָׁלוֹם.   ד. וַנַּמְלִיךְ מֶלֶךְ טוֹב עַל הָעָם. וַנַּלְבֵּשׁ אֹתוֹ בְּבִגְדֵי שַׁבָּת וַנִּתֶּן לוֹ כִּסֵּא כֶסֶף וַנְּבַקֵּשׁ מִמֶּנּוּ רַק לָסוּר מֵעֲבוֹדַת רֶשַׁע וְלַעֲשׂוֹת מַעֲשֵׂי שָׁלוֹם.   ה. וַיַּמְלִיכוּ הַכֹּהֲנִים מֶלֶךְ טוֹב עַל הָעָם. וַיַּלְבִּישׁוּ אֹתוֹ בְּבִגְדֵי שַׁבָּת וַיִּתְּנוּ לוֹ כִּסֵּא כֶסֶף וַיְבַקְשׁוּ מִמֶּנּוּ רַק לָסוּר מֵעֲבוֹדַת רֶשַׁע וְלַעֲשׂוֹת מַעֲשֵׂי שָׁלוֹם.

A TALL TALE: Daedalus and Icarus

And it came to pass in those days in the land of Greece there was a wicked king. There was also a wise man and his name was Daedalus and his son was Icarus. Daedalus was very wise. And he knew many things. And the king was afraid of him. He judged him and he put him with his son in prison.

Daedalus and Icarus lived in the midst of the prison in a a small place. They arose with the coming of the sun in the morning and they lay down with the going (down) of the sun in the night. Every day from morning until night Daedalus told in the ears of Icarus all the things under the sun. And from morning until night Icarus

(A TALL TALE continued)

listened to the words of his father and remembered them and they found favor in in his eyes.

And it came to pass after two years Icarus spoke to Daedalus saying: "If you are the wisest of all man(kind) and if everything is known to you why are you not able to bring us forth from this prison?" Daedalus replied to his son: "We are not able to go forth on (the) foot because the gates of the prison are not open. We are not able to go up on the gates and to go down from them because a big river is (all) around. Only the bird(s) that are able to go up in the heavens go forth from this place." And Icarus said: "My wise father, will you be able to free us from this prison? Will you be able to rescue us? It is true that the gates are not open and the river is around, but I will surely die if you will not find a way to take us to the outside."

The father and his son lifted their eyes toward the heavens and saw the bird(s) going up and going down there. And Daedalus said: "I will surely rescue you, we will not be destroyed in this place. From now, every day, I will see the bird and its wings until I will know how the bird crosses the heavens. And I will find a way to take us to the outside."

And thus he did. And it came to pass after a month Daedalus said to Icarus saying: "Go my son and go up on the roof! There the bird(s) drop many feather(s). Gather two thousand feather(s) and bring them to me!" Icarus did what his father said and he gathered two thousand feather(s) and he put them in the midst of a large container and he brought the container to his father. And Daedalus told his son: "You did well, my son. From these two thousand feather(s) I will make us wings like the wings of a bird. With wings we will be like bird(s) and then we will be able to go outside. And we will not return to the prison forever (ever again)." Daedalus prepared four wings according to his word, two big ones and two small ones for his son.

Daedalus took hold of (grasped) the wings in the his palms and he called in a big voice to the gods of Greece: "Bless please these wings in order that we may go up like bird(s) of the heavens." And Daedalus put his large wings on his arms. He went up and he stood on the roof. He lifted his arms and the wings were on them. The wind raised him up toward the heavens and he did not fall. Icarus saw his father in the heavens and he was not afraid. And Icarus called to his father saying: "Also I (me too)! Me too! Put wings on me now, and I will go up toward the heavens like you."

Daedalus heard the voice of Icarus and he returned to the roof. Daedalus put the little wings on the arms of his son. And Daedalus said to Icarus saying: "Be wise with your wings, my son! Cross the sky regularly (always) between the sun and the land or the sea in order that you will not fall. If you will go up near the sun you will surely die and if you will go down near the

land or the sea you will also die. See (watch) me and go up continually after me."

Daedalus and Icarus stood on the roof with wings on their arms. They lifted their wings and they went up on the wind toward the heavens. They crossed the heavens like bird(s) and they did not fall and they were not afraid. Icarus crossed after his father and they crossed between the sun and the land until the shore of the sea and then they crossed between the sun and the sea.

And Icarus was continually after (behind) his father but he said to himself: "I have more strengh than my father. I should be able to go up and go down on the wind." And Icarus did not obey (listen to the voice of) his father and he went down near the sea but he did not die.

And he went up toward the heavens. It found favor in his eyes to be higher than his father. And he went higher and higher and he said to himself: "I have more strength than my father and and more than the bird(s) around. I am like the gods of Greece."

He went up higher and higher until he was not able to see his father anymore. He said to himself: "If I am like the gods of Greece I will be able to speak to the sun." And he went up higher and higher and he was not afraid.

It came to pass in his going near the sun the feather(s) fell from his wings and the wings fell from his arms. And Icarus fell into the midst of the sea and he was never seen again.

Daedalus did not see his son behind him and he continued to cross the sea toward the house (home). And it came to pass in his coming to his house he saw and his son was not behind him. For two days Daedalus prepared the house for the sake of (when) his son would return. Every day he lifted his eyes upwards but Icarus was not returning. And it came to pass after two years Daedalus knew in his heart that his son had not obeyed him and he knew that his son had died. But Daedalus continued to lift his eyes towards the heavens until this (very) day.

And it came to pass with the death of Icarus the seed of Daedalus was cut off and no more children were born to him and his heart was broken and there was no son or daughter to inherit his possessions.

CHAPTER 29

Oral Review

1. Moses said to the children of Israel, saying: "May you remember the law." The word was said to the children of Israel and the law was remembered.
2. The young man gathered two hundred bulls and he guarded them in front of the border. Two hundred bulls were gathered and they were guarded in front of

(Oral Review continued)

your border.   3. The bird broke his wings and he fell from the heavens. The wings of the bird were broken and he was not seen in the heavens again.   4. I found the place and I built a house and my wife gave birth within it. The place was found and the house was built and my son was born within it.   5. I heard you with my two ears and also I saw you with my two eyes. You were heard with my ears and also you were seen with my eyes.   6. I knew that he did a sin and he killed his brother. It was known to me that a sin was done and the deed was remembered (for) two thousand years.   7. The commander fought with a wicked nation and he made a covenant with it (them). The commander fought with his brothers and afterwards he made a covenant with them lest he would be cut off from his people.   8. The prophet proclaimed words of righteousness and he gave judgements in the city of holiness. Words of righteousness were proclaimed and judgements were given in the city of holiness.   9. In a year or two years my father wrote a book and he gave it to me. The book was written for (in) two years and it was given to me after two days.   10. David arose in the morning and he opened his eyes and he walked to the shore of the sea. David arose with opened eyes and he walked to the sea and he was seen there.

Exercise 1

1. I was strong, I was strengthened, I strengthened, I strengthened myself, I will be strong, I will strengthen, I will strengthen I will strengthen myself 2. you walked (*m sg*), you walked back and forth, you praised, you praised yourself, you will walk, you will walk back and forth, you will praise, you will praise yourself 3. he worked, he prayed, he made holy, he made himself holy, he dedicated , he strengthened himself, he praised himself, he walked back and forth 4. he will work, he will pray, he will make holy, he will make himself holy, he will dedicate, he will strengthen himself, he will praise himself, he will walk back and forth 5. we made holy, we made ourselves holy, we dedicated, we prayed, we will make holy, we will make ourselves holy, we will dedicate 6. you worked (*m pl*), you walked, you were strong, you made holy, you will work, you will walk, you will be strong, you will make holy 7. they walked back and forth, they praised themselves, they strengthened themselves, they dedicated, they made themselves holy, they made holy, they prayed 8. they will walk back and forth, they will praise themselves, they will strengthen themselves, they will dedicate, they will make themselves holy, they will make holy, they will pray 9. to walk back and forth, to strengthen oneself, to pray, to make oneself holy, to dedicate, to make holy, to strengthen

Exercise 2

פָּעַל – See #10 on pages 370, 371, and 374.
פִּעֵל – See #5 on pages 376 and 377.

הִפְעִיל – See #2 on pages 378, 379, and 380.
הִתְפַּעֵל – See #3 on page 381.

Exercise 3

1. The children of Israel walked from Egypt and they crossed the sea and they walked back and forth in the desert for many years.   2. David was strong and therefore he was able to strengthen his son and the tribe of David strengthened itself forever.   3. We will pray and we will sanctify ourselves and we will say: "Praise the Lord."   4. And it will be if a person will praise the deeds of her (his) king and she (he) will find favor in the eyes of her (his) king and then she (he) will praise herself (himself) all the days of her (his) life.   5. Joseph was angry with his wife because the work of the house was not done.   6. The priests dedicated the young men to do good and they continued to strengthen them with words of the law.

Exercise 4

1.הִתְהַלֵּךְ מֹשֶׁה בַּמִּדְבָּר.   2. יְהַלְלוּ הַנְּבִיאִים אֶת עֲבוֹדַת הַצַּדִּיקִים.   3. הִתְחַזְּקוּ אֲבוֹתֶיךָ בְּדִבְרֵי תוֹרָה.   4. הַשָּׂרִים בָּנוּ פַּר זָהָב וְאָז עָבְדוּ אֹתוֹ.   5.בְּנֵי מִצְרַיִם הִתְפַּלְלוּ לַשֶּׁמֶשׁ.   6. הִתְקַדֵּשׁ הַכֹּהֵן בַּנָּהָר וַיִּתְפַּלֵּל יוֹמָיִם.

Exercise 5

1. Pharoh was angry with the children of Israel because they did not worship him. Pharoh was angry with the children of Israel because they did not worship him and they did not pray to him.   Pharoh was angry with them because they did not worship him and they did not pray to him but they were not broken.   2. Abraham was strong with strength of many people. Abraham was strong and he fought with a righteous heart. Abraham was strong and he fought but his sin was greater than the sins of all the people of the camp.   3. I sanctified myself in the waters of the river with all of my strength. I sanctified myself in the waters of the river and I strengthened myself with bread and with wine. I sanctified myself and I strengthened myself and it came to pass when I walked back and forth in front of the king, I found favor in his eyes.   4. Isaac walked to the house of Naomi. He walked to her house and he walked back and forth outside and he prayed. He walked to her house and he walked back and forth outside and he prayed that Naomi would come out and she will put her lips on his mouth.

Exercise 6

1. go! 2. to work 3. be guarded! 4. he commanded 5. we will hear 6. and he arose 7. be strong! 8. he will be called 9. he put 10. he will be seen/it appeared 11. he will judge 12. he was 13. you/she will fear 14. he smashed 15. she ate 16. he will be remembered 17. I will bring back 18. it will be said

(Exercise 6 continued)

19. he will live   20. to inherit   21. he will return
22. he was known   23. he established   24. he will come
25. he cut   26. and he heard   27. and I will establish
28. and he called   29. to drink   30. and you may love
31. to fight   32. and they lowered   33. I found   34. and
he spoke   35. they will die   36. and he counted   37. he
announced to me   38. and they crowned   39. save me!
40. walking back and forth   41. they announced
42. he will continue   43. he will erect   44. and they
gathered   45. he transferred   46. to raise   47. and I
will destroy   48. he begot   49. and he clothed   50. I
brought out   51. to guard   52. is opening   53. and he
prayed   54. and he sent   55. they strengthened
56. and he set free   57. and he strengthened himself
58. and he threw   59. and he saw   60. they were
broken   61. I broke   62. and he said   63. and he dwelt
64. and he lay down   65. they were gathered   66. is
crossing over   67. I brought   68. and you/she
begot/gave birth to   69. praise him!   70. are written
71. he will bless you   72. and he recounted   73. to tell
74. and you will make holy   75. and he hit   76. and he
came

A TALL TALE: Ali Baba

Baghdad was a great city and two brothers lived there. One of them was poor and his name was Ali Baba. And one of them was rich and his name was Cassim. Cassim did not work because he had much money but Ali Baba worked all of his days from the coming of the sun until the going (down) of the sun.

And it came to pass one day Ali Baba was working among the trees in the midst of the mountains and he saw a force of men coming toward him. Ali Baba was very afraid and he went up a tree to save his bones and his flesh from their hands. Ali Baba prayed and he said: "May they not see me please!" Ali Baba saw the men from his place on the tree and he counted them and there were forty men.

The captain of the forty walked to a large stone across from the tree where Ali Baba was sitting (there). And AliBaba heard the captain calling: "Open Sesame!" And behold the stone opened before him. The captain caused the forty to stand in front of the stone and he caused them to pass in the middle of it. The stone was closed after them.

Ali Baba was afraid lest the forty will come out and they will kill him. He continued to sit in the tree. And it came to pass in the going down of the sun the forty men came forth from the midst of the stone and the captain after them. The captain closed the stone saying: "Close Sesame!" And the stone was closed. The captain gathered his men all of them and caused them to go down from the mountains.

Ali Baba came down from the tree and stood in front of the stone and he called out: "Open Sesame!" The stone opened and Ali Baba crossed into its midst. And the stone closed after him.

Ali Baba lifted his eyes and he saw a large cave with much light. And in its midst there were stones of gold and bowls of silver and rich clothes and many other things. Ali Baba walked back and forth in the cave and he said to himself: "These men are thieves all of them. It is good that they did not find me. I have never seen things like these in my life. Behold there is very much silver and gold. I will take stones of gold and bowls of silver to my wife. The thieves will not know what I have taken from them."

Ali Baba grasped bowls of silver and stones of gold in his hands and he stood in front of the stone in the entrance of the cave and he called out: " Open Sesame!" And behold the stone was opened and Ali Baba went outside with all his things.

Ali Baba returned toward the house (home) and he gave the stones of gold and the bowls of silver to his wife. His wife said to him saying: "What are all these things? Did you find them or did you steal them? Did you kill a man to take them?" Ali Baba replied: "I will tell you everything if you will make a convenant with me and you will not tell to (any) man or woman or son or daughter what I have seen and what I have done." The wife replied: "I will make a covenant truly and I will not make known and I will not announce your words. Tell me now!"

Ali Baba told his wife that which he had seen, the cave and the forty thieves. And the wife of AliBaba kept the covenant and did not tell the doings of her husband. But she put one bowl of silver in the middle of her house in the place where it could be seen.

And it came to pass after two days the wife of Cassim came to the house of Ali Baba and she saw the bowl of silver. She did not say a thing to the wife of AliBaba. It was when the wife of Cassim returned home she said thus to Cassim: "Your brother was seen as a poor man, but today I saw a big bowl of silver in his house. Did he find it or did he steal it? Did he kill a man to take a bowl of silver like this? We are rich. Why do we not have a bowl of silver like your brother?" The wife of Cassim commanded him to strengthen himself with wine and to go to the house of his brother and to seek from him another bowl of silver like the bowl that she saw there.

Cassim strengthened himself with wine and arose and went out to the house of his brother. And it was in his coming (when he came) to the house of his brother he said to him: "You told me many times that you are poor. And here I am standing your house and seeing a bowl of silver. Did you find it or did you steal it? Did you kill a man to take it? Are you rich? Tell me now!" AliBaba said: "I will tell you everything. If you will make a covenant with me and you will not tell to (any) man what I saw and what I did and you will go only with me to the place of silver." And Cassim replied: "I will make a covenant and I will not tell and also I will only go with you."

(A TALL TALE continued)

Ali Baba told Cassim that which he saw, the cave and the forty thieves. Cassim sought to know more. And he said to his brother: "You did not tell me everything. What did the captain call out to open the stone? AliBaba loved his brother and he told him everything.

And it came to pass after these things Cassim boasted to himself saying: "How smart I am and how rich I will be. I will not keep the covenant with my brother. In the morning I will go to bring all the things from the cave to my house."

Cassim arose in the morning and prepared the animals in order that they will carry the gold and the silver. He strengthened himself and he ate fruit and bread and he went up toward the mountain. And it came to pass in his coming to the stone of the cave Cassim spoke to the stone saying: "Open Sesame!" And behold the stone was opened. The animals stood outside and Cassim crossed into the midst of the cave and the stone was closed after him. He lifted his eyes and he saw all of the things that he had heard about.

He walked back and forth in the cave and he praised everything saying: "How good is the silver! What a lot of gold! How beautiful are the clothes!" Cassim gathered bowls of silver and stones of gold and beautiful clothes in one place in the inside of the cave. He walked back and forth round about and he boasted to himself: "How smart I am and how rich I will be."

Cassim stood in front of the stone in the entrance of the cave in order that he might go out and he opened his mouth but he was not able to remember what to say. Cassim knew that he would not be able to go out or bring out his things if he would not remember. He was angry and he called out in a loud voice: "Open Stone!" And the stone was not opened. He strengthened his voice and he called out: "Open Abracadabra!" And the stone was not opened. Cassim was very angry and he called out again in he said: "Open Hocus Pocus!" But the stone was not opened. Cassim was afraid and he said: "What will I do? There is no water to drink in the cave and there is no bread to eat. I will surely die in this cave or the thieves will kill me What will I do?" Cassim fell on his face and he prayed to the gods of Baghdad saying: "Bless me and rescue me and bring me out from this cave. I will make a covenant to be a good man from now and forever if you will rescue me."

And it came to pass when Cassim was praying to his gods, the forty thieves returned to the cave. They came in the midst of the cave and they saw their things in one place in the center of the cave. They were angry. They lifted their eyes and they saw man lying down on the ground and praying. The forty thieves caused Cassim to stand on his feet and they hit him twice on his head and they threw stones upon him and they broke his bones and they caused him to fall on the ground and they killed him.

And it came to pass after these things the thieves went forth from the cave to do more evil deeds. And Cassim was dead on the ground of the cave.

Ali Baba came to the cave in the night and behold his brother was lying there and he was dead. Ali Baba knew that his brother did not keep the covenant and the forty thieves had found him and they had killed him. AliBaba returned his dead brother to his house.

And it came to pass when the forty returned to the cave, they did not find the man that they had killed. Then it became known to them that there is another man who knows (how) to open the stone of the cave.

Ali Baba remembered what was done to his brother and he turned away from the cave and from the silver and from the gold. Ali Baba went to the elders of Baghdad and said to them: "In the mountains a large cave will be found and in its midst there will be forty thieves who stole much gold from the houses of Baghdad. All of the stolen gold is kept in the cave. If all of us will go we will be able to strike (beat up) all the thieves and to return the gold to Baghdad." And thus they did.

Ali Baba and the people of Baghdad returned to their city with the gold and all of the other things. The nations in all the lands around heard that Ali Baba had saved the city of Baghdad from forty thieves. An altar was built in his honor and the people of Baghdad dedicated the altar to the gods of Baghdad. And the place of the altar was called with (by) the name of Ali Baba until this (very) day.

Chapter 30

Oral Review/Final Exam

Part I: Chapters 4-8

i. Abraham stood and he guarded a family. 2. There was no bread in the land and we took and we ate the animals from the field. 3. You sat with the brothers in the field and you saw the young men who guarded the young women. 4. David ruled over the people and he made war with the kings in Egypt and he was like a father to the people. 5. There was a war between Moab and Egypt. 6. "What did you do today?" "I sent the things that I took from the house." 7. I walked between the gates of the city until I saw the king. 8. You did what you said and we did not do what we said.

Part II: Chapters 9-12

1. David will walk to the mountains and there he will find gold. 2. If you will open the gates of the place, then you will see the faces of the people who lived there. 3. David will take the hands of Ruth, he will hear the voice of Ruth and then he will say: "I knew the soul of the woman." 4. The people of Egypt will take the

(Oral Review/Final Exam continued)

daughters to Jerusalem and there they will reside near the trees. 5. I will remember the names of the cities in the land because I will write the names in blood. 6. You might know that the son of David will rule until the days of peace. 7. Who will rule before David and what will he know about everything? 8. They crossed over the water, they went up towards the mountain, they stood there and also they made vessels of gold.

Part III: Chapters 13-16

1. The people went out to their road, their flock of sheep in front of them, the city behind them and the gold and the silver in their hand(s). 2. My soul went out to you, and I remembered your name because I loved you. 3. David is a wise young man and there is not a son better than him and there was not a wise man like him in the Torah. 4. I am the son and I have many slaves who will find in me a good heart forever and ever. 5. The evil chiefs did not hear the voice(s) of the great priests and they made war instead of peace. 6. This is the good king and these are the old chiefs who will take the evil ones from the city. 7. He found him in the desert and he took the gold from him. 8. Jacob had wise women and many children but he did not have bread in his house.

Part IV: Chapters 17-20

1. Only if you really obey me and you will keep my inheritance, I will give you my daughter. 2. David really went instead of his servant to see the judgements written in the stone. 3. Thus said the father saying: "Say only words of holiness, do good, give honor to the law." 4. He sent to him seven flocks and eight cattle and he gave them to the king as a gift. 5. You went to six of the judges sitting in the city. 6. When you went on your way from your house you were twenty years old. 7. And it came to pass in that year Aaron went up on the mountain and he made an altar. 8. Joseph will go on his way and he will see the Holy of Holies and he will open his mouth and he will say: "What is this?"

Part V: Chapters 21-23

1. I arose in the morning and I put my clothes on me and I went out from the entrance of the tent and then I commanded the servants to give me bread. 2. And you went to the war and you broke the heads of the people and you continually set free the slaves. 3. In the month of the famine we did not eat fruit and we did not drink wine and all of us sat in our house and we also spoke words of truth. 4. The elder will smash many stones in order that he will find the gold that he is seeking. 5. My father told me that he would bless me and then he would die but his words did not find favor in my eyes. 6. In the evening all of us lay down near the water. We heard the sound of the wind among the trees and we knew that life is good. 7. Here I am standing on the border, one foot in my land and one foot

in your land. 8. The king is not counting his money in front of his wife.

Part VI: Chapters 24-26

1. The leader of the army of Moab arose and he smote the army of Egypt and caused it to fall to the dust and established a holy altar. 2. I prepared for me and for my son bread and fruit to eat lest we would die from hunger. 3. After the death of Pharaoh his sons brought him outside and they returned his bones to the dust and then they returned to their home. 4. Joseph prepared his sword and he hit the evil one and he saved the young woman from him. 5. If you know all of the commandments of the scroll of the law and you announce them then you will be a prophet. 6. The young man transferred his flock of sheep to another field and he killed a ram on the way and he ate it. 7. I announced to my children and I told my brothers, saying: "Do not eat with the palms of your hands or with an open mouth."

Part VII: Chapters 27-29

1. Pharaoh was angry with them because they did not worship him and they did not pray to him and they were not broken. 2. Abraham was strong and he fought with all of his strength but his sin was greater than the sins of all of the people of the camp. 3. I made myself holy and I strengthened myself and it was when I walked back and forth in front of the king I found favor in his eyes. 4. David walked to the house of Naomi and he walked back and forth outside and he prayed that Naomi would come out and she would put her lips on his mouth. 5. The king was known as a man of strength and he ruled as a good man until he killed his brother and he was cut off from his people. 6. David fought with the nations around and he made a covenant with them in order that a city would be built and his name would be remembered. 7. You should not do a sin twice lest you will do it three times and then it will be done again many times. 8. The priest will go up toward Jerusalem every year and every two years he will raise a bull on the altar.